CHILD OF THE
HOLOCAUST

Jack Kuper

CHILD OF THE HOLOCAUST

A Jewish Child in Christian Disguise

The Robson Press

This edition published in Great Britain in 2013 by
The Robson Press (an imprint of Biteback Publishing Ltd)
Westminster Tower
3 Albert Embankment
London SE1 7SP

ISBN 978-1-84954-384-2

10 9 8 7 6 5 4 3 2 1

A CIP catalogue record for this book is available from the British Library.

Set in Caslon

Printed and bound in Great Britain by
CPI Group (UK) Ltd, Croydon CR0 4YY

CONTENTS

We know that a man can read Goethe or Rilke in the evening, that he can play Bach or Schubert, and go to his day's work at Auschwitz in the morning.
George Steiner

ONE

A heavy layer of mist covered the village of Kulik, disclosing a few chimneys and thatch roofs as if they were suspended in the air.

I sat in the back of the wagon, clutching the bag of food, and listened to the wheels turning and the horse's trot.

Mrs Pejzak sat in the front holding the reins, her back towards me. 'Giddy up,' she called out to the horse, hitting him across the back whenever he slowed down.

The horse too could barely be seen, and it seemed as if we were sitting on a cloud being pulled by some magic force.

Perhaps all this is a dream, I thought. When I wake I'll find Mrs Pejzak and Genia gone.

Every week on market day, Mrs Pejzak drove into Siedliszcze. She would sell some produce and buy a dress or pair of shoes, matches, oil, or a reel of thread. Usually Genia would accompany her and I'd be left behind to feed the pigs and the chickens, take care of the cows, and wait impatiently for their return with messages from my mother.

For the first time since leaving home I was now going to see my mother. There are so many things I want to tell her. She'll be so surprised; she probably doesn't even expect me!

What will she say when she unties the bundle and finds a loaf of bread, some potatoes, a small sack of flour, and three eggs?

I pressed this treasure against my body and could see my mother's dark eyes beaming with pride.

The same eyes weeks earlier had covered my cheeks with tears. 'He's only a child, Mrs Pejzak. How can I let him go?'

'I'm not a child any more,' I answered indignantly. 'I'm ten!'

'You're nine, Jankele.' My mother smiled. I lowered my head.

'Well, I'm almost ten, and don't call me Jankele; my name is Jakob.'

The mist lifted, and a slow-rising sun appeared. The countryside now visible was moving away from me revealing mud houses with small windows and crooked chimneys from which black smoke rose, here and there a cowhand taking his herd to pasture, a cock waking the village.

In a meadow, an old farmer was ploughing. By the roadside an angry dog barked, and over the road loomed an ancient dead tree. Under it rested a stone on a crudely made grave. Buried in the cold ground beneath was my grandfather, Shie Chuen the cobbler from Pawia Street in Warsaw, but for a split second I imagined he was running behind our wagon, wearing his brown leather coat and hat with earflaps. Icicles hung from his nostrils and beard, and his worn black boots were caked with snow. One hand held the burlap bag over his right shoulder, the other reached towards me, and he called, 'Jankele, wait! I need a ride into town.'

Several times Mrs Pejzak turned to look at me, and once, she tossed me a wink. I cracked a smile and began to sing a song Genia had taught me about an orphan named Jasio:

Driving the cows to pasture, Jasio plays the flute,
But what sad sounds drift, drift afar.

The shepherd boy plays but in his heart there is grief.
Why do you play so, Jasio? What troubles you?
Is your life on this earth so unbearable? Tell, tell me.

We now crossed a wooden bridge, entered the town, and were soon driving through winding narrow streets. It was unnaturally quiet; not a living creature to be seen, except a cat roaming the rooftops. Broken household articles littered the roads, and echoing through the streets was the horrible sound of uncontrolled laughter.

I was stunned. Mrs Pejzak lashed the horse, and ordered, 'Giddy up.' The horse began to gallop; the wagon jumped and shook along the cobbled road, then came to a sudden halt in the marketplace.

The stalls were not there. The square was deserted, and loose pillow feathers hung in the air like snowflakes in winter. Across the square two peasants lugged a chest of drawers out of a house. Another struggled with a mattress, a third a sewing machine; a young girl wrapped in a coat pirouetted like a ballerina.

An aged man, bent in half and clutching a tailor's dummy, suddenly materialised beside us.

'Praised be Jesus Christ!' said Mrs Pejzak.

And the man answered, 'For all the ages. Amen.'

'What's going on?' she asked.

'You should have been here earlier, sister. There's nothing left.' The old man's eyes slowly widened and he set the dummy down. 'In the middle of the night, the Germans took all the Jews away. They marched them out like a herd of cattle. There isn't one left.'

'Dear Jesus!' exclaimed Mrs Pejzak, and made the sign of the cross.

For a moment, I sat paralysed. Then I bolted off the wagon and ran. My feet pounded the cobbled road and carried me faster than I had ever imagined possible. The houses seemed to be removed from their foundations, and reclined at different angles; sometimes they appeared to sway from one side to the other and even turn upside down. Soon they were no more than fast-moving blurs passing in front of my eyes.

Mrs Pejzak. I've left Mrs Pejzak. Why am I even thinking about Mrs Pejzak? But what if she needs my help? What about Genia? Has she taken the cows to pasture? Why do I persist in thinking about these things?

The small crooked window of my home was now before me. I hoped to see my little brother Josele's face in it and hear him shout, 'Mama, Mama, Jankele is home!' But the glass was shattered and no one looked out from behind the pane.

Isn't it possible, I thought, that by some miracle, by some fortunate chance, by an act of God, my entire family was still inside? Perhaps they hid in the attic, or in the cellar, or under the bed. Or maybe the Germans who came to deport them took pity and spared them! It's possible. Why not?

The door lay broken, torn from its hinges. That's only for appearance, I consoled myself, to make it seem that no one lives here. It's possible; in fact, it's very clever.

I entered. Our two pots were still on the stove. A torn straw mattress lay on the floor, a sheet beside it. Several floorboards had been removed and, in the corner, crumpled and smudged, lay a small drawing of Tarzan swinging from a tree.

Uncle Shepsel, I thought. Will I ever see him draw again? Will his voice ever again keep me spellbound for hours with tales of cowboys and Indians in a distant land called America?

'Mama!' I whispered. 'Josele, Uncle Shepsel ... don't be afraid. It's safe to come out now.'

On the floor among the debris I recognised the two pieces of fur that once adorned my mother's coat pockets. I picked them up. 'Josele, Uncle Shepsel, Mama! Please come out. It's Jankele.'

I must cry. Why can't I cry? I'll think of onions, or the little bird I treasured once then found dead, its head crushed between two bars of the cage. I cried then ... why can't I cry now? I must cry. What else can I think of? Quickly, something heartrending has to come to my mind ...

Suddenly, I heard footsteps.

Perhaps it's my mother! It's possible ... why not? No, it's probably a German coming to get me. I'll hide ... but where? No, why hide? I want to be taken with the others. I'll go willingly.

I faced the door. Mrs Pejzak's stocky figure appeared. Her eyes were wet, her head tilted to one side. She made several attempts to say something but nothing came out. She scanned the room, examining the few articles, and finally said, 'Jakob, we might as well take these.' I remained silent. 'If we don't, some thieves will.' And she gathered the total sum of what remained of our household into the sheet.

She eyed the pieces of fur I was holding, but I enclosed them in my hand.

'My mother will be worried about me,' I finally said.

'She knows you're in good hands, my child,' answered Mrs Pejzak, tying the sheet.

'How will I manage on my own?'

She fell to her knees, held my face in the palms of her hands, and said, 'You're not alone. I'll look after you always.'

'There's no one left from my family.'

'You have your uncle, what's his name ...?'

'Moishe?' I reminded her.

'Oh yes, Moniek. Isn't he working for some farmer?'

My Uncle Moishe! How can I find him? What if he was home visiting and was also taken away? How can I find out? Where can I look? I have to find him.

My arm was pulled, and I found myself outside. More looters were now to be seen, with axes and saws, ransacking and fighting for the spoils.

On the outskirts of town we saw others carrying empty burlap bags, walking briskly towards Siedliszcze. As they passed us they shouted, 'Anything left there, or did you grab everything?'

Again I saw the tree, the grave, the stone; once more my grandfather, Shie Chuen the cobbler, from Pawia Street in Warsaw, was trudging along the snow-covered road.

Suddenly, out of the blinding snowstorm came three German soldiers on horseback, their faces in shadow. One drew his revolver and fired. My grandfather only wavered. The second German aimed. A bullet whistled through the air and found its target. The cobbler groaned, but still stood. The third bullet was the fatal one. The towering old man in the brown leather coat fell to the ground. The burlap bag flew through the air and out of it tumbled pieces of bread, a few frozen potatoes, and cobbler tools.

'Sing something, Kubus,' I heard Mrs Pejzak say.

'Kubus? My name isn't Kubus.'

'It's the same as Jakob,' she answered, 'only more fitting for a little boy like you.'

I turned my back to her and in choking tones began to sing:

Driving the cows to pasture, Kubus plays the flute,
But what sad sounds drift, drift afar.

The shepherd boy plays but in his heart there is grief.
Why do you play so, Kubus? What troubles you?
Is your life on this earth so unbearable? Tell, tell me.

And then the tears came, trickling in rivulets down my face.

'Poor boy, poor boy,' I heard Mrs Pejzak mutter to herself. The tears filled my eyes and blinded me. The road, the little houses with the straw roofs, seemed to melt.

IN THE EVENING, THE NEIGHBOURS would congregate in Mrs Pejzak's farmyard. Like Mrs Pejzak, most Kulik inhabitants were Ukrainian. They gossiped, exchanged news, and sang haunting songs. But no matter what the topic, the conversation would invariably lead to Jews.

During my first days at the Pejzaks' I had heard them complain about the opportunists, swindlers, and lice-infested herring merchants who chiselled and cheated them out of their produce and in turn sold them goods that fell apart after one outing to church. Now that the vendors had vanished, and with them market day, the evening conversations had a different slant.

'You have to travel as far as Lublin to put something on your back,' one ruddy-faced woman complained.

'Those Jews weren't all bad,' added another.

Slowly, one after another would reminisce about his or her favourite Jew who was different from the others.

'Moszek was all right; he sold me a coat twenty years ago and it still looks like the day it left his shop.'

And so it happened that Mrs Pejzak, a Ukrainian, filled the vacuum left by the deported Jews of Siedliszcze. With butter, eggs, bread, and other food, she travelled to the Warsaw

Ghetto, and when she returned days later, half the village of Kulik would congregate at her small one-room house, with a queue stretching from her door to the main road. It was hard to believe that for the little produce she took with her she was able to return with so much merchandise: coats, dresses, shoes, underwear, scarves, umbrellas, and socks, things made of lace, wool, fine cotton, embroidered pillowcases, rare jewellery, and countless other goods.

The Jews of Siedliszcze, or for that matter of any town, would have envied her for the brisk trade she carried on. The same day she returned, her suitcases would be emptied and a crowd of angry women would be told that everything was sold, but not to despair, there would be more in a week or two.

I looked at the items being carried out of the house, articles from the Warsaw Ghetto, bought with a portion of butter or a slice of bread, and would wonder who their owners were. Perhaps that scarf or that brooch or maybe this pair of shoes had once belonged to my grandmother, or to one of my aunts, or even to my own mother.

The trips continued. Now farm women from adjoining villages heard of Mrs Pejzak, and they too came running, looking for bargains. The queues grew longer, the bartering louder, and it was surprising to see how adept Mrs Pejzak became in her new profession.

She was no longer a simple, honest, farm woman, but reminded me more of the shrewd market hucksters I'd seen on the corner of Pawia and Smocza in Warsaw. If there was a hole in a dress and a prospective buyer pointed it out, Mrs Pejzak, laughing, would say, 'That's the style, my dear. It's for ventilation.' And the peasant, who had never worn such fine attire, took her word for it.

Two gloves of different colours were sold as the latest

style in Warsaw; costume jewellery magically transformed into pure gold or silver or rare diamonds from Africa; worn-out shoes, faded dresses, and dilapidated coats were sold for handsome sums, by a most unusual method.

'I know it's not in the best of shape, my dear,' Mrs Pejzak would affirm. Taking the customer aside, she would whisper confidentially into her ear, 'Would you like to guess who this coat belonged to?' The would-be buyer's eyes would open wide, as if expecting to hear the greatest revelation, whereupon Mrs Pejzak would utter a Jewish-sounding name. 'Mrs Zilberberg herself. Of course you've heard of her, my dear.'

The poor woman had never heard of Mrs Zilberberg, and neither had anyone else, but how could she confess her ignorance? In fact, she had no time to, for Mrs Pejzak would allow her only to take a breath and say, 'Is that a fact!' or 'You don't say!'

Whereupon Mrs Pejzak would jump in. 'You know, of course, how rich the Zilberbergs were! Who knows, maybe something's hidden in this lining, or in the heels of those shoes. I shouldn't really sell it before I examine it myself.' By such unorthodox methods, the merchandise in question was sold, and even though no one in the village ever found money, gold, or silver in linings or in the heels of their newly acquired shoes, no one who bought from Mrs Pejzak ever lost hope of becoming rich. Shoes were torn apart and examined; coats ripped open and searched for treasure, and then mended.

As time went on, the village of Kulik had a new look. On Sunday mornings the maidens and matrons on their way to church were now bedecked in the fashionable attire of the former Zilberbergs, the renowned Tiszmans, or the famous Chuen family, the shoe magnates from Pawia Street.

And so it was with the silk dress. It was indeed made of silk, beautiful pale-blue silk, with two delicate narrow straps that held the dress up at the shoulders. On the left side was embroidered a red rose with a green stem and two green leaves. In fact, Mrs Pejzak didn't intend to sell the dress and had put it aside for Genia, but as it lay there in the corner on the cot, a young girl with long straw-blonde braids, about Genia's height, caught sight of it. She wanted it. She had to have it. Was it real silk?

'Yes, it is,' Mrs Pejzak told her, and then dropped the name of the supposed owner. But the dress wasn't for sale. She had paid an exorbitant price for it, she informed the girl, and added that it was the only one of its kind. The more Mrs Pejzak tried to divert the girl's attention to other dresses, the more the girl fondled her braids, and her eyes never lost sight of the one on the cot. Finally Mrs Pejzak caved in and quoted an excessive price.

By this time Genia was furious with her mother for even thinking of selling the dress that was promised her, but Mrs Pejzak soothed her by explaining that it wasn't sold yet. Surely nobody would be crazy enough to pay what she was asking.

Taken aback by the price, the girl began to haggle. Mrs Pejzak refused to budge one grosz. The girl picked up the dress, held it up to her body, and gazed at the oval-shaped mirror on the wall. She put the dress down, sucked her thumb, meditating, then again picked up the dress and circled the room. In the end, she tossed the dress to Mrs Pejzak, accusing her of profiteering, and left. Mrs Pejzak winked at Genia, and her daughter's beautiful face lit up.

Shortly thereafter the girl returned, followed by her buxom mother. The mother fingered the dress and concluded it was out of the question. The girl cried. She had to have it. The father was summoned. He shifted his feet and scratched his back on the doorway and then said, 'No!'

Genia was crying, the girl was crying, the mother trying to reason with her daughter, her father shouting at both of them, and a laughing Mrs Pejzak was signalling to Genia. A bazaar-like tumult ensued. In the end, the mother extracted a bundle of bills from her bosom, counted and recounted, then paid, calling Mrs Pejzak every name under the sun. The girl wiped away the tears, the father grumbled under his breath, Mrs Pejzak diverted her attention to the next prospective buyers, and poor Genia sat in the corner crying.

The following Sunday before going to church, the girl with the long blonde braids came to show off her new dress, or perhaps she came only to make Genia jealous. Besides the dress, she wore a large straw hat with a bright blue ribbon and a pair of black-strapped low-heeled shoes. In her hand she clutched a pair of white gloves. From the distance she looked rather smart, and I could see Genia's burning eyes watching her approach. Greeting us, she bowed like a countess, and waited for our reaction. Mrs Pejzak showered compliments upon her, and even poor Genia had to admit she looked stunning.

'Kubus,' Mrs Pejzak called me to her side, 'Doesn't she look like a high-class Warsaw lady?'

I wasn't quite sure what she meant by that, but now that my opinion was needed I looked critically at her outfit. Whose dress was this, I wondered. How can this girl wear it? It's like wearing a dead person's memories. Whose eyes once gazed into a mirror and admired themselves in it? Now I looked even closer at the dress and thought how immodest this girl was. The silk was thin, transparent, so that I could see her torn underpants, and her bare firm breasts under it.

I couldn't recall anyone wearing such dresses in Warsaw, and yet the style looked familiar enough. Suddenly, my memory clicked in. Yes, my aunts and my mother too wore dresses like that, and as I tried to recall where, and on what occasions, a vivid picture flashed in my head.

'Yes, Mrs Pejzak,' I said, 'they do wear such dresses in Warsaw.' The girl beamed. As she turned to leave for church, Genia stuck her tongue out after her.

Did Mrs Pejzak know what she had sold this girl, or was she perhaps in the dark as well? Should I tell her, or keep silent? I decided to speak up, for no matter what Mrs Pejzak's reaction might be, I felt at least Genia would get some satisfaction.

'Mrs Pejzak,' I said, 'that isn't really a dress.'

She looked at me quizzically. 'No?'

'It's not a dress, it's a nightgown.'

'For sleeping, such fine silk?'

'Yes,' I answered.

Genia stifled a giggle followed by a smile that quickly transformed into peals of laughter.

Taking me aside, Mrs Pejzak murmured into my ear, 'Kubus, that isn't a nightgown, understand? That's a dress.'

I understood. 'It's not a nightgown, Mrs Pejzak; for sure it's a dress.'

THE SUMMER CAME. The days were long and hot, and the nights were short and sleepless, for my mind wandered and my body turned restlessly from side to side waiting for daybreak.

I slept in the barn on a bed of hay, but on exceptionally warm nights I made my sleeping place outside the barn on the haystack. I'd lie awake listening to the croak of the frogs coming from the nearby pond, and my eyes would gaze at the stars, trying to count them ... one ... two ... three ... four ... five ... Then my thoughts would wander to my mother, Josele,

Shepsel, and eventually to Moishe. Where was Moishe? If he's still alive, why hasn't he come looking for me? He knows where I am. It's been weeks and yet no sign of him.

Due to my sleepless nights I found it difficult to stay awake during the long stifling days. I would squat on the ground and slowly my head would drop, my eyes close, and I would doze. 'I must not fall asleep,' I told myself, 'for who knows where my cows could end up, and then what?' But I wasn't always in control of myself, especially on a day before a rainfall. I could feel a weakness overtaking me ...

I was in bed at home in Pulawy, clean sheets, a soft quilt, and a pillow of goose feathers. I was flying on clouds; my mother was reading me a bedtime story, *Little Red Riding Hood*, no – it was *Hansel and Gretel*. How would Hansel and Gretel find their way home? I was flying. It was so soft, so sweet, and so pleasant. Mrs Pejzak's voice or the feel of Genia's soft hand touching my face would wake me. My eyes would open and once again I was Kubus the cowherd, far away from home.

When the sun was directly above me I eagerly awaited Genia's arrival with lunch; boiled potatoes with pork cracklings and, in another dish, curdled milk or cold borsht. If a cow had to be diverted, Genia would jump to her feet, 'Eat in peace Kubus,' and she would perform the task. She ran briskly, with her feet bare and her colourful skirt almost carrying her into the air like a balloon. Genia looked forward to bringing me my food and usually stayed longer than was necessary.

In fact, she never left unless Mrs Pejzak called her, 'Genia, get home, you've got work to do!'

On days when the pasture field was close to the house, Genia would depart almost immediately after dropping off my midday meal, but when I was on grazing land far removed from Mrs Pejzak's voice, Genia was in her glory.

She was about thirteen or fourteen, with an inner beauty that only enhanced her outward appearance. She loved fun and had a burning love of life. What she wanted I hardly understood, but whatever it was, it didn't frighten or displease me in the least.

With lunch out of the way, her green eyes would scan the surrounding area, and once satisfied we were alone, she would proceed to tickle me. The first time this happened I giggled and laughed, and though I had the urge to tickle her, I resisted in case my hand touched her accidentally in a place where it might be embarrassing both for her and for me. But later, when she ridiculed me for being so meek and restrained, I tickled her too, always careful, though, to confine myself to her underarms. We giggled and laughed and chased each other around the field and stopped only when we saw her mother approaching from the distance, infuriated at Genia's long absence, or when a farmer returned to a nearby field after a belch-producing meal.

As the days progressed, so did our tickling. Instead of my armpits, Genia now explored other sensitive parts of my body: my neck, the soles of my feet, my back, my belly button, my knees, and finally between my legs. The first time this happened I was sure it was accidental, and pretended not to notice. But I was wrong. It was no accident. Genia repeatedly tickled me there, and eventually confined herself to that area. When I did not respond by tickling her in her private areas, she taunted and dared me, saying she wasn't ticklish there. I was embarrassed, but then, too, I wanted to show her that I was a man and would not fail to meet this challenge.

Before long I forgot the challenge and it became a matter of practice to tickle Genia between her legs and also on her breasts. I'd chase her, catch her, turn her over deep in the wheat field, and tickle her until she was exhausted from laughter. Then it was her turn. I'd run like a demon; she would catch me and almost tear my white cotton pants to shreds. We'd roll on the ground like a wheel down a hill; one moment I on top of her, the next she on top of me.

I told myself that what we were doing wasn't really wrong, but also that it wasn't entirely right. Why, I couldn't tell, and didn't intend to ask. Why spoil it? I thought. Genia seemed to enjoy it, so why deprive her of the pleasure. I didn't mind it either; in fact, as time went on, it was something to look forward to in the middle of the day. And these diversions made me forget bitter memories. For that I was grateful.

But when she would depart, guilt would set in, and I'd berate myself for forgetting even for a moment. What kind of a son am I? Imagine rolling in the grass with a Gentile farm girl, and even enjoying it, when, who knows where my family is at this moment! What would my mother think if she could see me?

One day while sitting on top of me holding me pinned to the ground, Genia didn't stop at tickling. She undid the lonely wooden button that held my pants up and proceeded to strip me. I couldn't stop laughing, but at the same time tried desperately to free myself. When I succeeded in throwing her off, she pulled at my pant legs, and had it not been for my firm hold at the top of my trousers I would have ended up naked. As I tried to do up the button, Genia ran towards me again. I held my pants tight and ran. She caught me, threw me down, and turned me over, then fought to finish what she had set out to do.

Squirming, I pleaded with her. 'Please Genia, that's enough! No! No!'

'What are you afraid of?' she smiled. 'I just want to look at it, that's all.'

I was shocked. 'What for?' I trembled.

'Well, I heard that Jews are circumcised.'

'So?' I said, perplexed.

'So I want to see how much is cut off.'

I held my pants tighter than ever. I wasn't going to be put on display. She would probably laugh once she saw it, I thought.

I now felt like a cripple, different from the others. As if, when I was eight days old, the rabbi had cut off one of my arms or legs. How mean, I thought, how unjust to inflict such punishment upon an infant and mark him for the rest of his life!

One day she surprised me by not instigating our noontime shenanigans. At first I was relieved but then began to worry. What was the reason for this change? Perhaps her mother was on to us. Even though I had wished many times to end our horseplay for good, now that it was her decision, I was hurt. And so I initiated the game, by pouncing on her, ready to do mischief.

'Stop,' Genia held me at bay. She explained it had nothing to do with me and that it was only temporary. Then she proceeded to tell me in great detail and with great pleasure that she had become a woman.

Since what she told me seemed so outlandish, I pointed out that I was not born on a farm, and that I had lived for at least a year in the big city of Warsaw. I knew something about life, and had never heard of such old wives' tales.

To prove me wrong, she immediately pulled up her skirt to demonstrate proof of her condition. 'Look here and see for yourself, you big ten-year-old from Warsaw who knows so much.'

I covered my eyes. 'I believe you, Genia.'

'No, you don't. Look, I don't mind,' she chuckled.

'I can't stand the sight of blood,' I said.

She lowered her skirt and, pursuing the topic, she said, 'Jewish girls have it sideways. You know that don't you, Kubus?'

'No, it's not true,' I protested. 'Their bodies are just like yours.'

'It's sideways, Kubus, that's a fact. Ask anyone, they'll tell you.' She pointed to the rear of a cow grazing nearby. 'You see, Kubus, that's the way normal women have it, but not Jewish women.' When I continued to vigorously protest she said, 'Why do you argue? Have you ever seen a Jewish girl naked?'

I hadn't, but I wasn't going to let her get away with it. Even if it was true, I had to defend what I felt was a terrible injustice that God inflicted upon Jewish women. For if the cows and the horses and everyone else in the whole world, man and beast alike, had it one way, why did God deem it necessary to set Jewish women apart?

'Sure I've seen it, many times,' I said, 'and it looks just like yours.' Hearing this, she laughed, and voiced a list of indictments against Jews. 'Jews kill Christian children during Passover, and use their blood to bake matzah. That's why the matzah has brown spots.'

'Where did you hear such lies?'

'In church,' she replied defiantly.

I tried to recall what matzah looked like and to my sorrow I remembered the brown spots. 'Those are the burned parts of the matzah,' I retorted. But she wouldn't accept that, and clarified that she didn't blame me for not knowing the truth. In fact, most Jews didn't know about it, only the elders, a very few chosen pious ones who are entrusted to carry out the deed.

I refused to accept that, but then I hadn't believed her about her womanhood and she proved me wrong. Maybe it was true, but how could it be? I remembered my father's father, Shloime Kuperblum, the baker from Pulawy, baking matzah during Passover and I couldn't recall him mixing blood into the dough.

'It's not your fault, Kubus,' she consoled me, 'but because of that, and because the Jews killed God's only son, our Lord Jesus Christ, the Germans are now repaying you.'

How horrible, I thought. If all this is true, then indeed there is good reason for our suffering. Why did we kill Jesus? This and many other questions plagued me. If only we had not killed Him and all those innocent infants, then I'd still have my mother and father and my brother Josele, and we'd all be back in Pulawy. I'd be going to Hebrew school, and every night my mother would tuck me into bed and read me fairy tales. Oh, how I wished that we had not committed those heinous crimes! But I argued emphatically that her stories were simply grandmother tales.

'That's a good one.' She dismissed me with a shrug. 'If so, then why can't Jews see the sun?'

Now what did she mean by that? I was sure I could always see the sun, but was it the sun I had been looking at all my life or something I only thought was the sun? 'I don't know who filled your head with such silliness,' I said.

'Ask anyone in the village and see if they tell you differently.'

'They're all ignorant,' I said defensively.

'All right then, Mr Educated,' she sneered, 'show me the sun.' I raised my arm and pointed it out. 'You saw me looking in that direction.' She took her rose-coloured kerchief off her head, tied it tightly around my eyes, then turned me several times to the left, then to the right, then to the left again, and again to the right. Dizzy, I was about to fall when she removed the blindfold. 'Now point.'

I blinked and without hesitation pointed to the sun. She

looked at the sun then at me, and said, 'You're a clever one. You felt the sun's rays on your face, that's how you know.'

I protested and tried desperately to convince her I could see the sun. Perhaps I was only trying to convince myself. At any rate I didn't have a chance. Mrs Pejzak's voice was suddenly heard, heaping all manner of invective at Genia for taking so long.

Genia scooped up the empty dishes and ran off saying, 'Wait for a cloudy day, my educated cowherd, when there are no warm rays to guide you. Wait till then.'

Impatiently I waited for such a day, when the sun was a circle of golden yellow, peeking from behind the clouds but yielding no heat. Once again I was blindfolded, turned like a spinning top, and pointed. After many more trials, Genia was eventually convinced. She took me in her arms, lifted me off the ground and kissed me, screaming with joy, 'It's a miracle, Kubus!' and ran off shouting, 'Mother, dear Mother! Dear Jesus! Kubus can see the sun!'

Besides Genia's noontime visits, I also had the company of another cowherd, whom I originally met during my first days at the Pejzaks', when I heard a flute being played and followed its sound to the next grazing field.

'Want to try it?' he asked when he had stopped. I reached for it, placed the flute between my lips and, fingering the holes, I blew. But what came out scared the cows, and so I handed it back.

'It's yours,' he said, 'I'll make me another.' He asked my name and revealed his, Wojciech. His head was almost clean-shaven, and he was barefoot, wearing torn pants and a soiled peasant shirt. He saw me staring at his bruised and scarred face, and thus offered an explanation: 'The bitch had nothing better to do,' he spat.

'The bitch?' I puzzled.

'My stepmother. No matter what I do it is no good. One of these days I'll punch her one, and knock her frickin' head off. The whore! Wait till my father gets back and I tell him everything.'

'Where is he?'

'In Germany,' he said, 'forced labour.'

I was tempted to tell him that my father was also away, in Russia, but I had second thoughts.

Wojciech and I would meet on days when our animals grazed in adjacent fields. Besides whittling flutes from willow branches with his sharp pocket knife, his specialty was killing frogs. With one blow he could bludgeon a bullfrog's head to smithereens. I was repulsed but pretended to admire him.

But his favourite topic was Genia, and he constantly prodded me with questions concerning her.

'I bet she would be good in the hay,' he told me one day. 'I'd like to break her in.' He looked at me, and then slapped me on the back. 'Or did you do that already, Kubus?'

I resented his remarks, in fact, I despised him for it. How could he talk like that about a girl? 'She has nice tits,' he continued. 'I'd love to pinch them.'

I wanted to defend Genia's honour. I wanted to strike him or at least sever my friendship with him, but he might think I was a sissy, and so I laughed along. But my laughter was filled with painful guilt.

This preyed on my conscience and every time I ran into Wojciech, I resolved to do something about it. Although about my own age, he was physically better developed, and had proved his might on occasion when jokingly he would twist my thumb or hold me on the ground, wrench my arms and legs, and say, 'Let's see if you can get up.'

I envied his strength and at the same time detested him for it: the way he could climb a high tree, the way he swam, and his self-assurance.

From him I also heard many indecent words and lewd songs. 'Who was that guy I saw Genia with last Sunday?' he would interrogate me. 'I bet he's getting into her, eh, Kubus?'

'I don't know,' I would reply.

He'd laugh, then, half-closing his eyes, he'd add, 'I bet he's in, but good.'

Sensing my ignorance, he explained to me in great detail and with much zest what went on between men and women. Even though I knew vaguely of these matters, his teaching clarified many things for me.

'Is that what Genia does?' I asked him one day.

'What do you think, stupid?'

I began thinking of all the boyfriends Genia had. There were so many of them, especially on Sunday. During the week one or two would show up in the evening and take Genia out for a swim in the pond or a walk in the fields, but on Sunday the farmyard was filled with young men in polished shoes and white shirts with ties.

I could see them coming across the fields from far away. The parade would start about noon and, when the sun had set, there would still be new ones coming, each desiring to hold her hand, or at least play with her kerchief. Genia laughed and joked with all of them, giving each and every one her personal attention, while Mrs Pejzak, beaming with pride, would busy herself with providing refreshments.

I now began to feel ashamed for Genia, but I couldn't entirely take my friend's word as to how Genia behaved. If it's true, I thought, then no wonder she's so popular, while some of her other girlfriends never received a single visitor. In the end I dispelled these negative thoughts from my mind and believed only the best of her. Certainly she flirted with all her boyfriends, but that's all, I convinced myself. I was certain she wouldn't even tickle one of them the way she did me.

I thought of confronting Genia, but I was embarrassed and feared she might think I was jealous. I wanted desperately to tell her about the gossip, and confess that I was incapable of defending her against such slander. But I didn't. For who knew what she would think of me then? In the end I resolved to continue the way I had, and say nothing.

Normally when Genia brought me lunch and Wojciech happened to be nearby, he would greet her and then busy himself with the frogs, or serenade us from afar. But on this day he joined us and made no move to leave. As I began to wolf down my lunch, he made obscene comments to Genia.

'Say, when will I have a chance to try you out, filly?'

Genia looked him up and down. 'When you stop wetting your pants, little boy.'

This humiliated him, especially in front of me. 'Any day you say, flower,' he went on. 'Let me show you how well I could roll you in the hay.'

Genia laughed and told him to get lost. I was embarrassed for her, but to my surprise she didn't seem to be uncomfortable and obviously knew how to handle him. In fact, she was getting the better of him. This infuriated him even more, and he began to deliver more hurtful indecencies.

'Why don't you let me pinch your tits, whore?'

Genia looked at him with disgust. 'Go tend your cows,' she said. 'Look, they're in someone's cabbage patch.'

'Cabbage is good for them,' he answered smugly. 'Well, what do you say? I'll make you feel good. I've seen my father doing it with that bitch.'

'Then go play with your dick,' said Genia.

I wanted to stand up and hit him, but just the mere thought made me tremble. And yet how could I just sit and do nothing? I had to show Genia I could stand up to him like a man.

One moment I imagined Genia being proud of me for my chivalry, and the next I could see my bleeding nose and feel a broken rib.

Impulsively, I got to my feet and reached for my stick. I intended to strike him, but now I was sorry I had stood up. Genia was looking at me, expectantly. Grinning, Wojciech sized me up, as if to say, Look who's going to defend the lady!

'Wojciech, why don't you leave us, please,' I asked.

'And who's going to make me? I'm staying right here, and let's see what you're going to do about it.'

His insult didn't bother me as much as Genia awaiting my next move. 'Come hit me,' he said mockingly, and stretched his arms out like a bird in flight.

I had no choice. I raised my cane and struck him lightly so as not to really hurt him. At that moment I realised I had not been afraid of being beaten. What really worried me was that if I hit him with all my might I could kill him.

He mocked me. 'You hardly touched me, you fly. Even the bitch hits harder than that.'

I struck him again, but with restraint.

He didn't laugh this time but said, 'Now, that hurt a little. Not much, mind you.'

Then I felt his fists smashing into my face and jabbing my body, but I didn't respond. I simply closed my eyes and accepted the blows.

When his energy was spent, he retreated, panting like a dog. Genia praised me for my courage and, while trying to stop the bleeding from my nose, told me what a licking I had given him. I knew that wasn't so.

From then on, Wojciech and I kept our distance. He stayed in his field and I in turn kept my back to him; but even then I could hear the insults he directed at me.

'Wait, they'll make soap out of you, you cut-off-dick Jew boy!'

THE EVENING WAS QUIET and warm, and only the crickets could be heard. Across the village, naphtha lamps were being lit, and now a faint glow of light appeared in the Pejzaks' window.

Night was about to descend. My two cows were resting in the stable from a weary day of chewing cud and swatting flies with their long tails. Mrs Pejzak and Genia had been out in the field that day weeding, and were now inside preparing supper.

I stood by the well washing my hands and face, and was reaching for the bristle brush to scrub my feet when from the abutting golden wheat field I heard a rustle. I turned and listened. But now it was quiet. It must be my imagination, I thought, and returned to my task. Again I heard a sound. Perhaps it's a dog, or bird, or a wild rabbit, I reasoned. But the distraction continued. I tried to ignore it, but suddenly I sensed I was being watched. I could feel something peering at me.

I wanted to rush into the house and inform Mrs Pejzak, but what if it's only my imagination? Or what if it was only a bird, or a cat? Then Genia and Mrs Pejzak would laugh at me and call me a city mouse.

I've got to be brave, act like a man, and not run like a child crying for help. I picked up my stick and, though my legs were trembling, I approached the wheat field and whispered, 'Who's there?' There was no reply. I stepped forward, trying to appear confident, but now that I was close I could hear the beat of a heart, and the eyes, even though I couldn't see them, were boring right through me. 'Come out, whoever you are!' I called, and hoped that a reply would not come. I was about to turn back when suddenly a figure rose up. Facing me was an unshaven man with fierce eyes, attired in a train conductor's uniform. It was obvious the costume didn't belong to him; the jacket hung loosely on his shoulders, the trousers were too short.

I had to ease my way out as one does when confronted by an unfriendly dog, and so I acted as if finding him there was the most natural thing.

His eyes shifted, and I could see he was trembling. At last he said something I couldn't understand. It sounded Ukrainian, and yet it wasn't. He repeated the same words slowly, enunciating every syllable, and gesturing with his hands. I guessed he was asking whether there was anyone inside the house.

'My employer and her daughter,' I replied in a blend of Polish and the Ukrainian I had picked up.

'No one else?' he bore into my eyes, as if squeezing a truthful answer out of me.

'No, I swear,' I reassured him. 'Do you want to see my employer?' I asked, and backed up towards the farmyard. 'I'll get her.'

I could feel him trailing me, and when I reached the house, I turned and caught a glimpse of him at the well, drinking from the pail like a parched animal. Rushing into the house, I bolted the door behind me, and shouted frantically, 'Quick! Look outside!'

Genia didn't react. Mrs Pejzak unlocked the door and looked out. The man was standing by the well staring at us.

I could now see his bare feet. Over one shoulder hung a pair of black leather boots. Who is this man? I wondered.

Certainly not a train conductor. He's not an escaped Jew either. Then a frightening thought struck me; he's a German disguised as a train conductor, and he's here to get me.

'Good evening,' said Mrs Pejzak at last. He answered her in that strange tongue. Mrs Pejzak slowly approached him. They exchanged a few words and then, led by Mrs Pejzak, both entered the house. His eyes scanned the room, and then he sat down.

By the flickering light of the lamp, I studied his face. He looked almost as old as my grandfather, the baker. Mrs Pejzak barked orders at Genia to set the table, to mash the potatoes, to cut some bread, to pour the milk.

At the slightest noise the stranger would jump up like a rabbit about to flee. At every such instance, Mrs Pejzak reassured him, and now, to my surprise, she too was speaking in that strange language. Some I could make out, but most was unfamiliar.

When the supper was placed on the table, the stranger, without crossing himself, unlike Mrs Pejzak and Genia, attacked what was placed in front of him. Genia cut more bread and, just as quickly, he devoured it. Again and again his glass was refilled, and long after we had finished eating, he continued.

At last he was content. He belched, and a faint smile sprouted on his face. It brought smiles to our faces. Then his mouth widened and he beamed, then giggled, and finally gave a healthy chuckle. We laughed, he laughed louder, we joined in, and gradually the house exploded in peals of laughter. But why I laughed I didn't know, any more than they did.

Later on he sat quietly answering the questions Mrs Pejzak hurled. As the clock on the windowsill ticked away, he began to yawn. Mrs Pejzak turned to me.

'Kubus, show him to the barn.'

Was he going to sleep with me? What if he plans to kill me?

Mrs Pejzak lit the lantern and handed it to me. The man rose, kissed Mrs Pejzak's hand, bowed, and said, 'Good night!'

I led him to the barn and pointed to the sleeping area. He curled up. The night wasn't warm enough to sleep outside and there wasn't room for me inside the house. I debated for a moment, and then ran back to the house. The door was already bolted. I knocked. Mrs Pejzak's leery voice came from inside, 'What is it?'

'It's Kubus,' I whispered. The door opened and Mrs Pejzak, half-undressed, and combing her long hair, faced me. Stuttering, my eyes filled with fear, I implored, 'Who is that man?'

'Go to sleep, Kubus.'

'Mrs Pejzak,' I whined, 'He's a German soldier, sent here to kill me.'

She drew me to her. 'Not to worry, Kubus.' But when that did not suffice, she asked, 'Can you keep a secret?' I nodded. 'He's a Russian soldier. He escaped from the prisoner-of-war camp in Chelm. But no one must know he's here. No one, do you understand?'

I was relieved and happy, and returned to the barn. How exciting, I thought, an escaped prisoner sleeping with me. The fact that he was Russian made me feel safer than ever. My father had told me that the Russians were kind to the Jews and treated them well. That's why my father had fled to Russia.

The man extended his hand, 'Ivan!'

I offered him my hand, 'Kubus.'

He turned on his side and closed his eyes. I blew out the lantern and sank into the hay, but my active mind prevented me from sleep.

Mentally, I projected a conversation: 'Do you by chance know Zelik Kuperblum?'

'What does he look like?'

'Well, he ...'

What did my father look like? I tried to visualise him, but his image refused to be focused.

I now saw myself as a child of five or six. Out of a fog, a stranger in a raincoat and creased fedora hat approaches me. He stares at me with the bluest eyes. He offers me a cluster of grapes, picks me up, hugs me, and kisses me. 'Do you know who I am?' he asks. I tremble but I'm afraid to cry. The precious grapes fall from my hand and I shake my head. 'I'm your father,' and he presses my face against his, irritating my young skin with his unshaven face.

I see his silhouette at the workbench, a sharp tool in his hand, cutting leather for the upper part of shoes and whistling Schubert's *Serenade*.

He is in bed with earphones, listening to the muffled sounds of a symphony orchestra on his homemade radio.

I'm running with him, bombs are falling from German planes.

He's digging through the rubble of what was once our Pulawy apartment, hoping to retrieve his precious sewing machine.

Then his hands are busily building a birdcage out of wooden dowels.

And then I feel his lips upon my cheek and faintly I hear his voice, 'Goodbye, Jankele my darling child. I'll send for all of you.'

He's framed against the doorway and then I see only the doorway ...

Digging deeper into my memory, I recalled that my father

had a scar on his left cheek from a tooth operation many years back.

One thought led to another and before long I began to suspect that not only did this Russian escapee know my father, but also maybe he *was* my father. It's possible, I encouraged myself. He looks older. But that could be due to his beard, I reasoned. But then, if he is my father, surely he would have recognised me! How could he? He hasn't seen me for such a long time and wouldn't expect to find his son Jankele in such a place. It's possible, I kept repeating. But is it possible? After all, this man's name is Ivan. Maybe he changed his name! Sure, that's it, he changed his name. If he shaves his beard and reveals a scar on his left cheek, then I'll know for sure.

The next morning when I opened my eyes, Ivan was still sleeping, snoring heavily. I ate breakfast, unhitched my cows, and drove them to a parcel of grazing land far from the house.

Sitting cross-legged on the wet morning dew, my eyes were on the animals but my thoughts centred on Ivan. Perhaps he'd already shaved by now. But what if he doesn't shave? How will I know? I could ask him if he'd ever been to Pulawy, and if his answer is 'yes,' then I'll casually ask if he has a boy named Jankele. If he is indeed my father, I reasoned, he'll embrace me, lift me into the air, and cover me with kisses.

I was waiting impatiently for noon and Genia's arrival. The sun seemed to play tricks with me that day, staying in the same place. I was hoping to learn more about Ivan from Genia. But when at last the sun was above me, as hard as I looked I couldn't see Genia's figure in the distance. Something had happened. Perhaps the Germans had discovered Ivan and arrested Mrs Pejzak and Genia as well.

By the time the sun had eventually passed the noontime position, with still no sign of Genia, I decided to drive my two cows home. I was about to set out when, in a cloud of dust along the road, I saw Genia's dancing feet coming towards me. She raced faster than at any other time.

Panting, she almost threw the food at me and apologised for being late. As I sat down to eat, she said, 'Kubus, don't forget to bring the dishes home.'

Surprised, I asked, 'You're leaving?'

She pinched my cheek, 'Mother needs me,' and turned to go.

'Genia,' I shouted after her. 'What about the Russian?'

'What about him?' She flew off like a bird.

I couldn't eat, waiting impatiently for the day to end. But the sun continued to frustrate me, refusing to set. And so when it was still some distance from the earth, I made my way back, running all the way.

'Why so early, Kubus?' Mrs Pejzak was visibly annoyed.

'It feels like rain. I didn't want us to be caught in it.'

'Rain?' she grimaced. 'Without a cloud in sight?' I cast my eyes to the ground. 'All right, take them in for the night, but don't let it happen again.'

I drove the cows into the stable and tied them up.

I wonder where he is. Probably in the house. I'll go and look. First, I'll wash up.

As I headed to the well, I heard a swishing sound coming from the hay. I stopped to listen, and then tiptoed to where it was coming from. Genia lay in my sleeping place, and beside her, with his arms around her, reclined a young man. He wore a clean cotton shirt, open at the neck, and white cotton trousers. His hair was combed neatly to the back, and his face was free of whiskers. I looked closer and recognised Ivan.

They both acknowledged me, not disturbed in the least by my presence.

'Home so early?' Genia asked.

I turned and ran out, slamming the barn door behind me.

'Don't run away, Kubus, come and join us,' her voice pursued me. Then I heard her laugh and say to Ivan, 'He's jealous.' And then they both laughed.

SUDDENLY GENIA SEEMED to be grown up, and this made me feel more like a child. She was constantly preoccupied with Ivan. The Sunday visits of other young men came to an abrupt end, but instead, as if they had fallen out of the sky, a new group congregated in Mrs Pejzak's farmyard on Sundays and sometimes in the evenings during the week. Most were about Ivan's age, though a few were older, and they too were Russian prisoner escapees. There were Nikolai, Dimitri, Joska, Boris, Juri, Sergei, Sasza and others.

Some, like Ivan, were billeted with families in the village, while the less fortunate roamed the fields by day and slept in the forest by night.

While tending my cows, I would meet new ones almost daily. Sometimes alone, other times in pairs or more, wandering aimlessly like lost sheep. I'd scrutinise their faces, constantly searching for a scar, and I'd ask each one the same question, 'Do you know Zelik Kuperblum?'

I was met with blank stares. My questions led to questions of their own and, reclining on the grass, they would listen to my story and urge me to continue when I stopped for a moment.

I welcomed their company and interest, and was only too happy to let them share my lunch. When the food was gone, the stories over, and evening about to descend, they would disappear with a promise to look for my father.

Occasionally, a trio would show up looking for Ivan. He

would don a raincoat, under which he would hide a rifle, and the group would depart. Ivan would return in the early morning, sometimes inebriated and sometimes bruised.

Where do they go? Why do they carry rifles?

Once, Ivan described in detail a night's adventure: an ambush, a truck full of German soldiers, rat ... tat ... tat ... tat ... the truck turns over, the Germans try to flee, but there is Sasza or Juri with a grenade, he hurls it ... the German bastards are shredded into small pieces.

On other missions an informer is shot asleep in his own bed, a garrison is set on fire, and so on.

These accounts fascinated me, and I admired Ivan and his pals for their courage and felt that at long last someone was taking revenge for all the atrocities the Germans had perpetrated against us.

I would clearly picture the blood gushing over the roadside and could almost hear the ghastly screams of pain shattering the still of the night. But other times I felt sorry for the ambushed victims.

Perhaps they were the good ones, innocent ordinary soldiers who had mothers and fathers back home.

Then my other self would say, Good Germans? What's the matter with you, Jankele? After all that's happened, how can you have such naive thoughts?

But some *are* decent.

I'd like to meet one.

What about the one in Lublin?

In Lublin?

The one by the truck, when they were deporting us, remember?

Yes, I remember. He was shoving you onto the truck, as if you were cattle. Is that what you call decent?

He offered me and Josele candy. Now if he was as bad as you say, why would he give us candy?

Candy? It was poison, you fool. That's why Mommy wouldn't let you take it. Did you forget so soon?

I remembered the scene vividly, and could clearly picture the German soldier with his outstretched hand offering us the bonbons.

'Take, please take,' he pleaded. My mother drew us nearer to her, holding our hands in hers, so that we couldn't reach. 'Please take it. Let your children have it,' he begged. But my mother just stared at him and held us tighter. 'Why?' he finally asked.

'It must be poison,' my mother replied.

The sweets dropped from his hand. 'I have two sons of my own. Your children remind me of them. I wonder if I'll ever see them again,' and with a slam he closed the rear of the truck, then shouted to the driver, 'Filled up, take it away.' As the truck started to move, he turned his back to us, and from the distance I could sense he was crying.

I felt sorry for him and for his children.

Shame on you, shame! I heard the voice within me again. Go on; feel sorry for the German and for his children. You should feel sorry for your own family and yourself instead. All right, maybe this one had a beating heart, but he's the only one.

And so I argued with myself and only brought the argument to a satisfactory conclusion when I told myself that the German soldier with the bonbons was not among those killed last night. I was certain that he was still alive. Probably on leave visiting his children at home. Ivan and his companions only kill the bad ones, the ones that mistreated us. And now, again, I was glad, I was satisfied. They were getting what was coming to them.

But in front of my eyes I could now see the smiling face

of another German soldier. Rudi was combing his blond hair, admiring himself in a small mirror hanging on the side of an army lorry. I was cleaning his motorcycle, covered with mud from the previous day's manoeuvres. The encampment where he was stationed on the outskirts of Siedliszcze had been a public school before the occupation. Almost daily Rudi went on manoeuvres and I not only kept his motorcycle sparking, but also polished his boots, brushed his uniform, and rinsed out his canteen.

'Your name is Jakob,' he once mused, 'a good biblical name.' And he threw me a loaf of bread. 'For your mother.' Quite often he stuffed my pockets with food to take home.

The bread my mother accepted without comment, but the pork sausage she disposed of, even though we were starving, and forbade me to ever bring it home again.

I stood by the gate and watched truckloads of the German army leaving the former school. I catch a glimpse of Rudi. His motorcycle glistens, his boots shine, and his uniform is spotless. I feel proud of my efforts. He sees me and pulls over to the curb. He forces a nervous smile.

'Where are you off to?' I ask.

His face tenses. 'To the Russian front. Come along Jakob. I could use your help.'

'I can't leave my mother,' I answer.

'Move on!' shouts the soldier directing the convoy.

'Will I ever see you again?' I ask.

He reaches into a pouch and hands me three chocolate bars. 'I doubt if I'll ever come back.'

There you go again, said the voice within.

I closed my eyes and vowed not to think about it any more.

MANY A SUNDAY, MRS PEJZAK'S HOUSE was filled with song and laughter. The vodka poured freely and she served perogy with sour cream to the assembled Soviet soldiers.

Genia would not confine herself to Ivan alone; she sat on everybody's knees and gave all of them kisses with little prompting. Her mother, pleased beyond description, urged everyone to fill their bellies.

This is more exciting than my Uncle Shepsel's cowboy tales, I told myself, and here I am in their midst, helping them polish guns, lending my voice to their songs, and occasionally taking a sip of their vodka. In time, I even began to believe that I too was part of this daring band.

Apart from Ivan, the one I liked best was a different Ivan, Ivan Bialykonie, but we called him Vanja. He was tall with curly black hair, a camel nose, and large dark eyes. He wore a heavy long earth-coloured coat, under which he normally hid his rifle. He was lively, full of stories, songs, and jokes, but on occasion I observed him brooding.

Whenever the opportunity presented itself, I would hurl all sorts of questions at him about life in Russia.

'Is it true that Jews are well treated there? I heard that there are Jews in the Soviet army, and some are officers, even generals.'

Vanja would roll a cigarette, light up, and present his answers.

I was mesmerised by his own history; the town he came from, the school he had attended, and the girl he had loved and left behind.

'What about your family?' I inquired.

Looking into my eyes, he said, 'Kubus, I, like you, have no family. I'm an orphan; I've always been one.'

'What happened to your father and mother?'

He shrugged. 'I don't know, I never knew them. I grew up in an orphanage.' Then he pointed to his nose. 'You see this?' I nodded my head. 'It's a real hooker, isn't it? It could be that I'm one of your tribe.'

Is he telling me the truth or is he saying this only to comfort me?

'You speak Yiddish?' I asked.

He shook his head.

We became good friends, and every time we saw each other, he had a little present for me: a bullet shell, a shiny button, anything that came his way.

He also taught me a song, with which he identified himself. From then on, I abandoned the song about Kubus the cowherd, and Vanja's haunting melody now echoed throughout the fields of Kulik:

Forgotten and abandoned,
In my very young years
I became an orphan
Without happiness in my life.

There, far in the valley,
There a nightingale sings a song;
I'm a guy on foreign soil
I've forgotten my friends.

When I die, I will die
And they'll bury me,
My relatives won't know
Where my grave is.

No one will come to visit,

My resting place,
Only a nightingale will sing
In the early spring.

He will sing and whistle,
And then fly away,
And the unattended grave
Will remain lonely once more.

'Tonight, Kubus, we're going to pay a visit to your town,' Ivan announced one evening. He ruffled my hair, and left to rendezvous with the others.

I couldn't sleep that night waiting for his return, but there was no sign of him. The night passed and still he was not back.

The next day a story circulated in the village: the previous night while a well-known collaborator of Siedliszcze was asleep in his elaborate bed, with fine quilts and fluffy pillows, partisans snuck into his residence, stripped his wife, tied her up, and then beat her with a horse whip. They destroyed all the furnishings, looted the valuables, dragged him into the market square, and strung him up on a post.

Mrs Pejzak kept sending me out to keep an eye on the road for an approaching figure. The third or fourth time I ventured out, I saw a man wearing a homburg hat, a heavy long coat, and full leather boots.

I ran back to report. Mrs Pejzak followed me out. The dignitary was entering the farmyard. Only when he was upon us did we realise that this stylishly dressed gentleman was no other than our own Ivan.

'What do you think of the new me?' he inquired, twirling a cane with a silver handle. Mrs Pejzak gasped, I was stunned; both of us were happy to see him.

'Feel the fur,' he indicated the collar. 'Fox.'

That night Ivan tossed and talked in his sleep. I listened to his senseless mutterings and wondered how one human being could allow himself to kill another. What does it feel like to watch a man die?

Then I tried to imagine what it would be like to have a gun pointed at one's face, and know that this is the end. What goes through a man's mind at such a moment? What does he think? Or does he think? What did the collaborator of Siedliszcze think when he felt the noose around his neck? God, I prayed, I hope I never find out!

DAYS TURNED INTO NIGHTS and nights into days. The trees had blossomed, borne their fruits, and were now bare. The wheat had matured and was ready to be harvested.

Thus the summer came to an end, and with it Mrs Pejzak's excursions to the Warsaw Ghetto. There was too much work to be done on the farm, and entering and leaving the ghetto had become costly and dangerous. On her last trip she was caught, arrested, and interrogated for hours; only a large bribe saved her from being transported to an unknown destination.

Furthermore, her transactions were not as profitable as they had been at the start, for by now the town of Siedliszcze had come back to life. Poles from the villages and other towns had moved into the emptied homes and stores, and again once a week, there was market day in town.

According to Mrs Pejzak and Genia, who drove in now and then, it was not the same. I tried to imagine what the town now looked like. Who occupies our room? Who looks through the window where I once peered waiting for my grandfather, the cobbler, to come home from his daily journey to the nearby villages in search of work and food? And the people who walk the streets, what do they look like? And what do they talk about? And what do they think?

I pictured German soldiers parading to and fro, their rifles hanging from their shoulders. I could see the officer, meticulously outfitted, strutting like a wound-up robot ... one ... two ... three ... automatically raising his left arm, bending it at the elbow, bringing his wrist to eye level and consulting his watch. The arm lowered ... one ... two ... three ... and pacing stiffly on. But here in the village, a few kilometres from town, not one German in sight.

One day upon returning from pasture I was surprised to find a young blond man of about eighteen or nineteen rummaging through a suitcase and extracting a lady's hat, which he handed to Genia. She showered him with kisses.

'Oh, Staszek! Just what I've always wanted,' and she quickly pranced over to the mirror to admire herself.

Next he produced a shawl from the same suitcase, handing it to Mrs Pejzak, who unfurled it, and said, 'You shouldn't have, Staszu. It looks so expensive,' and she took her turn hugging and planting kisses.

I stood in the doorway unobserved, assessing the guest. He was attired in a smart blue suit, polished shoes, white shirt, and blue tie. He was tanned, with closely clipped fingernails free of dirt. Next, a bottle and glasses found their way to the table. Mrs Pejzak poured, raised her glass, and saluted the guest, 'Thank you Lord Jesus for bringing my boy home safe and sound,' and the three downed the vodka.

It was only then that her son noticed me and looked inquisitively to his mother. She turned to see where he was focusing. 'This is Kubus.'

'Whose boy is he?' he asked.

'He's a good boy,' she answered and quickly went on to divert the attention from me. 'Oh how we missed you! Did those Huns work you hard?'

'Mother, you should see their farms. They have machines for everything. Even for milking cows. You wouldn't believe how well people live. Paved roads everywhere, and apple trees for all to pick to their heart's content. And almost everyone owns a bicycle.'

He blew his nose into a white handkerchief and not onto his sleeve, then continued, 'I tell you mother, this Hitler isn't all bad. When he's finished off the Yids, and puts the Pollacks in their place, he'll give us back our Ukraine. We'll be masters of our own house, at last.' Naturally, I didn't believe these tales of paved roads, free apples, high living, and especially the bicycle crap. But quickly my doubts were dispelled when he passed around photographs: the farm he worked on was indeed impressive. There was Staszek driving a tractor ... and Staszek sportily dressed on a bicycle, along a paved road flanked by fruit trees. And again Staszek with a smiling maiden, both on horseback.

Shameful thoughts invaded my mind, but hard as I tried to ignore them or drive them away, they refused to depart. Perhaps Staszek is right; Hitler is indeed a good man and is out to save the world; bringing machinery, paved roads, and bicycles to every human being on earth. That's good. If only he would let us share in this Garden of Eden.

Why, I questioned, is he exterminating us? There must be a reason. Perhaps Genia was right, it's God's will. We killed Jesus Christ and now the Lord has sent Hitler to avenge His only son's death. Or perhaps, I thought, it has nothing to do with Jesus!

Maybe we are inferior and stand in the way of progress; paved roads, free apples, and bicycles. Perhaps that's what it is.

We're not like other people at all. We speak a different language, have a different alphabet, celebrate different holidays, and eat different foods, so in fact we are different. Why is our Sabbath on Saturday instead of Sunday? And worst of all, why do we circumcise little boys and make them suffer? It's cruel. And why do we ... No. I mustn't think of that.

You'd better think of it ...

I can't, it's a lie.

Is it?

Sure it is.

It's true! Jews kill Christian children for Passover.

It's a lie!

But deep in my heart I felt ashamed, deeply ashamed for my doubts.

Food appeared on the table and Mrs Pejzak motioned for me to join them. Hesitantly, I sat down, fidgeting uncomfortably and staring at the ceiling as the others crossed themselves. When I cast my eyes down, Staszek's gaze was fixed upon me with a furrowed brow and narrowed eyes. Taking note of it, and attempting to preserve the happy occasion, Mrs Pejzak once more raised her glass.

'To your happy return, son,' and she and Genia downed theirs.

His eyes still glued on me, he slowly lifted his glass and sipped his drink. The spoon dropped from my shaking fingers.

Something outside now caught Staszek's attention. He stood up, and looking out the window, he said, as if to himself, 'While we're celebrating here, some crafty son of a bitch is helping himself to hay in our meadow.'

Genia peeked over his shoulder and laughed. 'That's Ivan. He is haying.'

'Ivan?' he turned to her. 'Who is Ivan?'

In the days that followed there were countless quarrels on account of Ivan and me. Mrs Pejzak reminded her son that she was still the boss in her house, and he countered by accusing her of the danger in which she placed not only herself and her family, but her surrounding neighbours as well.

She held him against her bosom. 'Dear Jesus! Holy Mother! Staszu, what have they done to you?'

When the bickering failed, he resorted to threats. Pointing at me, he raged, 'If he doesn't leave, I'll tie him to the horse's tail and deliver him to the Gestapo personally.' Mrs Pejzak rushed to my side and hugged me protectively. 'The boy stays. He's part of this family,' she glared at him scornfully.

Ivan offered to leave, but Genia's crying and her mother's pleas stopped him. Perhaps I too should at least make a move to avert a family tragedy! But what if they don't stop me? Then what? Where would I go?

'Go and inform your Gestapo friends,' she hissed. 'We're not afraid.'

Jumping on the horse, Staszek galloped off in a flurry.

The rest of the day we spent in torment, waiting for Staszek's return or the Gestapo's arrival. Mrs Pejzak assured us that her son's threats were hollow.

I was not so sure, but I reasoned that by informing he would also implicate his own family. Nevertheless, the outcome was not yet clear. Who knows, I thought, what human beings are capable of?

Late in the evening Staszek came back, leaving the tired horse for me to attend to. He strode into the house, sat down at the table, and ate his cold supper. He didn't utter a word, nor we to him. The silence was deafening.

Not surprisingly, the Sunday get-togethers with Ivan's compatriots stopped.

Mrs Pejzak continued to stand up to her son, but I sensed that she was now frightened of him. On occasion, she referred to him as a fascist, a traitor, and for sure not the son she once carried in her belly.

'Your father would turn in his grave if he knew you now,' she told him.

Staszek screamed at me, shouted orders, and called me every despicable name with the word 'Jew' in it.

With Ivan he was more tolerant. He rarely spoke to him, and mostly ignored him.

The other Ivan, the one we called Vanja, and some of the others, I saw only fleetingly in the fields, but none dared to come into the house, or even close to the farmyard.

Even in spite of Mrs Pejzak's firm resistance, Staszek had indeed succeeded in changing things.

IT HAD RAINED THAT DAY; heavy, merciless rain poured down from a leaden sky, and in late afternoon it stopped as suddenly as it had begun. The clouds moved swiftly, breaking up into smaller puffs, and eventually disappeared; all that was left was a grey, even-coloured sky. It was too late to take the cows to pasture so Mrs Pejzak told me to join her and the others in the potato field.

For me this was a holiday, and a rainy day was like a day of rest. I used to pray for rain, heavy rain, torrential rain. If only it would rain forever, never stopping, and then I would never have to take my two mischievous cows to pasture.

Digging potatoes was a reprieve. We'd walk along the rows, yank out the plants, dig into the earth with our fingers, and scoop up the golden beauties from the ever-giving earth.

Staszek worked faster than any of us; when he'd completed two rows, we'd still be on the first, with me at the end. 'This is hard work, eh? Not like selling herring, is it, Jew boy?'

Suddenly a shot rang out and a bullet whistled above our heads. We stopped work, and looked about. Another shot was heard. 'Probably one of your comrades got drunk,' sneered Staszek, but Ivan ignored him. Soon another shot, then another was heard, and then Staszek pointed, 'Look! Over there!'

In the distance a line of silhouetted soldiers were coming over the hill towards us.

'He's right. It's our boys,' said Ivan.

'Whoever it is, it doesn't concern us. Just continue working,' said Mrs Pejzak, and so we did, though the bullets were now flying over our heads, and the armed men in the distance were moving ever closer.

And when they were almost upon us, it became evident that they were German soldiers and Ukrainian Black Shirts, fully equipped for battle.

'Quick Ivan, you must hide,' warned Mrs Pejzak, and, dragging him by the arm, she headed for the farmyard.

I ran after them, Genia following. 'Mrs Pejzak,' I called after her, 'shouldn't I hide as well?'

'I'll tell them you're my son.'

In a corner of the barn Ivan removed some rubbish, lifted a trap door, kissed Genia, and jumped into a hole that I never knew existed. Mrs Pejzak shut the trap door and, with great urgency, we piled a mound of our freshly dug potatoes on top.

By the time we emerged from the barn we were confronted by a group of soldiers approaching the farmyard, Staszek sharing a laugh with them.

What if he tells them who I am? I'll deny it. But if they pull down my pants? Then what? The rabbi who circumcised me flashed through my mind. I imagined an old man with a long beard and black caftan, holding a large, razor-sharp knife in his hand. I hated him, despised him. He was the cause of my predicament.

Mrs Pejzak faked a welcoming smile, while Genia busied herself feeding the chickens, as if the soldiers' presence was of no consequence.

Nevertheless, as they entered the farmyard, Mrs Pejzak panicked, and whispered in a trembling voice, 'Run, Kubus! Hide.'

My heart beat like a drum and in a split second I surveyed the surroundings. It was too late to find a safe haven in the barn, in the house, and in the farmyard. I opened the picket gate that led to the back fields. I thought I heard one of the soldiers calling after me but I didn't dare respond. I just kept walking.

At any second I will be pierced with a bullet in my back. I could see myself falling into an everlasting sleep. Where will they bury me?

I reached the back of the house and, to my dismay, found a German soldier armed with grenades, as well as a cocked automatic rifle. He was tiptoeing near the back window and peering inside. I swallowed hard and forced a smile, and began to whistle. He didn't even glance at me. I continued along a footpath dividing a field of wheat from a field of alfalfa. Plucking a stem of wheat, I stuck it between my teeth and continued further and further away from the house towards the river.

Bullets zoomed past me. But I kept my eyes focused ahead and walked at a slow steady pace, never looking back.

I'm safe, I concluded, the farm is far behind me. Then I hurled myself into a wheat field and lay panting. My heart was beating so loud that the vibration shook my whole body. The slightest sound of a bird or a field mouse made me jump as I imagined a German aiming a gun at me. Any moment the expelled bullet will penetrate my heart.

Why are you shaking like that? You'd better take hold of yourself, an inner voice advised. That's right, nothing to be afraid of, just lie still. All this too will pass. The soldiers will leave and you'll go back to the house.

I heard voices, German voices. It's your imagination, you fool!

But they kept coming closer and closer, and soon I was able to decipher certain words. I've got to see who's there.

Lie still you idiot.

I raised my head.

Below, where the river flowed peacefully, a German battalion was crossing the narrow water, making a game of jumping over. One plunged into the stream, eliciting convulsive laughter from the rest. Those already on this side were heading in my direction. I looked left and right and saw soldiers fanned out along the bank of the river as far as my eyes could see.

They moved ever so slowly, methodically searching every stack of hay, stabbing every bush with their mounted bayonets.

This is the end, I am trapped. They'll question me, look into my eyes, and see a little Jew boy staring back at them. But just to be sure, they'll pull down my trousers, and laugh. That will be the last sound I'll ever hear.

Not far off, a horse was grazing and a plough lay idle in the middle of a partly ploughed field. A wagon was nearby. I approached, fearing not only the oncoming enemy but also the horse.

'Please, horsey, don't kick me. Be kind,' I pleaded, and reached out and touched him. He didn't flinch. 'That's a good horse.' I patted him on his forehead, then fetched his harness, and managed to put it on. I led him to the plough, hitched him to it, gripped the handles, and yelled, 'Giddy up.'

Ploughing had looked easy enough when I observed others do it, but now I realised it was indeed a skill to be learned.

The horse began to trot, but the plough slid along the top of the ground, refusing to submerge. I then pushed the handles with all my strength, forcing the blade into the earth. It went too deep; the plough keeled over. The horse stopped. The soldiers were almost upon me. I backed up the horse and started again.

Miraculously, the plough moved along at the proper depth. Trying to appear nonchalant and whistling Vanja's song, I walked behind the plough, snapping the reins whenever the horse hesitated.

Although I didn't raise my head, I could see from the side of my eye a multitude of gazing eyes surrounding me.

'You!' a German voice thundered. I continued to bark orders and swear at the poor horse. After a few more angry shouts in German, I brought the horse to a standstill and looked up, feigning surprise at their presence.

A fat-faced sweating one approached me; others followed behind him. 'What are you?' he asked suspiciously in German.

Even though I did understand him, I answered him in Polish, 'I don't understand.'

'Are you Ukrainian?' he asked, looking at my dark hair.

Again I responded in Polish, 'I don't understand, I speak only Polish.'

He looked into my dark eyes, 'Are you a Jew?' he asked with a grin. Again I played stupid. 'Do you know of any Russians hiding in the village?' he continued to probe.

This time I resorted to an idiotic laugh.

'Look at this imbecile!' he remarked to his buddies. 'Laughing at himself.' And they moved on.

'Giddy up,' I called out to the horse and resumed ploughing.

I didn't dare lift my eyes from the plough until much later when I had finished the entire field.

There was no one to be seen, but shots could be heard coming from the direction of the village. I set the exhausted and confused horse free and patted him affectionately.

'Thank you, horsey, I'll never forget you for this.' The horse snorted and, a few paces later, relieved himself. Then he trotted to a grassy area and began to graze.

I lay down on the ground but, feeling vulnerable, I walked to a stack of wheat and burrowed my way in. Soon enough I realised it afforded no protection against a stray bullet. Then I spotted my sanctuary – the deserted wagon.

I hoisted myself onto the rear, my feet dangling between the two back wheels. I surveyed the landscape, matter-of-factly reclined, turned on my stomach, and wiggled to the centre.

Should a bullet come my way, I'll be safe. But soon it became evident that the wagon's wooden sides offered no defence. But by now I couldn't think of anywhere else to hide, so I closed my eyes and reconciled myself to fate. If I was hit, I didn't want to see the bullet, and each time I heard one whistle by I'd wonder if I was still alive.

At long last when the shooting came to an end, I opened my eyes, raised my head, and saw that night had fallen. Little stars were shimmering in the sky and all around was darkness. I could hear the horse still grazing but couldn't see him. In the distance, flickering naphtha lamps could be seen.

I climbed down. Perhaps what is before me is not the village of Kulik, but the land of the dead. I took a few steps.

'I'm alive!' I said aloud. Perhaps I'd better wait. The Germans are probably still in the village. Maybe they've discovered Ivan's hiding hole. What about Vanja? Where did he go? What should I do? Wait here? Why isn't Genia looking for me? I know why. They've found Ivan and shot everyone. No! They would never find Ivan. Poor Vanja, what if they caught him? Not only is he an escapee, but probably Jewish to boot. How could they tell? I wonder if he's circumcised!

I waited patiently, listening to the sounds of the night: a dog barking here and there, a wild rabbit running through the field. It was cold and I shivered in my thin cotton trousers and light shirt. I had to find out what had happened. I began to walk briskly, finding my way more by instinct than by vision.

The small flickering light of the naphtha lamp guided me to the back window of the house. Someone is home; I encouraged myself, and peeked in.

Except for Mrs Pejzak asleep on the cot, there was no one else inside. Treading softly, I walked to the front and opened the door. The squeaking of the rusted hinges propelled Mrs Pejzak to a sitting position and she yelped.

She rubbed her eyes, 'Your supper's on the stove,' and she went back to sleep.

I had forgotten about eating, but now I realised how hungry I was. On the stove I found some cold potato patties left from the day before. I poured myself a glass of buttermilk and sat.

Where are the others? I'd better not ask. I looked at Mrs Pejzak turning restlessly.

By the time I was into my fourth potato patty, the sound of an approaching motorcar made me jump out of my seat, and I ran to the door. My intention was to head back to the field, but it was too late. The car had come to a stop in the farmyard and a Ukrainian Black Shirt got out.

I stopped in my tracks, smiled, and casually returned to finish my meal.

The Black Shirt entered, walking briskly, the sound of his leather boots striking terror in me. He looked around the room, then, with the riding crop in his hand, he whipped Mrs Pejzak's behind. She jumped up, swearing.

'Where's the boss of the house?' he asked in Ukrainian.

'I'm the boss here,' replied Mrs Pejzak.

'I mean the man of the house,' he said, his face expressionless. 'Your husband.'

'My husband is dead. I have a son,' said Mrs Pejzak.

'Where is he?' he snapped.

'He's in the field. What is it you want with him?'

'Get him!' he snapped.

Mrs Pejzak struggled to get to her feet.

If she leaves, his attention will surely focus on me. I jumped up and offered, 'I'll fetch Staszek,' not waiting for a reply.

I dashed out and into the barn, untied the cows, and drove them to pasture in the dark of the night. As I passed the potato field I heard Staszek and Genia conversing.

'Staszek!' I called out.

'Is that you, Kubus?' asked Genia.

'Yes,' I answered, and then one of the cows mooed.

'Are those our cows?' Staszek's angry voice bellowed.

'Yes,' I answered meekly.

'Where in hell are you taking the cows at this time of night?' he growled.

'To pasture,' I yelled back. 'They've been in all day; some fresh grass will do them good.'

'You crazy herring merchant, take the cows back,' he snarled.

'It was your mother's idea,' I lied.

'She's as crazy as you are,' he shot back.

'By the way, Staszek, there's someone at the house waiting to talk to you. Right away.'

I lashed the cows again and again, and ran behind them and when I finally stopped, I didn't know on whose land they were grazing, or if they were snacking on grass or perhaps nibbling on someone's cabbage heads.

I clutched my frail body, trembling from the night's chill.

Much later I heard Genia's voice, 'Kubus! Kubus!' Perhaps it's a trick! I knew Genia would never willingly betray me. But what if she was forced to? Maybe the Black Shirt is treading quietly behind her, waiting for the sound of my voice. 'Kubus! Where are you?' She was closer now. The chewing and mooing of the cows finally led her to me. 'Kubus, why didn't you answer?'

How could I tell her what I had been thinking? 'Is he gone?' I asked.

'Yes, don't be afraid,' she consoled me.

'What did he want with Staszek?'

'A lot of questions, that's all.'

We started driving the cows back, their bellies now swollen. 'Did they find Ivan?' I asked, afraid of the answer.

'Let's hope he's still all right in there,' she said.

When we returned, Mrs Pejzak and Staszek were in the barn feverishly removing the potatoes over Ivan's hiding place. They opened the trap door, and there, in a hole hardly big enough for one to squat, was Ivan, unconscious.

We pulled him out, poured vodka down his throat, and a few moments later he revived. Soon he was his old self, lying in the hay, embracing Genia.

THE FOLLOWING DAY WAS SUNNY and warm, the sky was clear, and the sun covered the village and its surrounding fields with bright rays of light.

I started to take the cows to pasture but Mrs Pejzak stopped me. That morning a neighbour have brought news that the fascists had spent the night in the village hunting and interrogating. They had found many fugitives in hiding, and had killed some in the fields who were trying to escape.

I sat at the table but I couldn't hear the conversation, for my mind wandered. Weeks and months have passed and my Uncle Moishe has not shown up. What has become of him? Vanja, my friend Vanja. Is it possible that he is ... No! I'd better not think of it.

My father, God only knows his fate. And my mother, Josele, and my Uncle Shepsel; they are lost. But why am I so sure? I should not write them off so easily. There's still hope. I've got to have hope.

Ivan sat quietly on a cot listening to consoling words from Genia. I noted his pale face. Does he feel the same as I do? I caught Staszek's gaze and felt uneasy.

Suddenly there was a knock on the door. We froze and looked at each other. There was nowhere to run and hide now. A revolver suddenly appeared in Ivan's hand and he stationed himself at the side of the door.

How daring! Could I do that?

He motioned for one of us to open the door. A trembling Staszek couldn't take his eyes off Ivan's gun. Genia covered her mouth with her hands to prevent herself from screaming.

The scene reminded me so much of the cowboy tales told to me by my Uncle Shepsel. But somehow it wasn't quite the same. The excitement and adventure were missing. I wasn't thrilled, I was terrified.

The knock was repeated, now a little louder. Mrs Pejzak opened the door with quivering hands. I expected to see a German or a Black Shirt, suspiciously looking at me, 'You're a Jew!'

'No!' I imagined my answer.

'Then pull your pants down.' And at that moment Ivan would squeeze the trigger. The soldier would drop to the floor, his blood gushing like water from a fountain. And then ...

A man with a heavy moustache and large bulging eyes stood in the doorway. He removed a straw hat from his head and pressed it against his chest. Then with his sleeve, he wiped the perspiration from his almost bald pate, and in a stuttering voice said, 'Praised be Jesus Christ.'

'For all the ages. Amen,' replied the Pejzaks in unison.

Mrs Pejzak rushed to the threshold, blocking him from entering further.

'I've been sent by the reeve,' he stopped, cleared his throat, and asked for a glass of water. Genia handed it to him; he swallowed it in one gulp, and then continued, 'You're to come to church at noon.'

'Why? Is it Sunday?' asked Mrs Pejzak.

'It's an order from them. Those who don't show will pay with their lives.' And he departed, running to the next farm.

Mrs Pejzak slammed the door, Ivan lowered his revolver, and I began to worry anew.

It was immediately decided that Ivan would return to his usual place, and the rest of us would go to church.

Staszek washed and dressed for the occasion as if he was going to a wedding.

Solemnly, as if marching behind a coffin, we left the farmyard. When we reached the main road we saw other families heading in the same direction. Unexpectedly, Mrs Pejzak pushed me gently.

'Kubus, go and hide somewhere, my child.'

'Where?'

'Wherever the good Lord Jesus will lead you. Go child.' She turned to catch up with her offspring.

Gazing at their backs and feeling abandoned, I thought of heading to the nearby forest. But I knew the forest would be the first place they would comb for partisans. I thought of the fields and considered running there, but again I decided against it. I looked around and there was not a soul to be seen. Where then?

'I have to get off the open road,' I said out loud, and headed back to the farm.

In the yard the chickens welcomed me with their cackling. How I envied them! They didn't have to run. Perhaps I could hide with them! I darted into the small putrid chicken coop, covered with droppings. It offered no concealment.

Next I hurried into the house intending to hide under the bed. But that was too obvious. Scanning the room my eyes rested on the trap door leading to the attic. With the help of a ladder I climbed up.

I had never explored there before. For a moment I forgot my reason for venturing there now. Then I remembered; I debated if I should hide here or perhaps there, or under the pile of grain, or inside the trunk ... Yes, that's a good idea. I clambered in and closed the lid on top of me. A terrible musty odour penetrated my lungs, but I was safe.

Then I remembered the ladder. How am I to get rid of it?

Quickly I scrambled down, left the house, and headed for the barn. Upon seeing me, the cows lowed as if complaining that I had neglected to take them to pasture. Perhaps in the hay? I'll bury myself. But what if they probe with their bayonets, or worse, set the barn on fire?

Passing the mound of potatoes, I envied Ivan. He was safe in that hole. I can't waste much more time; they may be on their way this very minute. Maybe even inside the farmyard already.

As I shut the door behind me, I saw my shelter staring me

in the face. On the opposite side of the farmyard was the root cellar: a deep rectangular dugout, covered with a thatched roof. It resembled a miniature house with only the roof showing, and its walls were deep into the ground. In the summer it functioned as a cooler, to keep milk, cheese, and butter from spoiling, but its main purpose was to store potatoes during the winter months. Luck would have it that it was empty.

I slid through the opening, feet first, and jumped down, squatting in a corner.

The ground was chilly and damp, and the air was pungent. I studied the earth beneath my feet, the walls around me, and gazed at countless minute bugs and insects busily engaged in their own safe world. I envied them, for they were free.

If only I could be a little bug! A small ugly insect, in fact anything at all but a Jew. If only I could be a cow, a horse, a bird in the trees, or a frog in the pond! Anything at all – I'd have a better chance of survival.

Why did God create Jews anyway? There seems to be no reason for our existence. I travelled from one thought to another, not daring to move at all, not even to brush off a fly when one landed on my nose. I was glued to the earth.

Outside I could hear the birds chirp and sing sweetly; the crows cawed in the fields and the cows in the barn mooed now and then, and the rooster gave a loud cock-a-doodle-doo. Periodically I heard the bark of a dog somewhere in the distance, but otherwise it was quiet.

What must have been hours later, the sound of approaching footsteps reached my ears. Perhaps I'm only imagining, or perhaps the Pejzaks have returned!

I listened, but didn't move. The footsteps came closer, and closer, and then I heard voices. Two soldiers were conversing in German. Their every step was like a gunshot.

The barn door opened. Silence. Then their voices. The door to the house opened ... footsteps running up the ladder ... some other sound ... then their voices again coming from the farmyard. The door to the chicken coop opened, more conversation ... laughter ... more footsteps ... now far away ... now closer ... closer ... closer ... and to my horror the shadow of a soldier fell into my dungeon and crept up the wall as he bent down peering in.

I could hear him breathing. Does he see me? He must see me. Even if he doesn't, he must hear my heart pounding like a drum. The shadow shifted ever so slightly. What is he waiting for? Why doesn't he order me to come out? Perhaps he's afraid! Perhaps he can't hear my heart, after all! Wait a minute; I know what he's up to: he'll simply throw in a grenade. If he does, I'll catch it, and toss it right back. I've got to be on guard.

Oh, God, what am I to do? I have to sneeze. I could feel it coming. Why doesn't he throw the grenade and be over with it?

'Something there?' asked the other.

'Just bugs,' came the reply.

'Let's get to the next shit hole.'

The shadow straightened itself and disappeared. I heard footsteps moving away, and then silence. I swallowed my sneeze.

Why did he leave? Surely he must have sensed that someone was here. Perhaps he mistook me for a partisan and was as frightened of me as I was of him! Or maybe they haven't left. It's a trap. They are trying to lure me into the open. I have to deceive them to the end.

By now my knees were giving way. Soon I couldn't feel them at all, as if they had been disconnected from the rest of my body. I was numb. Perhaps the German has thrown the grenade and I am dead! That's why I can't feel my legs. If so, then there's no reason to fear death. It's quite sudden and painless.

Alive or dead, I remained in the same position and lost all sense of time and sound. I heard nothing, saw nothing, and eventually thought of nothing.

'Kubus! Kubus! Where are you?' Genia's sweet voice woke me from my deadened state. Then I heard Mrs Pejzak's voice calling, but still I didn't answer. Then Genia was sobbing. 'They must have found him, Mama, they've found him! He's probably dead,' she cried hysterically.

'So they found him,' said Staszek.

I attempted to stand but my legs kept buckling under me. I crawled over to the opening, and saw that night had fallen.

'Holy Mother, Kubus is alive!' cried Genia.

'My prayers have been answered. Jesus saved you,' said Mrs Pejzak.

'Afraid, eh? I bet you shit your pants,' laughed Staszek, but no one laughed with him.

Later inside the house, after Staszek had drunk too much, he turned to his mother and, pointing at Ivan and me, he said, 'Mother, tell them what they did to the Pundiks.'

A distraught and weeping Mrs Pejzak looked at her son with disgust, 'Staszek!'

'I'll tell them,' and he picked up the bottle of vodka.

'Shut up!' said Genia.

He emptied what was left in the bottle into his mouth and, ignoring Genia, addressed us directly. 'They cut Pundik's tongue out; pulled out his teeth one by one with pliers; ripped the skin off his body; pulled out his fingernails and toenails. Then they gouged his eyes out one at a time with a hot iron.'

'Stop! Stop! I beg you,' sobbed his mother.

But Staszek was just warming up and relishing it. 'They locked his family in their house and set it on fire. God, they screamed! We were forced to watch. Those who refused were shot on the spot.'

Mrs Pejzak wept uncontrollably.

By now good and drunk, her son collapsed in a chair, covered his eyes with his hands, and sobbed hysterically. 'That's what they'll do to us when they find a Jew and a communist here.'

Ivan, who had sat silently throughout, now said quietly, as if to himself, 'I'll leave.'

Mrs Pejzak threw her arms around him, holding him tightly, and cried, 'How can I let you go? You're like a son to me. Better than a son, much better than my own.' And she continued to weep until the naphtha in the lamp burned out.

The next day we received reports of the death of Nicolai, Dmitri, Boris, Juri, Sergei, Sasza, and countless others, but there was no word of Vanja. We listened with heavy hearts to the way our friends had met death: some in the fields, others in the forest defending themselves to their last bullet, and still others found hiding in an attic or haystack.

I wanted to cry, but hard as I tried, I couldn't coax the tears to flow. Sadly I recalled the many Sundays that those who were now dead had sat at our table and brought a smidgeon of joy into our lives. But where was Vanja? Was he safe? Or ... His song rang through my mind.

In the evening, an old woman who lived at the edge of the forest paid us a visit. 'One of them was shot in the bushes near my house,' she informed in a shrill voice. 'He's still lying there.' And now a silly grin crossed her face, as if she took delight in bringing us this sordid news. With much gusto she proceeded to relate how a bullet had struck the runaway

Russian in the back, how he had limped for a while, returned the fire, and finally fell.

Staszek turned his back on her and, since it wasn't safe for Ivan to be seen, Genia and I followed the woman. On the way, I prayed silently and begged God that it shouldn't be Vanja lying dead in the bushes. But God ignored me, or perhaps He didn't understand me, or else I didn't pray hard enough, for when we reached the body, we recognised the face with the hooked nose.

We dug, but the soil was hard, full of rocks and tree roots, as if the earth was refusing to receive him.

Somehow we managed and laid our friend Vanja to rest. Genia knelt, crossed herself, and silently prayed. I thought of joining her, but I didn't know the prayer for the occasion. And at the same time I wondered if there was, after all, anyone in heaven who listened.

And so I just stared at the freshly dug grave in silence and thought how accurately Vanja's song had predicted his fate.

There, far in the valley,
There a nightingale sings a song.

But where is the nightingale? I looked about, hoping there would be one. On the branch of a young poplar tree, I spotted a bird. I wasn't at all sure if it was a nightingale, and it probably wasn't, but I took it to be one. The tiny bird hopped from branch to branch and finally stopped and chirped, but I imagined that it sang. How could Vanja have known?

The next day Ivan left. He wore the collaborator's lavish attire. Under the coat bulged his rifle.

'Going somewhere?' I asked as he passed me in the pasture.

He stopped. 'I'm going away for good, Kubus.'

'Where to?'

'I don't know.' He offered me his hand. 'Goodbye.'

'Goodbye,' I answered, and followed his gait across the field towards the river until he disappeared.

The countryside was deserted. A cool breeze blew. Gone were my friends forever; gone were their songs, their stories, and their promise to find my father. Only Vanja's song remained.

There far in the valley,
There a nightingale sings a song;
I'm a guy on foreign soil
I've forgotten my friends.

TWO

In the late afternoon of a cold autumn day, I caught sight of an approaching figure in the distance. The walk was familiar, the feet shuffling rather than walking. It couldn't be! I thought. And yet I wanted it to be ... How I hoped that it would indeed be my Uncle Moishe! How wonderful it would be to have someone, anyone!

Perhaps it is Moishe! But once the figure comes closer it will be some stranger. How many times before had I imagined someone in the distance to be Moishe, only to be disappointed?

I was so accustomed to this that on this chilly day as I sat on the grass, my legs crossed under me, my eyes on the approaching stranger, I refused even to stand up. And yet, the walk was so much like his. Unmistakably Moishe, my Uncle Moishe! But why risk being hurt again?

I sat. The figure came closer and now stood in front of me. I looked at my Uncle Moishe, barefoot, shabbily attired. I wanted to jump up and kiss him, hug him; I wanted to laugh, sing, but I simply sat there, choking with onrushing tears.

He sat down beside me, and we started to cry. I wanted to stop the tears; I tried desperately, but they were out of control.

Finally when there were no more tears to be had, we sat looking at each other, as if in a trance.

'I knew you'd come looking for me, Moishe,' I said, to break the long silence.

'I would have come sooner,' he answered, 'but they wouldn't give me a day off.'

'I'm so happy to see you, Uncle Moishe. You'll have to come more often and I'll visit you.'

Moishe nodded, forcing a smile. 'Don't worry, Jankele, everything will be all right.'

'When do you have to leave?' I asked.

'Oh, not until later, maybe not even till tomorrow.'

'Good!' I cheered. 'Then you'll sleep over.'

'Will they mind?'

'I'll speak to Mrs Pejzak.'

And she readily agreed.

It felt good to have my Uncle Moishe beside me in the barn. We lay awake for a long time reminiscing of our days in Warsaw.

In the morning we ate garlic soup for breakfast. Moishe thanked Mrs Pejzak for her hospitality and kissed her hand when saying goodbye. She giggled and invited him to drop in whenever he was free.

Moishe accompanied me as I drove the cows to pasture, and when we got there, we both sat down on the wet dew, and Moishe pulled out a deck of playing cards and entertained me with some amazing card tricks. After exhausting his repertoire, we got into composing silly limericks:

Hitler is a shit,
He is really bad,
Like a fly,

He will die,
We'll piss on his head.
Cut him into pieces,
Even chop his dink,
The dogs will eat,
The pile of shit,
While we dance and sing.

'Are you still here?' asked Genia, looking at Moishe when she brought my lunch.

'I'm going,' he answered.

We shared the food, and after Genia left, I urged him to leave.

'What's the matter, Jankele, you're tired of me?'

'I wish you would never have to go, Moishe,' I said, 'but I'm afraid they'll punish you for being late.'

'So I'll be punished,' he shrugged.

'Please, Uncle Moishe, go. Tell me where you are and I'll come visit you next week.' He didn't respond.

Late in the afternoon he still hadn't made a move, and finally, he said, 'The truth is, Jankele, I have nowhere to go.'

'What about your job?'

'They don't want me.'

'But why? What did you do?'

'Nothing, Jankele. They're afraid. But don't worry, I'll find another job, maybe even around here. This way we'll see each other more often.'

'Uncle Moishe,' I hugged him, 'that would be wonderful.'

'Do you think Mrs Pejzak could use another hand?'

'I'll ask her,' I said, and I ran off.

Mrs Pejzak listened to my sales pitch; what a good worker my uncle was and what big muscles he had, and after all he was thirteen and capable of greater tasks than I. Mrs Pejzak was amused.

'We'll find something for him to do.'

'Oh! Mrs Pejzak, thank you, thank you.' I jogged back to the field. 'Moishe! Moishe!' I yelled, leaping into the air.

He lifted me onto his shoulders, just the way he did on my first days in Warsaw when showing me the sights.

'Giddy up, horsey!' I yelled, and he galloped around the field until he fell from exhaustion and I on top of him. We rolled on the grass and laughed. The cows stopped grazing and stared at us.

How good it felt not to be alone!

EVERY DAY ANOTHER PLOT of land was cleared of its crop, and now the fields were bare, waiting for the spring. The trees shed their leaves, and the winds grew fierce. On some days it was even too cold to take the cows to pasture.

Mrs Pejzak was pleased with most of her harvest but she complained bitterly about the cabbage. She said, 'There's no justice in this world. Across the river a son of a bitch has a wonderful crop of cabbage, every head as big as a pumpkin.' Staszek looked at her critically and she turned on him. 'Don't look at me like that; I'm only saying what nice cabbage there is to be had, and if you want cabbage soup this winter it wouldn't hurt to help ourselves to some of it.'

On a moonless night we set out with burlap bags under our arms and long, sharp knives in our hands. We could barely see where we were going and silently had to feel our way along, without as much as a whisper.

Staszek, Moishe, and I let our knives loose at the cabbage, and after three trips the patch lay bare.

In the house, Mrs Pejzak and Genia were shredding and pressing the cabbage into barrels so as to immediately obliterate any evidence. Drunk with victory, Mrs Pejzak slapped our backs. 'This is only the beginning.'

From the start I was aware that what we were doing was wrong, but there was a certain excitement about it that I savoured, and so I looked forward to this diversion and hoped it would continue. And it did.

Our next raid took us to an isolated property not far from our farm. When we got back, I was too late to go to sleep. Instead, we sat at the window and looked across the fields at the neighbour's ravaged cabbage patch.

Once the sun came up, a figure appeared there, then another. We heard conversation. Then more people came, and later we heard a woman wailing.

What if they find out? What will happen to us?

At the end of the day when I saw a man bringing his horse and wagon to a halt in our farmyard, I was terrified.

'How is life treating you, Abraham?' He smiled at me as he descended from the wagon and entered the house. Later Mrs Pejzak led him into the barn. There was some haggling; he gave her some bills, loaded one of our pigs onto his cart, and, snapping the reigns, drove off.

'Why are you shaking so?' Mrs Pejzak asked.

'I thought he came looking for his cabbage.'

'What cabbage?' asked Mrs Pejzak, straight faced.

'The cabbage we snatched,' I said innocently.

'Kubus!' exclaimed Mrs Pejzak. 'What are you saying? What cabbage?'

'But, Mrs Pejzak,' I protested, 'the cabbage in the barrels.'

'That's sauerkraut from our garden, Kubus. Thank Jesus, we had a very good crop.'

DRESSED IN A SHORT LEATHER COAT with a scarf around his neck, Mr Kowal's bachelor son was making his way towards our farm. Looking at him reminded me how cold it was, and that winter was on its way.

He had never been particularly warm towards me, but friendly enough. Now as he entered the farmyard he avoided greeting me. 'Where's the boss?' he asked, without looking at me.

'In the house,' I said.

From inside I heard voices, low unintelligible voices. Shortly after, he departed without even a glance in my direction.

When I entered the house I found Mrs Pejzak seated at the table, with teary eyes. She pulled me to her and held me tightly against her.

'Dear Jesus,' she murmured. 'Please guide me. What shall I do?' She released her hold, bit her tongue, and broke down crying hysterically.

Frightened, I ran out to the field where Moishe and Staszek were spreading manure. 'Moishe! Moishe!' I screamed, and fell into his arms.

'What has happened?' Staszek asked, alarmed.

'It's your mother.'

Staszek dropped the pitchfork and ran to the house. We followed, and found his mother kneeling in front of the gold-framed Holy Mary. Mrs Pejzak stood, dried her eyes with the end of her apron, and only then the cause of her sorrow unfolded in broken sentences, interrupted with more tears.

The Germans had issued a decree that commanded every farmer employing a Jew to deliver the Jew to the Gestapo within forty-eight hours. Anyone disobeying the order would be shot, together with his family and ten surrounding neighbours.

Now I realised the Kowal's concern; they lived only a few properties away.

When she had finished, Mrs Pejzak joined our stony silence. And that's how the rest of that particular day was spent.

Moishe and I avoided looking at each other. Genia had heard the news in the village, and when she came home, she too was numb. None of us had an appetite that evening and so, in deadly silence, we went to sleep.

When we arrived for breakfast in the morning, Mrs Pejzak was mending my coat.

Seeing it now, I recalled the day my mother had taken me to the tailor to have it made for Passover. I must have been about seven years old. It had been a great occasion. Now three years later, the sleeves were too short and the coat so tight I couldn't connect the buttons to the button holes. Seeing the problem, Mrs Pejzak solved it by fetching a length of rope and tied it around my waist.

'They would have to kill me before I'd lead you to your deaths,' she said, 'but at the same time I have to think of my own family.'

'When do we have to leave?' asked Moishe without emotion.

'Right away,' came the reply. 'I've prepared food for you.' And she handed me a sack containing a loaf of bread, a bottle of milk, and two chunks of pork fat.

'Where should we go?' I asked.

She didn't face me. 'I don't know. You'll have to decide.'

I wanted to cry but then I looked at Moishe. He was calm and collected. He has a plan, I thought, and so I too calmed down. I said goodbye to Genia. She grabbed me and kissed me on the cheek, then fell onto the cot, stifling the sound of her sorrow. Mrs Pejzak walked us outside.

'What are your plans?' she inquired.

'We'll see,' Moishe said, smiling. And I marvelled at his confidence.

'Listen to me,' she said. 'I've done everything in my power. If I could, I'd keep the two of you for as long as you'd want to stay, but what can I do? Your presence here endangers the entire village. Your tragedy is not of our making. It's the Germans who have brought this upon you. Your fate is sealed. Why don't you go to Chelm? There's a ghetto there. You'll be safer among your own. If you wander around these parts, sooner or later they'll find you and then you'll implicate us. Give yourselves up, for our sake.'

I should have been appalled by her insensitivity, but I wasn't. I understood the overpowering instinct for survival; nevertheless, I *was* sickened. That same Mrs Pejzak, who had fed me, bathed me, who had once even told me that she thought of me as her own son, that same woman was now ready to sacrifice me.

Moishe listened attentively, thanked her, and then to my astonishment said, 'I think that's a good idea. We'll go to Chelm.'

'No!' I jumped in. 'We will not give ourselves up.'

'Don't you understand, Kubus ...?' Mrs Pejzak pleaded.

'No! We are going to live!'

She turned to Moishe. 'Take care of him, you're older.'

We started down the back road.

'May the good Lord Jesus look after you,' I heard her whisper, but I didn't turn back. As we passed Staszek in the field, he pretended not to see us, as though we were invisible.

The day was extremely cold and we shivered in our rags. Moishe had acquired an old, torn suit jacket that didn't protect him from the bitter wind. The fields were almost deserted and the naked trees played a melancholy symphony as they bent in the wind.

'She's right!' said Moishe. 'There's nowhere for us to go except to Chelm.'

'No!' I protested. 'If we give ourselves up they'll kill us.'

We had reached the river. Several boys bundled in heavy garments were sitting around a glowing fire baking potatoes. Their cows were close by, enjoying the last blades of grass before the snow. One of the cowherds recognised me and invited us to join them. We sat down, warmed ourselves, and later filled our stomachs with freshly baked potatoes, washing them down with the milk Mrs Pejzak had given us.

We cherished every second by the fire, knowing it would end only too soon. At dusk the boys drove their cows home saying, 'See you tomorrow.'

How I envied them for having somewhere, anywhere, to go! We tried to keep the fire alive, but soon night fell and we began to look for a place to sleep. How cosy and warm Mrs Pejzak's barn seemed now! What we wouldn't have given to sleep there that night!

'Look, Jankele!' exclaimed Moishe, pointing to a haystack. We burrowed our way in and fell asleep.

In the morning, we waited anxiously for the cowherds to arrive, but hung around in vain. It was too cold even for the cows. We sat in the haystack, savouring the remains of our provisions and looking across the naked fields without a soul in sight. Even from this distance, we could see the Pejzak farm, and now and then we caught glimpses of Mrs Pejzak, Genia, and Staszek.

To break the monotony, we busied ourselves with more

Hitler limericks. Moishe entertained me with card tricks and I serenaded him on the flute Wojciech had given me. At the end of the third day, our stomachs growling from hunger and our bodies stiff from the cold, Moishe suddenly announced, 'Wait here.'

'Where are you going?'

'I'll be back shortly.'

'Let me go with you, Uncle Moishe.'

'You stay, Jankele,' and he left. I sat waiting but when, what seemed hours later, my Uncle Moishe still hadn't returned, I began to worry that he had deserted me, or worse, that perhaps he had been caught.

Along the horizon, lamps flickered in windows. To have a home, a mother, a bed, I mused. To belong to someone, to be loved, to be cared for, to have a piece of dry, black bread. How lucky some people are!

'Jankele,' I suddenly heard Moishe calling. From under his coat he produced half a loaf of bread, and from his pockets, a few raw potatoes and frozen sugar beets.

We wolfed down the bread, leaving the rest for later. We had cheated death for another day.

After weeks of this existence, Staszek searched us out. Once again he threatened to personally drag us to the Gestapo unless we left the area immediately. We listened without protest and were frightened, but much as we wished to oblige, we had no place to go.

One very bright moonlit night, soon after, we were awakened by voices, whispers, coughing, then heavy stabs all around us. Hands reached from all directions and held us firmly. Suddenly we found ourselves faced by about a half dozen pitchforks.

'Kubus!' I heard a voice. 'Who is your friend?'

'My uncle,' I replied, studying the man's face. I recalled having helped him once build a fence. He had offered to pay me and I had refused. I remembered how grateful he had been.

'Blow the bugle!' ordered one of the pitchfork holders.

'No!' voiced another. 'Look at them. There's nothing to be had.'

'Got any gold?' a new voice joined in. 'If you give it to us, we'll let you go. If not, I'll blow this horn and a horse and buggy will come running to deliver you to the Krauts in Chelm.'

'We have nothing,' said Moishe.

'What was your father, a moneylender?'

Now a toothless one stepped forward to search us, but the farmer I knew shoved him aside, and said to us, 'Our job is to make sure this village is free of Jews and partisans. If the Germans catch you here, Kulik will be reduced to ashes. We'll let you go this time, only if you promise to clear out of this district. But God help you if we find you here again.' We spent the rest of that night talking and pondering. Moishe pressed on about going to the Chelm Ghetto. I had no alternative plan to offer but still refused to surrender.

'Let's go into the forest then,' said Moishe, 'and join the partisans.'

I had heard how the Germans combed the woods for what they referred to as bandits. 'Not the forest,' I said, 'it's not safe.' We argued and argued, and in the end decided to explore a different region. And so in the morning we crossed the river into the next village, but when night fell and we were hungry, tired, and had nowhere to sleep, we returned to our haystack.

Our nights were now sleepless, with the fear the vigilantes and the pitchforks would return, but several nights passed without incident.

Then Staszek showed up, but this time with bread in his

hands. To our amazement, he was unusually sympathetic. While we devoured the loaf, picking up every crumb that fell, he asked us to help him.

'I need some lumber to repair the barn,' he said. 'There are a lot of good trees in the forest, but the forest ranger keeps a sharp eye during the day. If you boys would give me a hand tonight, I'd let you sleep in the barn and feed you some tasty grub.'

We were overjoyed with this turn of events. At dusk we entered Mrs Pejzak's house again. How good it felt to be in a warm place, with a fire burning in the stove!

'Hit the hay,' said Staszek when we had finished eating. 'We have a busy night ahead of us.'

We lay down in our familiar sleeping quarter. That it was only for one night didn't seem to matter; our stomachs were full, and our bodies thawed. It felt good to be alive.

Staszek was to wake us at midnight. The excitement of doing something illegal and potentially dangerous returned. For one night we weren't homeless wanderers. There was purpose in our being.

Neither asleep nor awake, I heard the barn door open and a voice whisper, 'Moniek!' It's Staszek coming to wake us, I thought. 'Moniek!' But it wasn't Staszek's voice. I opened my eyes, a beam of light flashed across the rafters. 'Moniek!'

Moishe turned in his sleep, jerked his head, and yelled out, 'All right, Staszek we're ...'

My hand descended over his mouth, muzzling him, and he began to struggle. The light was now upon us with hands reaching for us. We scurried like a pair of barn mice trying to find shelter.

'I've got the big one,' I heard a voice. 'Get the other.' Feet and hands all around me, and then a beam of light blinded me. Firm calloused hands gripped my throat.

'This time we're not letting you go. Blow the bugle!'

'Please, please, I don't want to die,' I begged. 'Please let us go,' my voice echoed through the barn.

'Blow the bloody bugle, I said,' the same voice commanded. I cried hysterically. Moishe remained calm.

They left the barn, locking us in.

A door opened and slammed, a vicious argument ensued, and then we heard Mrs Pejzak's voice pleading for our lives and cursing Staszek, pouring every imaginable misfortune onto his head.

'We have to be rid of those two lice, Mother, once and for all,' he was yelling.

'You scum!' she shouted at him. 'How could you have ever been born from my belly?'

Then it was quiet. I waited for the bugle to shatter the silence, and foresaw two white horses pulling a wagon driven by a brutal, husky peasant. Like a couple of hogs being taken to slaughter, we were being delivered to Chelm. On the way villagers stopped and stared. What a horrible end! We were herded to the Gestapo, ordered to dig our own graves, shot, and ... there was no ... and ... that was it. That's all forever ... no one will ever know, remember, or care.

The door opened, and I fell to my knees and cried, 'Please let us go, we haven't done anything. We have nothing to give you. Take mercy, please let us go!'

A hand pulled me up, forcing me to my feet. I looked into the face of my acquaintance. 'Stop crying, Kubus!' he said. I tried and choked on my tears. 'We warned you before, but you didn't listen.'

'We had nowhere to go.'

'This is your last warning,' and he released me.

I grabbed Moishe by his coat sleeve and we ran out.

Mrs Pejzak intercepted us. 'I beg you, have mercy on me and don't show your faces here again.'

We took off and ran and ran until we were almost upon the river, and there stood the haystack. Instinctively we approached and crawled into our nest, exhausted and still shaking.

Above us the moon shone brightly, like a searchlight pointing us out. I was determined that we abandon the haystack and move on.

'We'll be picked up in no time at all,' said Moishe. 'Look at us, a couple of runaway Jews.'

When I stood my ground and refused to be swayed, he said, 'We would stand a better chance if we separated.' I was shocked. 'Let's try it for a few days,' he said. 'We'll meet here at the end of the week.'

'Promise me you'll come back,' I implored.

'Don't worry, Jankele, I wouldn't abandon you.'

He turned left and I right. We drifted away from each other, two lost figures on a vast, deserted early-morning freezing landscape.

FOR THE FIRST PART OF THE DAY I meandered in the fields, but by late afternoon hunger drove me to the village across the river. To my amazement, I was ignored by those I encountered. Dogs barked and sometimes chased after me; otherwise I attracted no attention.

By the time I had reached the last house of the village I resolved to enter and ask for food. Then fear overtook me and I imagined being chased with a stick or apprehended, bound, and driven to the Gestapo.

In spite of that, I approached. It looked like a well-to-do farm: a huge barn and separate stable. A restrained dog's barking brought a man out. I wanted to turn and run, but something told me I didn't need to be afraid.

I neared him; he pulled a pipe from his pocket, and eyed me with suspicion.

'Could I have something to eat?' I asked. He lit the pipe, then said, 'Follow me,' and led me inside the house.

An old man with a full head of white hair sat at the window staring out. A fire burned in the stove and the aroma of food permeated the air.

'Take off your coat,' said the man. I removed my hat and coat and looked around. My aching feet were swollen. My shoes were too small, forcing my toes to curl under.

'Over there.' He pointed to a round table in the centre of the room. I sat down, and next when I looked up, he was carrying a plate of soup and a chunk of black bread. I shifted my eyes from him to the old man; they in turn were watching me.

Obviously he knows I'm a Jew, I thought. That's why he doesn't question me. I bit into the bread and was picking up the spoon when his voice distracted me. 'Don't you cross yourself before eating?' The spoon fell into my soup, and quickly I made the sign of the cross. I guess he doesn't suspect.

'What do they call you?' inquired the older one in a hoarse voice.

I raised my eyes, pausing for a moment and answered, 'Kubus.'

'What?' shouted the old man, turning an ear in my direction.

'Kubus,' I repeated.

'Louder,' said the younger one. 'My father's almost deaf.' And addressing his father he thundered, 'They call him Kubus!' Either the old man still didn't hear or he simply gave up. He turned back to face the window as if waiting for a messenger who would never arrive. The son reached for a log and fed the fire. 'Where are you off to, boy?' I wasn't prepared for this, and almost choked on the last spoonful of soup. 'Looking for work perhaps?'

'Yes, yes,' I nodded.

'I need someone to help me around the house and assist my father, and come spring, to look after the cows.'

'That I know how to do well,' I said with a beaming face.

'Really?'

'I looked after two cows this past summer.'

'Where?'

'In the next village. In Kulik. The Pejzak family.'

'Oh? Why aren't you there now?'

I had blundered. I should never have mentioned the Pejzaks, but now it was too late, and he was waiting for a response.

'I would rather not talk about it,' I finally said.

He sat down opposite me and refilled his pipe. 'That's all right; you don't have to tell me.' I was relieved. 'Very well, Kubus, you're hired.' He extended his hand and I shook it.

When it was time to retire for the night, I began to undress, feeling uneasy as my employer and his father were also readying themselves for bed. So as to blend in, I imitated their every move. When they were down to their winter underwear, they knelt at the side of their beds. Quickly, I too fell to my knees. From the corner of my eye I watched them and mimed their every gesture to the minutest detail; lips moving silently, hands in a praying position, and eyes closed. They crossed themselves, and got under the covers.

I followed suit. 'Blow out the light, boy,' grunted the old man. I walked over to the table and extinguished the naphtha lamp and then lay down on the floor on a burlap bag filled with straw.

How fortunate I am! There must indeed be a God in heaven.

The crackling of the fire beside me, and the heat it produced, induced me to sleep. But as I wallowed in my new-found comfort, my thoughts turned to Moishe and I felt guilty. Where is he right now? Is he sleeping beside a burning stove? Is his stomach full like mine? Is he still alive? If only he had come along, then both of us would have found this shelter.

From Moishe, my thoughts roamed in other directions: I was in danger of betraying myself. What if I dream and in my sleep I should speak Yiddish? I have to start thinking in Polish, dreaming in Polish. But what if I succeed so well and forget my name, my father's name, my mother's name? No, I won't forget.

Dear God, then immediately I qualified, dear *Jewish* God, make sure I don't dream and speak Yiddish tonight. I know I've been breaking the laws – eating pork, not covering my head and as you have witnessed, kneeling and crossing myself. But you know dear God, I'm only pretending. My heart isn't in it.

Outside, the wind lashed without mercy and the branches on the trees were beating against the window panes. When day broke there was snow on the ground and frost on the windows. I looked across the white, deserted vista and wondered where my Uncle Moishe was.

Nothing eventful occurred during the first days. I rose in the mornings, made the sign of the cross before each meal, mouthed my prayers at my bedside, and did everything else I could to appear devout. I peeled potatoes, swept the house, fed the pigs and other animals, and generally made myself useful. Both father and son were pleased with me and praised me generously.

On the fifth day of my stay, the son donned his Sunday clothes and announced, 'I'm going to church. I would take you along, but I don't like leaving father alone.'

He returned early in the evening, covered in fresh snow and with his nose red from frost. He warmed his hands by the stove, helped himself to the soup from the day before, and inquired if everything was in order. He filled and lit his pipe, and spent the rest of the evening puffing on it, refilling, and puffing again. Then it was time for bed. Again the three of us got undressed and knelt to say our nightly prayers. By this time I had mastered their mannerisms. I crossed myself, when unexpectedly a voice rang out.

'Why don't you say your prayers aloud, Kubus?' My employer was towering over me.

'It's private. I never say prayers out loud.'

'Just this once, perhaps you'd be good enough to recite the Lord's Prayer.'

'I'd rather not, sir,' my face turning crimson.

'Is it possible you don't know it?'

'Of course I do,' I forced a chuckle.

'Then let's hear it.' A knowing smile glued itself to his face. 'Stand up, boy, I know all about you.'

'I know the prayer, sir!' I raised my voice slightly.

'I was in Kulik today.' My heart dropped. 'I spoke to Mrs Pejzak.' I lowered my head.

'You'll leave first thing tomorrow.' He blew out the lamp and went to bed.

I couldn't sleep. When day broke, I dressed and, while they were still snoring, I unlatched the door and faced the elements.

It's all for the best, I reasoned. God knows what He's doing, and tomorrow I have to meet Moishe anyway.

I headed in the direction of the haystack.

THE RIVER WAS FROZEN, but as I began to cross it, the ice gave way and I slid into the deep, freezing water. I fought with all the strength I possessed and didn't possess, and miraculously managed to rescue myself.

I continued on to our agreed rendezvous, resembling a frosted scarecrow, icicles hanging from my body. And when I reached the field where the haystack had been, it was gone. Everything was gone. Only snow, snow all around as far as my eyes could see. Even the little houses in the distance looked like mounds of snow with smoke emanating from the tops.

I have to find shelter. But where? Who will have me? What about Moishe? I was expecting him the next day. If I leave, he won't know where to look for me. But if I stay, I'll freeze to death.

Longingly I stared at the Pejzaks' farm. I'll hide in the barn, I mused. They don't have to know that I'm there. It was difficult trudging through the deep snow, but I managed to reach the back of the barn and peeked in through a gap. No one was there. I pried a loose board with my frozen fingers and barely squeezed through. The cows resting in their steaming dung were warm and content and so I chose to join them under the trough, waiting for the day to pass. Tomorrow Moishe will come!

Slowly the ice on my apparel melted, leaving me drenched. Suddenly, the door opened.

'On your feet, Princess.' It was Mrs Pejzak's voice.

But the cow just lay there. Mrs Pejzak kicked her backside and Princess obeyed. She pulled up a stool and began to milk.

From my vantage point I couldn't see her face, only her hands working the cow's udders, but I could also see right up Mrs Pejzak's skirt. I was aghast. In this bitter cold, she wasn't wearing underpants. I felt ashamed for peeping, but in truth I had experienced a certain thrill. I was tempted to call out to her. In spite of her instructions, I knew she'd be pleased to see me, but I feared frightening her.

If only I was a cow instead of a Jew, then I could stay here all winter, I mused.

By noon I began to feel cramped. My eyes wandered, surveying the barn, and finally rested on the ladder that led to the loft. There I dug a hole in the straw, crawled in like a fox, and fell asleep.

I was awakened by the grating of the barn door opening. Below me, making her way to the pigsty with a lamp and a bucket was Genia, humming a familiar Ukrainian melody. How I would have loved to call out to her! But for her sake, I denied myself the pleasure. She emptied the contents of the bucket into the trough, and after patting one of the cows, went back out. If only I had signalled her, I admonished myself; she would have brought me food.

The whiff of the pigs' feed reached my nostrils, drawing me towards them. The swine were jostling one another, fighting for every morsel. How appetizing the still-warm boiled potatoes looked! Not giving it a second thought, I wedged myself between two of them, and partook in their feast.

I had made a kill and now thought of myself as a wild animal, a rat perhaps.

'What's this, Daddy?'

'A trap, Jankele, to catch a big ugly rat,' said my father. The next morning the spring had sprung, and inside the cage my father had made was a monstrous rodent. What a revolting creature! We drowned him. How cruel! I now thought. Who knows what went through that rat's mind when we flung him into the smelly pond!

Recalling my feelings towards rats, I now knew what my enemies thought of me. What careful traps were they setting for me?

Starting before daylight the next day, I kept watch through a knot hole in a barn board so as not to miss Moishe. Outside it was calm and clear; I had a good view of the fields, the river, and where the haystack once stood. I reasoned that once I spotted him I would break out of the barn. The door to the barn opened and closed several times. When I heard some-one whistling, I sneaked a glance and saw Staszek grooming the horse. I refocused my eyes through the lookout and saw my uncle shuffling his way in my direction.

'Moishe!' I screamed excitedly.

Staszek's whistling stopped abruptly and, before I realised what I had done, his hands were gripping my ankles, pulling me down the ladder.

'You conniving vermin!' he yelled, twisting my arms behind my back and kicking me out of the barn.

At this point Moishe entered the farmyard and I fell into his arms. At about the same time, Mrs Pejzak and Genia suddenly appeared.

'Quick, come,' Mrs Pejzak ordered. 'Someone may see you.' And she shooed us into the house like chicks into a coop. Staszek yelled, 'Mother, if they stay here, I am ...' She slammed the door in his face.

'My Staszu is right, boys,' she said. 'It's too dangerous here. The Germans are snooping every day.' Then she pointed to the table for us to sit. Her trembling hands placed food in front of us. 'You can stay overnight in the barn,' she offered.

'Don't you think it's dangerous, Mrs Pejzak?' asked Moishe, with a grin. 'On the way here I saw a truckload of Germans headed in this direction.' Mrs Pejzak could hardly speak, as if she was dumbstruck. Moishe broke into laughter. 'Look how afraid you are. You're shaking.'

'Get out,' she became unhinged. 'Go! Remember, I've been kind to you. Don't give them our name.'

'I was just having a little fun with you,' said Moishe. 'Go! Go! Leave me in peace!' and forcefully she pushed us out the door.

We rounded the corner of the house and headed towards the river without a word until we reached the spot where the haystack once stood. All around was snow and ice, as far as the eye could see.

'Where to now?' I asked.

'To Chelm,' came the reply. 'There's no escape, Jankele.'

'I won't go.'

'You'll go where I tell you to go, understand?'

'I don't have to listen to you,' I rebutted in anger.

'Look, you squirt, I'm your uncle and don't you ever forget that.'

'That doesn't give you the right to lead me to my death.'

'A little respect. After all, I am older than you and therefore I should be the one who makes all the decisions.'

'You're not much older, you're only thirteen,' I said.

'But I *am* older.'

'That doesn't make you smarter. Why did you have to frighten Mrs Pejzak? We could have had a warm meal and stayed the night there. But, no, you had to play the clown. I was doing all right without you, and the minute you show up I'm out in the cold again.' I regretted saying that, but I didn't apologise, for I feared it would weaken my stance.

Moishe fell into a long silence, after which he said, 'Perhaps I am in your way, Jankele. Maybe you'd be better off without me. You don't look so Jewish. They see me coming, they let the dogs loose. What I've been through these last few days is worse than death.'

'Nothing is worse than death,' I answered.

'I envy you, Jankele; you still have such a strong will to live.'

'We'll live, Uncle Moishe,' I said, 'or at least, let's try.'

'I'm going to Chelm; come with me.'

'No!' I said. I reasoned that he wouldn't leave me. All I had to do was stand firm. 'Go if you like,' I countered.

Moishe reached into his pocket and handed me his soiled deck of cards. 'Jankele, here's something to remember me by. I won't need them anymore.'

Another ploy of his. It's all part of his act, I thought. If I pretend to be unconcerned, he won't go. To impress upon him how adamant my position was, I offered him a parting present; the two fur pieces from my mother's coat. And he played his role to the end and accepted them.

'Goodbye.'

'Goodbye,' I answered, as if I didn't care.

We turned sharply and walked away from each other in opposite directions. I restrained myself from looking back. He'll come running after me any moment. Perhaps he's already following me! I turned to steal a glance.

A small, hunched figure, shuffling rather than walking, reached the river, jumped across, stopped, and looked back. Immediately I turned and walked on. When I looked again, my Uncle Moishe was nowhere to be seen.

One of my voices instilled me with hope. He'll come back; all you have to do is wait. By now, he's probably on the other side of the river expecting you to come running after him.

Let him wait. I'm not giving in.

By midday, my body was frozen and I had no feeling in my fingers or toes. My voice rose and echoed through the barren landscape, 'Moishe! Moishe!'

BY STAYING IN THE FIELD much longer I risked freezing to death, but I vowed never to return to the Pejzaks'. I began to walk. I should have cried; I wanted to cry. In fact, I felt there was something wrong with me for not crying. But in place of tears, I began to sing.

I had a vision of myself as a partisan with a rifle under my garment. The next German I see, I'll shoot. How thrilling! How daring! Nothing and no one can harm me. Soon I was marching instead of walking, swinging my arms, singing Vanja's song at the top of my voice. I had forgotten who I was, and what I was looking for. I didn't feel the cold, the hunger, or the sorrow.

'Jew boy!' a voice spoiled my delusions. I ignored it. It didn't mean me. 'Jew boy!' Staring me in the face was the old woman who told us about Vanja, carrying a load of firewood on her bent back. Her shrivelled face and sunken eyes made her appear as the messenger of death. 'Jew boy, run for your life. They're in the village.' I stood gaping at her. 'Hundreds of them. Germans and their Ukrainian collaborator pigs; they're searching under every bed. Run! Hide! Or you'll be dead before the day is over.' She moved to touch me, but I drew back. 'Poor Jew boy,' she muttered, and continued on her way.

I was no longer the fearless partisan. Looking about, I found myself on the Kulik village road, familiar houses all around. I was known here; anyone could have recognised me. Luckily I wasn't far from a dilapidated house I knew of. I rushed in and found it stacked with wheat. I climbed to the top of the heap, and again like a rat, burrowed in. Perhaps they won't find me here! But what if they have dogs? They could sniff me out.

Several shots rang out in the distance. I tunnelled deeper. More shots, voices, shouting, footsteps. I imagined someone with eyes like a cat looking through the splintered window or missing door, ready to leap if I stirred or murmured.

How many times had I witnessed this very scene? A cat waiting patiently, endlessly, for the mouse to stick its head out. I closed my eyes and prayed that if I were shot I should be spared witnessing the one pulling the trigger.

Is he still there? How long will he wait? Perhaps it's only my imagination.

When at long last I opened my eyes and looked out, night had fallen. The village was as quiet as a graveyard, yet I was afraid to move. I filled my empty stomach with kernels of wheat and retreated to my hole.

Three days went by. The wheat, even though abundant, did not satiate my hunger. At times I regretted not having listened to Moishe. Outside, streaks of smoke were rising from the chimneys towards the sky. Oh, to sit near a burning stove! I mused. I rubbed my hands, trying to make my blood flow again. I could hardly move my legs or the rest of my body. I had lost all touch and taste.

Footsteps in the snow made me stick my neck out, and when they came closer, I recognised Mrs Pejzak's oldest son, who lived only a few properties away from her.

'Jan!' I called out.

He turned, startled. 'Kubus!' he gasped. 'What are you doing here?'

'I'm hungry,' I answered.

'Wait!' and he disappeared.

Now I could have kicked myself for revealing myself. I didn't know him all that well and the enemy had many guises. So I decided to flee. When I reached the open threshold, Jan reappeared.

He pushed me, 'Get back inside.' From under his coat he extracted a round loaf of bread and threw it at me like a football.

'Are they gone?' I asked.

'I'll find out.' And he left.

I retreated into my lair and simply stared at the bread, admiring it. It must have been weeks old, as it was as hard as stone. I tried to bite off a piece, and lost some crumbs. I searched until I found them deep in the straw. Finally I attacked the loaf, taking tiny bites and chewing slowly, turning each mouthful dozens of times before swallowing. After devouring half of the loaf, my stomach still growled. Just one more morsel, I thought, and treated myself to another bite, then another, and another, until there was little left. This, I was determined to save. But the voice in my stomach kept urging: don't deny yourself. Go ahead. Enjoy it.

What about tomorrow?

Tomorrow? the voice mocked. How sure you are of yourself. What makes you think you'll still be alive by tomorrow?

I reached for the remaining piece and devoured it.

When the sky turned dark, I heard, 'Kubus come out!'

'Is it safe?' I asked.

'They're gone,' he whispered and led me to his house. In the corner of the room sat his wife, her breast exposed, feeding a new-born infant.

I removed my hat and nodded to her.

'You'll find a sleeping place up there,' Jan pointed to a ladder leading to the attic. I climbed up.

I bedded down on the foul-smelling straw and, to keep my hands warm, I slid them into my pants and cupped my genitals. Rats and mice danced all around me, as if I were Gulliver from *Gulliver's Travels*.

The door of the attic opened once or twice a day, and Jan would appear with a bowl of soup or a heel of dry bread.

One evening he invited me down. When the meagre meal was over and his wife was clearing the table, he turned to me. 'If you had some money or valuables, I'd be able to keep you on.'

I knew he was impoverished. His farm consisted of a small plot of land, an old cow that gave hardly any milk, and a few scrawny chickens.

'I have nothing,' I answered.

'Didn't your parents leave you their gold?' he asked.

'Gold? We were very poor.'

He glanced at his wife, then back to me. 'You're too young to know, Kubus. All Jews have gold.'

Did my parents or grandparents have gold? If so, why were we so penniless? How many times, even before the war, did I go to bed hungry? How many times did I have to cry for one grosz to buy a candy? Did my parents lie to me? Were they in fact wealthy like all Jews are supposed to be?

'When you find out where they buried it, Kubus, then come and see us. You're a good boy; we'd like to save you.' I departed the next day. As I trekked in the deep snow, I saw coins, diamonds, and gold glittering all about me. When I scooped them up and held them in my hands they simply melted and turned into water.

NIGHT WAS DRAWING NEAR when I found myself in foreign territory; a dog barked here, a cow mooed there, a voice shouted, someone laughed. In front of me was an endless winding road visible only because of tracks left by a sleigh that had passed earlier.

No sign of Uncle Moishe. A terrible guilt gripped me. I should have clung to him and never let him go. Isn't it possible he maybe changed his mind and never went to Chelm? Wouldn't it be something if we ran into each other? I now resolved to find him.

My eyes continued to search; my feet continued to trudge, filling my undersized shoes with snow that drenched my feet.

Many kilometres later I arrived at the entrance of the village where Moishe had worked. If I could find his former boss, perhaps he could lead me to my uncle. Then a further thought presented itself: Moishe is there, of course! Where else? How can I locate that farmer?

At the side of the road, a young boy about my own age was aiming at a bird with a slingshot. He pulled the rubber band, a stone shot up into a tree, and a sparrow fell beside me. He ran to it, snatched it from the snow, and, holding it up for me to admire, said, 'That's the third one today.'

'Why do you kill birds?' I asked.

He was taken aback. 'For fun, stupid,' and he eyed me suspiciously.

That's why Wojciech killed frogs, for fun, and this one killed birds for fun. Others killed Jews for fun.

I then excavated the memory of a German officer in Pulawy who couldn't eat his lunch unless he killed two Jews for fun.

I pitied the dead bird in the boy's hands, its head limp, eyes closed, blood trickling from its beak.

One day I may look like that. Who knows who may seek some fun, seeing me wandering along the road, and ...?

'Three birds is nothing,' I said. 'I put away at least twenty a day.' He looked sceptical.

'If you're such a good shot, here,' and he extended his weapon for me to take.

'Oh, not with this,' and I waved my hand as if shooing away a fly. 'I have a special slingshot, with a device so that even a blind man couldn't miss the target.' It was getting dark and so I quickly changed the subject. 'Perhaps you can help me? I'm looking for a relative who lives in this village.'

'What's his name?'

'That's just it, I forgot. I only know he's got four cows and a horse.'

'That's not much help,' said the boy.

'Last summer, he had a Jew boy helping out.'

The boy's eyes lit up. 'I'll show you,' and he led me to a house. Along the way he showed me where he lived.

I approached and knocked on the door. A voice beckoned me to enter.

Sitting by the open fire was an elderly woman darning socks. A back door opened and her husband entered with an armful of split logs. They stared at me.

'I am Kubus,' I introduced myself. The man dropped the load, and removed his coat and hat. Obviously my name didn't register with them. 'Moniek is my uncle.' They looked at each other, and then back at me. The man rushed to the window and drew a curtain. 'What do you want?'

'I am looking for him and I thought you might know where to find him.'

Nervously, the man paced the room, and then whispered into the wife's ear. While he threw fresh logs on the fire, she poured a glass of milk and cut a slice of bread.

'Eat,' she said, setting it on the table. I sat down and ate.

'Some days ago,' began the man, 'Moniek stopped here. We fed him and he left us this.' He displayed the two pieces of fur.

I finished eating. The rest of the loaf lay before me, but I couldn't bring myself to ask for another slice. The room was so cosy, so inviting, and so to prolong my stay I engaged them in further conversation for a few minutes.

'We're glad you looked us up, but don't come here again. It's too dangerous.' I found myself rising and putting my hat on. 'Go to Chelm. You'll find your uncle there.'

Behind me the door was bolted. Facing me was the night, waiting to swallow me up.

I passed the farmhouse where the boy with the slingshot lived and imagined him on his knees saying his prayers, getting ready for bed, or already asleep, under the goose-feather bedding, with his head on a soft pillow. I walked, not because I had a destination, but rather because it was warmer to move than to stand still.

Soon the lights in the windows were dimmed and even the dogs retired for the night. My feet tramped in the snow. My eyes on the stars above, I counted them; one ... two ... three ... a few more steps, another house, eleven ... twelve ... more ... more snow, a turn of the road, snow ... snow. Thirty-six ... thirty-seven ... and suddenly I fell into a pit. Quickly, I wiped the snow off my face and looked around. The road was not to be seen. Nothing was to be seen except for the stars in heaven.

A terrible melancholy took hold of me from which I could not free myself. Moishe was right; there is no escape. At that moment death would have come as a welcome relief. Please dear God, let me drift into an everlasting sleep, I prayed. The snow felt warm; I lay back and buried myself in it, as if it was bedding.

Above the stars twinkled, went out of focus, and then disappeared.

BRILLIANT RAYS OF WINTER sun woke me, and when I opened my eyes I was glad that God hadn't been swayed by my prayer of the previous night.

Quickly, I brushed off the snow and headed towards a road. Soon a new village appeared on the horizon. To an onlooker, I must have looked like a peasant boy delivering an urgent message to a known destination, and yet I had no idea where I was headed.

It occurred to me to go to Chelm, but I feared for my life, and in the end I accepted the loss of Moishe the way I had my previous losses. I addressed myself to my immediate needs: food and shelter. I was a wild animal on the lookout for easy prey.

As I walked and looked down at my cramped shoes, they dissolved into my grandfather Shie Chuen's boots. Perhaps he walked along this very road. He most likely knew every house, every farmer by name, and every curve of this road and all the other roads in these parts.

Now, more than ever, I realised the shame and humiliation my grandfather must have felt to keep us alive. And yet he never complained; only revealing his good fortune but never his bad luck. How many times must he have stumbled and fallen on ice or snow! How many times must he have been called abusive names! Yet he invariably greeted us with a caring smile. My poor grandfather ...

How our eyes were glued to the frosted window that night, waiting for his return! To at least see his shadow or hear the sound of his footsteps! But night fell and darkened the gloomy streets of Siedliszcze, and though we sat up waiting till the small hours, his knock on our door never came. It seemed impossible to me then. It was as if the man with the burlap bag had been swallowed somewhere inside a village, or else had grown wings and had vanished behind the clouds.

It saddened my mother greatly that her father, a proud man, should be reduced to begging, and she would often cry upon his return home, tired and worn after a gruelling day.

'There is no shame in begging,' he would say, 'the shame is in stealing.' And when saying it, he would invariably look at me, to stamp the message onto my young mind, and file it there forever.

Now I walked in his shoes, in his footsteps, resorting to begging as well. But how to enter a home and ask for a piece of bread or a place to sleep, I didn't know.

I made many attempts at approaching doors but shame and mostly fear made me hesitate.

Then my grandfather's words rang in my head, like bells in a church, and I resolved to enter the next house.

Arming myself with courage, I said, 'I won't be afraid; I'll go in and keep my head up high.' Yet at the next house I looked for an excuse.

You're afraid, eh? said my voice.

I'm not afraid. That farmhouse looked too poor. I doubt if those living there have enough for themselves.

Then what's wrong with that one? My other self asked, referring to a prosperous-looking estate.

I'll give it a try, just watch. And, trembling, I undid the gate and suddenly three chained dogs announced my presence. Keeping an eye on the animals, I opened the door and entered. The house was dark and looked unoccupied. As my eyes acclimatised themselves to the absence of light, a hunchback, sitting in the corner, became visible. He turned, opened his mouth, and said what sounded like, 'Get out, Jew!'

I fled and, kilometres away, in my mind's eye I could still see the man's rotten teeth, and hear the growling dogs.

Coward, my inner voice laughed. How frightened you are! Why did you run?

He called me Jew boy and told me to get out.

Nothing of the sort. He said, what is it you wanted?

I'll try again, I said, and this time I'll succeed. I shouldn't be afraid of people, I reasoned. After all, the worst they can do is refuse me.

I had come to an old house in dire need of repair. Poor farmers, I observed. Needy people are usually kinder so I decided to enter and was greeted by a cloud of steam.

'Come in and close the door,' a woman's voice was heard.

She was washing clothes. On the stove water was boiling in a metal cauldron, and at a shaky table by the window sat three children, two of them snotty nosed and crying.

'I'm hungry,' I said. 'Could you give me something to eat?'

'We're all hungry,' answered the woman. I started to leave. 'Don't go away,' she shouted. 'If you wait I'll make supper as soon as I'm through with this.'

'I'll wait,' I answered.

'Then take off your coat and see if you can shut my brats up.'

I recalled how my Uncle Shepsel used to divert Josele's and my hunger with drawings of Tarzan, cowboys, and clowns. I now performed that same magic. On a piece of brittle paper I sketched a bird perched on a branch. The children marvelled and asked for more. I drew a cow with a cowherd and a dog beside them.

'Draw some soldiers,' one child requested. I drew German soldiers with rifles ready to shoot.

'What are they shooting?' asked another before I had finished.

'I'll show you,' I said, and continued to draw a man facing the soldiers. To my consternation, I had included an armband with the Star of David on the sleeve.

The kids laughed, and then one said, 'I know, that's a Jew.'

'That's right,' I answered, and though my heart was aching, I too laughed.

'You'll have to leave now,' said the woman when we had finished eating and she was preparing her children for bed. I thanked her and reached for my coat, when the children started to scream.

'Let him stay.'

'I have nowhere to put him,' the mother threw her hands in the air.

'I can sleep in the barn,' I offered.

'It's too cold there.'

'I don't mind,' I answered, displaying my best smile.

'We want him to sleep with us,' begged the youngest.

Fatigued, she surrendered. 'But only for one night.'

The children cheered.

That night and the following night, I slept on the floor in a crowded but warm house, and when finally I did leave, I left the children as I had found them, crying. But this time they weren't crying for food, they were crying for me.

DEEP INSIDE, THE SHAME STILL LINGERED, but I tried to ignore it. In time I learned not simply to beg for food or lodging, but offered to work. In some cases I'd be given a task to perform, but most stared at me blankly and said, 'Work, in the wintertime?' But taking pity on me, they'd ask, 'Are you hungry?'

'Yes,' I'd answer though at times my stomach was full, and what I really needed was shelter. Once my hat and coat were off and I had been fed, I endeared myself by offering to split logs, feed pigs, peel potatoes, or rock a cradle. Where there were older children, I'd request paper and pencil and start drawing.

In this manner the day would pass, and when night would fall, very few had the heart to throw me out. The next day after the morning meal, I would move on to the next house, and often I'd be given another breakfast.

In time, I enlarged my repertoire by telling stories to children, tales my mother had read to me, and others that I made up as I went along. I also learned how to diaper babies and put them to sleep with a lullaby.

My young tenor voice attracted enough attention to be invited to evening gatherings of neighbours.

They'd applaud and ask for encores. To add spice to my performance, I played the flute and added the card tricks I learned from Uncle Moishe. Even the very simple ones held my audiences spellbound, and they began to believe I was blessed with godly spirits.

Whenever I was questioned about my past I fabricated a tale of a witch-like stepmother who beat me endlessly, and claimed that my father, a farmer, had been taken away to Germany on forced labour.

After listening to this saga, one asked, 'Why did you leave home?'

'I couldn't stand the beatings,' I answered him.

He smiled and said, 'It's all right, you don't have to lie to me. I can tell you're a Jewish child.'

When I protested vigorously, he told me he was a Sabotnik, a Seventh Day Adventist, and knew what it was like to be persecuted for one's religious beliefs. With bible in hand, he read passages aloud, and went to great pains to explain how the Jews had erred by not accepting Christ. 'That is the reason for your grief.'

I nodded my head as if I understood, and accepted his teaching. What would my mother think of me now, I worried. But God knew I was just pretending.

In the morning as I was leaving, he counselled, 'Believe in Christ and He'll save you. It's never too late.'

GRADUALLY I BECAME AWARE of a constant itch all over my body. I felt as if I was being devoured.

When we had first arrived in Siedliszcze and had been billeted in a public house, two families to one room, the lice were not only crawling in my hair and under my armpits, but also marching up the wall. But the plague that kept me awake nightly now was even worse.

My hunger experience did not compare to the suffering I now endured with these torturous vermin. Sitting at a table in a warm house, I would suddenly feel them eating away at me, but I didn't dare scratch, for the discovery that I was infested would have resulted in being instantly booted out, even though my hosts themselves probably had an ample supply of their own.

I'd suffer silently through the day, waiting for night to come, and then under cover, I'd work feverishly to rid myself of the agony. It was a hopeless battle. No matter how many I executed between the nails of my thumbs, the more they were attracted to me.

One day behind a barn, in desperation, I took off my coat and shook it. I was sickened by the multitude of lice that had tumbled from my garment and were now crawling in the snow. Oh, to have a bath and a change of clothes! I dreamed. But where? In the summer I could have stopped at a stagnant pond or stream, but this was winter.

My suffering reached such torment that one night I cried because of it. It had rained the last time I had a bath. Mrs Pejzak boiled four pots of water and she poured them into a wooden tub, and ordered me to undress. Genia was in the room. How shy I was! I began to undress with my eyes on the floor. When I looked up all eyes were on me.

'Come on, Kubus,' said Genia. 'The water will get cold.'

I dropped my trousers and got into the basin with my back to them. Mrs Pejzak scrubbed me from head to toe except my privates, which I kept covered with my hands.

'Don't worry, Kubus.' Mrs Pejzak laughed. 'You can let go, I won't bite it off.' And the room shook with laughter.

When I got dressed and headed for the barn, Mrs Pejzak said, 'It's raining, why don't you sleep in the house tonight?'

'With me,' added Genia, beckoning me. 'Come, Kubus!' I bolted out the door. When I reached the barn sopping wet, I could still hear them laughing.

Now as I recalled that incident, I longed to relive it. To bathe in warm water; to have a clean, lice-free shirt; to have my hair washed and combed! And the more I thought about it, the more I was tempted to visit the Pejzaks again.

One moonlit night I found myself crossing the river. Gently I knocked on the door and waited. There was silence, and from the darkened interior I heard snoring. My second knock brought a tired voice to my ears.

'Who's there?'

'Kubus!' I answered.

The door opened and Mrs Pejzak stood in the doorway,

her sheepskin coat wrapped around her body, her hair dishevelled, and her eyes only half-opened.

'Holy Mother!' she uttered, clutching her head. 'You're still alive, thank God for that!' She inquired about Moishe. 'Go to the barn my child,' she said. 'I'll bring you some food, and then you must leave.'

'I'm not hungry.'

'No?' She looked surprised.

'I came to have a bath.'

'Holy Mother! You poor child, how can I give you a bath? Staszek is out and could be back any minute, and if he should find you, it would be disastrous.' She began to weep. 'He is with the vigilantes; those brave heroes with pitchforks and bugle.' She wiped the tears and blew her nose on the end of her sleeve. 'They're bandits, Kubus, worse than the Germans. If he finds you here, Kubus ... he'll ... ' She suddenly looked past my shoulder. 'Listen!' she said. 'It's Staszek; he's coming down the road.'

The familiar terror gripped me and I turned and ran, and once again found myself inside the root cellar now full of potatoes, with just enough space for me to lie flat on my belly.

Staszek's footsteps came closer and closer, and then the door to the house opened and closed. I didn't move.

Some time later Mrs Pejzak whispered, 'He's asleep.' I wriggled out backwards on all fours. She shoved a parcel into my hands. 'Take this and go.'

'Goodbye,' I whispered.

On the other side of the river I stopped to examine the offering; a pair of Staszek's winter underwear unfolded in my hands.

In the next village I eyed a man's shirt dangling on a

clothesline. Quick as a fox, I had it off and was headed for a place to change.

How fortunate I felt! But that night my body itched. My companions had returned. To add to this discomfort, I awoke one morning with a rash on my hands. In the crevices between my fingers were little itchy pimples that when I scratched, opened, spread, and itched worse than before.

Wherever I went now, I tried to keep my hands out of sight, mostly in my pockets. That wasn't always possible.

'Out, you're diseased!' my hosts would shout, and I'd be thrown out like a rabid dog.

Word spread quickly that the beggar boy with the golden voice and the deck of cards was contaminated, and many doors were now slammed in my face. Once again I went hungry and slept in barns, spending my nights hunting for lice and scratching in the crevices of my body.

On one such night I heard the door to the barn open, and saw a shadow approaching. There was a rustle in the hay and later, heavy breathing. I lay motionless, in dreadful agony.

In the morning, a man's face popped out of the hay like a jack-in-the-box. Unshaven, wild eyed, wearing a tattered coat and feet wrapped in rags, he was startled upon seeing me. For a moment I feared he might attack me. We stared at each other.

'Boy, could you bring me a piece of bread?' he said in a cracked voice,

From his accent I knew immediately he was a Jew.

'Where am I to get bread?'

'Ask your mother for a small piece, just some crust will do.'

'I too am hungry,' I said.

Puzzled, he questioned me, his eyes boring into my own.

'I don't belong here,' I explained. 'I too am on the run,' I blurted out in Yiddish.

His eyes widened in their sockets. 'I don't believe it! You look and sound just like one of them. I wouldn't have guessed in a million years.'

I then displayed the rosary around my neck that I had pilfered off a night dresser, and falling to my knees, crossed myself and recited: 'Our Father who art in heaven – '

He allowed himself a slight chuckle. 'A perfect disguise!' and he rubbed his eyes. 'It's so much easier when you're young,' he sighed.

'I wonder what my mother would think if she saw me now!'

'She would probably be happy just to know you're still alive,' he said, and he looked at me sorrowfully.

'I'm forgetting my Yiddish. I've started to dream in Polish. I'm worried I'll forget my real name. You think God will forgive me for what I'm doing, or does He know I'm only pretending?' I asked him.

'God,' he looked at the rafters above. 'Our God is deaf and blind, or a figment of our imagination.'

Is that why there are no pictures of Him? They have pictures of their Jesus.'

It felt good to have found someone of my own kind, but then I feared that he might attach himself to me and with his looks and accent, betray both of us. I was ashamed for my selfish thoughts.

He noticed me clawing at my skin, and asked, 'What's with your hands?'

'Just an itch,' I answered. 'The more I scratch, the more they itch.'

Alarmed, he jumped to his feet. 'Between your legs and underarms also?'

I nodded. He quickly recoiled. 'You have scabies, child. It's contagious, you need medicine. But where will you get medicine in this forsaken place?'

'Do you know what kind?' I asked.

'Of course, I know. I'm a doctor.' He moved to leave and I ran after him. He raised his hands to keep me at bay. 'Don't touch me!'

'Wait!' I called after him. 'Let's talk some more.'

'There's nothing to talk about,' and he vanished from my sight forever.

A PAIR OF LADIES' BLACK GLOVES was drying on a fence. I picked off the first, but when I reached for the second, I heard the creaking of a door and fled. Several days later I stole another glove, this time a red one; unfortunately, it too was for the left hand.

With covered hands, and a different identity, I now moved into new territory and resumed my career with drawings, music, stories, and magic. Because I never removed the gloves, even when eating, I attracted attention.

'A dog bit me,' was my standard reply.

Everything within reach would attach itself to my gloved fingers. My pockets were filled with trivia: a pair of rusty scissors, a comb with missing teeth, a bent nail, a frayed prayer book.

One evening when I knocked on a door I was greeted by a fancy lady attired in a long dress and smelling of perfume.

'Who is it?' another woman's voice called from inside.

'A cute little Jew boy,' she answered.

Two other women almost identically dressed and of about the same age were suddenly in front of me, and now the three of them were looking me over.

'What do you want?' asked one of them.

'I'm hungry,' I answered.

'Come in, we're just baking bread, but then you'll have to leave.'

I scanned the room. Now and then one of the ladies would exit into another room from which the aroma of baking permeated. In the corner stood a piano with sheet music on its ledge. One lady sat down and began to play 'The Last Sunday'. The melody filtered through, awakening fragments of memory.

I was lost in recollection when one of the ladies suddenly yelped, 'Look! He's coming.' The playing stopped abruptly and all three stared out of the window.

Through the frosted pane, the shape of a man in a heavy jacket and fur hat could be seen. 'What do we do with him?' asked one, in panic, pointing to me.

'He has to leave,' cried another.

'It's too late,' said the third.

'He can't stay here.'

'Quick! He's by the barn. There's no time to think.'

I was thrust into the other room. It was dark and the heat from the oven transformed the room to an inferno. My body began to itch beyond endurance. I scratched but held myself back from screaming.

Voices reached me, and from their conversation I gathered that the three ladies were sisters. The gentleman, a well-to-do widower, was courting the three spinsters. He told foul stories. They laughed. The piano was heard. There was a tinkling of glasses. The visitor sang, rather poorly. And then someone remembered the bread. One of the sisters offered to check the oven, and the visitor, now inebriated, insisted on accompanying her. The others tried to hold him back, but couldn't stop him. The door burst open and I jumped behind it.

'So hot in here!' exclaimed the lady, opening the oven door.

'It's hot wherever you are, my lamb!' said the suitor, his smelly breath almost upon me. There was a bit of shuffling, something fell to the floor with a terrifying clatter, followed by the sound of a kiss. The lady giggled.

'Come, you devil, the bread isn't done yet,' she said, and they left.

'It's getting late,' I heard one of the spinsters say.

'Let it be late,' answered the widower with a slur. 'Let's live while we're still young,' and he broke into a new song, more off key than before.

I hadn't eaten that day and now felt faint. I reached into the oven, yanked out a chunk of a half-baked loaf and stuffed it into my mouth, burning my lips. After more songs and much more laughter, I opened the oven door again and devoured another serving of steaming dough. When at long last the drunken guest had been escorted to the door, the sisters came rushing in.

In place of three loaves, they pulled out two. I was grateful that they didn't reprimand me, and even more so for allowing me to stay the night.

I tried but couldn't sleep. The knowledge that two loaves of bread were lying in a cupboard within an arm's reach prevented me from even closing my eyes. Although my stomach was full now, I feared tomorrow. Without hesitation I opened the cupboard and snatched a loaf, then broke off a piece. In this fashion the second loaf disappeared. I still couldn't sleep waiting for dawn to come, and when it did, I slipped my coat on, and hid the third loaf under it. I unbolted the door and headed out.

TO ADD TO MY TRIBULATIONS, in midwinter I began to wet myself at night. Not only did I have to hide my infestation and diseased hands, but a wet floor every morning as well. When bedding for the night, I'd dread the thought of waking. For I knew that in the morning a smelly puddle of water would embarrass me and infuriate my hosts. And so I'd rise early and flee.

Some nights, sleep would overtake me and in my slumber I'd dream I had to urinate. Out of nowhere a large, golden basin would materialise. I'd empty my bladder and sigh with relief, only to awake to reality in the morning.

In desperation I tried several remedies without success, the last of which was a bottle attached to my penis. In the morning the bottle was empty, but the bedding was wet as usual.

An angry voice awakened me one night. I opened my eyes staring at my host. 'You're pissing on my floor,' he shouted.

'I'm sorry,' I apologised. 'It's never happened before.'

'I can cure you of this, boy,' he told me, and lit the naphtha lamp as it was still quite dark.

In a low voice so as not to awaken his wife, he said, 'I think you're a Jew.'

'You're mistaken,' I said without much emotion.

'You don't have to fear me,' he continued, 'I won't betray you. If you're not a Jew you can stay with us and be our son.'

'I'm not a Jew. What gave you that idea?'

'I have to be sure,' he said. 'Let's see if you're circumcised.' His wife stirred in her sleep and then woke.

'I don't mind,' I said, 'but your wife ...'

He led me into a lean-to. 'Pull down your pants.'

I unbuttoned my fly and dropped the trousers. Perhaps he can't tell the difference, I thought. Or perhaps in the morning light my penis will look like his, or perhaps God will intervene and blind him!

'Just as I thought,' he said. 'You're cut off.'

'Perhaps I'm cut off without knowing it. But I'm no Jew,' I answered stoically, buttoning up my pants.

'What's with this?' and he pointed to my gloves.

'A dog bit me.'

'Let's see,' he said, pulling them off. 'There's a cure for dog bites.'

Obviously I fooled him this time, I thought.

'Piss on them three times a day,' he advised, 'and in several weeks they'll be healed.'

For lack of a better cure I took his advice and for weeks urinated on my hands, but without success.

IF I SURVIVE, I THOUGHT, I'll come back here, gather all the villagers, and present them with a monument for their kindness. I longed for that day, imagining myself surrounded, and observing their surprised faces, hearing me declare, 'I'm a Jew!'

The snow began to melt; here and there a patch of green could be seen. The roads turned to mud and the sky brightened. Winter's end was in sight, but there seemed no end to my struggle to survive.

One day my wanderings from one village to another brought me to Chojeniec. I scanned the farmhouses and debated which to enter. On the right stood a prosperous-looking structure with a barn and large stable; on my left, smoke was coming out of the chimney of a small, well-kept hut set far back from the road. I approached the door. A young woman appeared and, without asking me what I wanted, invited me in.

At the end of the room by the light of a naphtha lamp, a young man was hammering small nails into a shoe sole.

'Take off your coat and sit down,' said the vivacious woman as she closed the door behind me.

'And what brings you here?' asked the young man.

Removing my coat I said, 'I'm looking for work.'

'You must be hungry,' and he called to his wife. 'Marisia, bring some of that tasty krupnik of yours.'

I watched him work. He reminded me so much of my own father making shoe uppers. My father. I wonder where he is! Our little flat in Pulawy, Josele, my mother, my father's mandolin playing. If only I could wake and find it was only a terrible dream!

Between spoonfuls of the barley, bean, and mushroom soup, I repeated my customary orphan story; my father working in Germany on forced labour, the terrible beatings I endured from my stepmother, and how in the end, unable to bear it any longer, I ran away from home.

The man dropped his hammer and listened, his mouth half open and his eyes upon me. His wife sat in the corner, wiping the tears from her eyes. At the end of my sad tale, the young cobbler rolled a cigarette, lit it, and then asked me my name.

'Kubus,' I answered.

'Kubus what?'

'Nowicki,' I responded without hesitation, not sure where it came from, but I must have come across someone with it.

'And I am Kazimierz Rutkowski,' and he joined me at the table. 'Well, Kubus, you won't have to wander any longer.'

I looked up. 'You need someone?' I asked hopefully.

He looked at his wife, then back at me. 'I wish we had more room, we'd keep you on. I know what it's like to be alone in this world. I too was an orphan, kicked from house to house. This is the first place I can call my home.' He took a deep puff on his cigarette, exhaled, and then continued.

'But I have a wealthy relative, and he's a fine gentleman, and now that summer is coming, he'll need a boy like you to look after things.'

'Where does he live?' I asked.

'In Majdan, near Siedliszcze.'

When I lay down to sleep, in the darkness of the room I could make out the cobbler's tools and paper patterns in the company of worn-out shoes in need of repair, and others that were already mended.

It wasn't a great leap to my father's workroom, where he was whistling Schubert's *Serenade* as he stood over the workbench cutting shoe uppers out of smooth leather skins, and occasionally lifting his head to steal a look at the church across the street or to wave to a person passing by.

'When will you make Jankele a pair of sandals?' my mother would nag.

'I'll get around to it,' he'd answer, and continue to whistle.

Then, catching sight of the barefoot, red-haired orphan, he called him in. Puzzled, the boy waited in the doorway.

'Come in,' my father motioned for him to sit. 'Let me have your feet,' and he took his measurements, telling him to come back in a week's time.

'What about Jankele?' my mother pleaded.

'Is Jankele an orphan?' He threw her a look and returned to Schubert.

My mother instilled in me the fear of God. Though she was not terribly pious, nevertheless she carried on the tradition. Friday nights she lit and blessed candles, abstained from cooking on the Sabbath, prepared food according to law, and guarded her two sets of dishes, one for milk and the other for meat.

My father did not interfere with her beliefs, but he had

abandoned religion when he was fifteen after being exposed
to books by the great masters. Thus he never covered his head
at the table, and didn't attend synagogue, not even on the
high holy days. This created friction between them, especially
concerning my upbringing.

I tended to lean towards my mother. On Friday evenings
when I'd go to the nearby synagogue and sip from the cup of
wine that was being passed around, I'd be questioned, 'Where
is your father? How come he isn't here?'

'He's sick,' I'd answer with shame.

'Sick again? What is it this time?' they'd tease.

'He has a toothache,' I would reply, and move on, only to
be confronted by another.

'And what's the matter with your father tonight?'

'He's sick.'

'Don't tell me, I know, a toothache. Will he be here next
week?'

'He'll be here for sure if he doesn't get sick.'

'Please, Daddy, all my friends' fathers are there, but not
you,' I'd cry.

The shame of having an atheist for a father was more than
I could bear.

He'd hold me on his knees and say, 'To be good to others,
to be strong and healthy and live a clean life, that's what's
important. And not sitting in a smelly old room, bending
your head in prayer, with words one doesn't understand.
Someday when you grow up you'll realise how the masses are
poisoned with fairy tales of a God who doesn't exist, so as to
make them forget how hungry they are.'

I listened, but refused to accept his teachings, for I could
clearly picture an enormous old man with a long white
beard reclining on a cloud and watching my every move and

listening to my every thought. I believed that everything was written down in a gigantic book. That when it thundered, God was angry. That when it rained, He was urinating, and when it snowed, His wife was changing the goose feathers in the bedding. I felt sad that my father did not believe in God, and feared that God would one day punish him for it.

Many a cold winter night our home came to life. In his workroom, my father carried on heated political debates with friends. And always, perhaps as a sign of protest, there were slices of smoked ham lying on wrapping paper, for my mother forbade her plates to be contaminated by the forbidden food.

In the other half of the room, the kitchen, my mother, two musical companions, and I would carry on with a singsong. Shie, the barber, my mother, and I would sing, and Kisel, the street musician, would accompany us on the mandolin. Between songs my mother served potato latkes and hot tea with lemon in a glass.

My father was gentle with me – never laid a hand on me. Yet, I feared him. So much so that one day, returning home from school, when I saw him coming, I took off.

He called, 'Jankele!' and pursued me. I ran like a demon, turning one corner, another, his footsteps and voice trailing, 'Jankele!' In the marketplace I managed to give him the slip, but now feared returning home, wondering what bad deed I was guilty of, and what kind of punishment awaited me.

When night ultimately brought me to the door, trembling with fear, he was sitting at the workbench, his eyes filled with tears.

'Why did you run from me?' he asked. 'I wanted to give you a few groszy to buy chocolate.'

'Jankele! Jankele!' the voice segued into him whistling Shubert's *Serenade*.

Outside the cobbler Rutkowski's window the wind whistled its own tune.

In the morning his wife asked if I slept well.

'Oh yes,' I assured her.

'You were dreaming,' she said, 'and talking in your sleep.'

'Oh, what did I say?'

'You kept repeating over and over, "My name is Kubus Nowicki, I'm a Pole."'

The game is up, I worried. They know.

After breakfasting on bowls of gruel, Mr Rutkowski and I set out for Majdan. The ice covering the roads was now melting, causing the poor horse to slip several times. Along the way the cobbler offered me words of hope; that someday when I would grow into manhood, I'd have my own family and farm. He shared the story of his sad life, of how his parents met death in a fire while he was still an infant, and how he had found his own way in life.

Before noon we turned off the road into a small, neatly kept farmyard and brought the horse to a halt. 'This is my cousin's place,' he said proudly. 'What do you think of it?'

'It looks fine to me,' I answered as we descended the wagon.

'He's a good man, you'll like him. Come.'

A petite, meticulously dressed woman met us at the door. The interior of the house had a clinical look about it; everything in its own place and not a speck of dust anywhere.

'I brought you a boy,' said the cobbler.

She looked me over and said, 'How wonderful! Wherever did you find him?'

'An orphan. His name is Kubus Nowicki.'

'Bolek will be delighted,' she said, leading us into the kitchen where a fire burned in the stove.

'Where is Bolek?'

She looked at me, then at him, and as if uttering some secret code. 'On business,' slipped out of her mouth.

'And Lucja?'

'Here she comes now,' she pointed at the window.

A girl about the same age as Genia fell into the cobbler's arms, asking him endless questions as he helped her off with her coat. I was introduced to her.

'I have to get back,' said Mr Rutkowski when we had finished lunch, and he shook my hand warmly and wished me good luck.

Unlike Genia, Lucja behaved as if I didn't exist, and when she did address me, she never looked me straight in the eye.

In the evening, the man of the house arrived. Mother and daughter ran out to greet him and helped unhitch the horse. Watching them through the window, it was hard to make out what they were saying, but from gestures I guessed they were informing him of my presence.

The door opened and, framed between his wife and daughter, stood the master of the house. He wore a dark suit that was neither green nor blue, but something in between, a shirt and tie, and polished black shoes; his hair was cut and combed neatly. He hardly looked the proverbial farmer, but more a city doctor. His face had a kind demeanour with a perpetual smile attached to it. I took to him immediately. He extended his hand and introduced himself: 'Boleslaw Gogulka. I offered him my gloved right hand. He shook it warmly and held on. 'Why the gloves?'

'My hands are always cold.' Our eyes locked and now, at close range, I recognised him and understood the reason for his stare. He was the man who had bought a pig from Mrs Pejzak and had referred to me as Abraham.

'What do you call yourself?' he asked.

I responded with a somewhat unsure voice, 'Kubus Nowicki.'

'Kubus Nowicki. That's a nice name, a very nice name.'

He knows who you are, cautioned a voice.

Not so, the other voice contradicted.

The first laughed. Oh, what an optimist you are! The man is no fool, he's recognised you.

He looks kind.

So that's how you judge people? How do you know if the ones who took your mother, brother, and uncle away didn't look kind as well?

Somehow I trust him.

Very well, wait till tomorrow, said the other voice, when he'll leave on some pretence and return with the Gestapo.

The two voices continued to bicker, long after I lay down for the night.

You can't trust anyone, the first voice was adamant. Especially those who look kind and smile. Have you forgotten that scoundrel in Warsaw? Remember how he smiled? And he was one of us. A Jew, a friend, and look what he did.

My mind voyaged back to the day when that very man, an old acquaintance of my grandfather's, stepped into our basement apartment on Pawia Street and confided, 'Shie Chuen, my old friend, I'm clearing out of the ghetto.' My grandfather was happy for him.

'But how?'

'Don't ask. All it takes is money. Plenty of it. But in this case it will cost a good pair of boots. And that's what brings me here.'

My grandmother served him tea with lemon in a glass and then my grandfather proceeded to show him a selection of remodelled footwear. 'That's all you have Shie? Only old junk?'

'What is it you're looking for?' my grandfather queried. 'New boots you won't find in the ghetto; surely you know that we had to hand over all new leather to the Hitlerites.'

'But I figured a clever man like you might still have a piece hidden here or there. And, after all, I am a friend. And I'm willing to pay top price.'

My grandfather turned the dining table upside down, reached for his hammer, and began removing nails from boards that formed a false bottom. 'Is this what you're looking for?'

The smiling customer walked across to the overturned table; his eyes popped as he knelt to finger several skins. 'That's more like it,' he said with an even bigger smile.

'Quick, brown or black, and let me close the vault,' said my grandfather.

'Shie, do me a favour; let me bring the fixer who's getting me out of here and let him decide. After all, he'll be wearing them.

'I can't keep this in the open much longer.'

'Who's talking about long, Shie?' And he left.

Within minutes a black limousine drove into the court-yard and out of it sprang several leather-clad Gestapo types led by the long-time smiling friend. They smashed into the apartment and, without a word, the Hitlerites began to slap and kick my poor grandfather. He fell and got up, but each time he staggered to his feet, he was hit again.

'How could you do this to me?' he asked, his face bleeding. 'I'm your friend.'

The informer stood in the corner of the room, munching on chocolate-covered plums. My grandfather's question made him laugh.

'Don't be so naive, Shie Chuen; just before Passover I turned my own father in.'

I was now convinced that Boleslaw Gogulka knew who I was and that come morning, he would turn me in.

Leave now! Go! The voice within me urged, but my eyes closed and I succumbed to sleep.

When I awoke, Mrs Gogulka and Lucja were busy with house chores. I asked if the man of the house was still sleeping and was informed he had left hours ago.

'Where to?' I wanted to know.

They looked at each other as if considering the question. 'To Siedliszcze,' Mrs Gogulka finally answered.

My heart jumped.

'You relax, Kubus. There won't be much for you to do until all the snow melts.'

I took a walk around the farmyard, chopped some wood, and pulled up a bucket of water from the well; then I entered the barn and introduced myself to the animals, still debating if I should pick up my coat and run. But the house was warm, the bedding soft and fluffy; there was plenty to eat, and my new hosts seemed kind. If I wasn't recognised, then this might well be a good home to wait out my time.

As my mind wandered, I suddenly heard a car's motor. I rushed to the barn door and looked out. A German car was making its way along the slushy road.

I've been betrayed!

Don't say I didn't warn you. You should have listened to me. You can't trust a kind face or any other face.

The car came to a stop at the entrance to the Gogulka farm. If I run out, I'm as good as dead. I withdrew into the barn.

I waited behind the open door, peering out between the hinges. Two German soldiers emerged from the vehicle and headed towards the house. As they passed the barn I caught a glimmer of their revolvers swinging from their hips. I heard a knock on the door, the door opening, conversation, and then Mrs Gogulka's voice hollering, 'Kubus!'

I began to pray, 'Dear God, if you can hear me, please help. I don't want to die. Dear God, please save me.' It suddenly occurred to me that perhaps the Jewish God got very old and died, or possibly He did hear our cries, but didn't care. I could think of so many people who prayed to Him and He never answered. Didn't my mother believe in Him? He obviously didn't respond to her prayers. And all those rabbis and scholars who did nothing else but pray day and night? What were their sins? What about all those people I used to see in the synagogue?

'Kubus!' Mrs Gogulka's voice interrupted my musings.

I fell to my knees and closed my eyes, 'Dear Jesus,' I trembled, 'Save me and I'll believe in you.'

'Kubus!' I left the barn and faced the two Germans as if I was pleased to see them.

Where is Mr Gogulka? Where is my betrayer? Probably in the car, munching on a chocolate-covered plum bonbon, ashamed to face me.

'Kubus,' Mrs Gogulka pointed to a house surrounded by tall trees. 'Run over to our neighbour and ask them if they have some extra eggs.'

'Eggs?'

'These gentlemen want to purchase some eggs.'

'Sure,' I said, and I flew off. In no time I was back. The soldiers paid, patted me on the head, and drove off. I re-entered the barn, closing the door behind me. Leaning against the wall, I cried.

Jesus saved you, whispered one of the voices.

Nobody saved you, said the other. There was nothing to be saved from. They came to buy eggs, not to look for Jews.

They came for you, but Jesus intervened and made them ask for eggs instead.

I felt deeply ashamed. I had indeed saved my life, but by doing so I had crossed the line. I had betrayed my mother's God, my God, and the God for which my grandfathers had died. I now saw myself as an outcast; small, despicable, loathsome, and unworthy. A betrayer!

I remembered the cool summer evenings in Pulawy when neighbours would gather on our doorsteps: Kisel strumming his mandolin, a fat bald-headed man, the tailor from down the street, and others, waiting for the night's cool air. I recalled a barefoot woman in peasant clothes approaching. The music and talk halted, and all eyes gawked at her. As she passed, one or two of the group would spit on the pavement, aiming at her footprints.

My father was aghast at the neighbours' behaviour and I hungered for answers. My mother explained that this woman had once been a nice Jewish girl, her father a learned and pious man. Then she fell in love with a farmer in the village across the bridge. They married and she converted to Christianity. From then on, I too spat when I saw her walk by.

God will never forgive her for this sin, I thought then. Now I had visions of myself being spat upon by my mother, my grandfathers, my brother Josele, and almost everyone I had ever known, except perhaps my father. Convert! Christ lover! I could almost hear their hostile voices. Humiliated and frightened, I said to myself, 'I was only pretending, I am still a Jew. I don't believe in Jesus Christ!'

Suddenly a shot rang out, followed by another and another. Am I still alive? When I saw no blood and felt no pain, I looked out to see what was happening, and spotted the German car heading towards Siedliszcze.

When Mr Gogulka returned that evening, his wife unfolded the day's events.

'Oh, yes,' he said, scooping a potato from the common bowl. 'I heard about it.'

'Who were they shooting at?' asked his daughter. 'Remember that collaborator in Siedliszcze who was strung up by some Russian partisans? Well, it seems they got some fugitive who was wearing that villain's apparel, and also had his cane with the silver handle.'

My heart jumped. Genia's Ivan was dead.

ON MY THIRD DAY with the Gogulkas, I removed my gloves to inspect the sores. By chance Lucja noticed, and when I caught her stare, she turned her eyes. Soon after, I heard her whispering to her mother. Immediately I put the gloves back on.

That night when the man of the house came home, there were more whispers coming from the other room. I gazed out the window and wondered where my feet would carry me next, when Mr Gogulka appeared.

Smiling and in good humour, he asked me if I was happy being with them. And then, as if out of casual curiosity, he looked at my gloved hands and said, 'I understand you have a rash, Kubus.' I was tempted to tell him the dog story, but because of the calm way he confronted me, I couldn't lie to him. And so I didn't answer. 'Nothing to worry, son,' he assured me. 'If it's a rash, we'll cure it.' Still I didn't respond. He reached for my hands and gently pulled off the mismatched soiled gloves. 'You poor soul! How you must suffer!' I turned my eyes from him, humbled by his kindness. He patted me and said, 'Tomorrow I'll get you medicine.' With that he threw the gloves into the fire. I lifted my head. He was smiling at me. I smiled back.

The following evening he came home with a jar of ointment. The women of the house were ushered out of the main room after which Mr Gogulka rolled up his shirt sleeves and poured hot water into a barrel.

'Start undressing!' he said to me.

'Everything?' I questioned.

'Everything,' came the sharp reply.

I hesitated.

'What's the matter, Kubus, don't you like to bathe?' he smiled broadly.

'It's not that,' I answered.

'What is it then?'

Ever so slowly I began to undress, all along thinking how to get into the barrel without exposing my privates. When I was down to Staszek's long underwear, way too large for me, I began to fidget.

'Come, come,' he called, 'the water will get cold.'

I had begun to undo the button on my fly, when Mr Gogulka went out to get more firewood. I rapidly dropped the underwear and dove into the water.

Re-entering, he gathered my clothing and threw it into the still-warm oven, then with a rough brush and a bar of soap he scrubbed me vigorously and then ordered me out of the water. How am I going to manage this? I manoeuvred myself in such a way that he could see only my back, but no sooner did I feel a sense of victory than his hands were upon me with a large towel, drying my body energetically. I kept turning my back to him.

'Will you please stand still, boy.' He raised his voice in slight annoyance.

I closed my eyes. He was now drying my legs, and gradually moving up to my groin.

I was sure he saw it. Any moment he'll stop and say, 'Why, you're a Jew!' But to my surprise he said nothing; instead, he poured the ointment into his right palm and applied it into all the crevices of my body.

When I was in bed I wondered how was it possible for him not to have noticed what set me apart. And, when for the next six days the same treatment was repeated, and Mr Gogulka still hadn't made any mention of it, I came to the conclusion that his knowledge in such matters was limited.

At last my body was free of those tormenting sores and lice. I could now sleep peacefully and eat my meals without having to hide my hands.

In no time at all I was part of the Gogulka family, and at times I had to remind myself who I really was. I had also, I realised somewhat sadly, forgotten Yiddish, and now both thought and dreamed in Polish.

I teased Lucja as if she was my older sister and even argued and pretended to be at odds with her. She also treated me like a sibling. But on occasion, when I would not obey her, she would remind me that I was only a servant.

Her girlfriends would visit on Sundays and encourage me to sing.

'You'll be a heartbreaker when you grow up,' they'd say, and ask for more songs. It seemed I never stopped singing, not only on Sundays, but throughout the week as well, from dawn to dusk.

'How come you always sing?' Mr Gogulka asked one day. 'They say a Gypsy sings when he's hungry. Are you hungry?'

'No, I sing because I'm happy,' I replied.

'I wish Lucja had an ear like yours,' he said. Lucja was

tone deaf and this troubled her father. She was given music lessons, but nothing came of it.

Mrs Gogulka too, treated me in a motherly fashion; sewing shirts and pants especially for me, and dishing out second helpings onto my plate. 'You're a growing boy,' she'd remark. I still wet my bed, but instead of disgracing me, Mr Gogulka began waking me in the middle of the night, in hopes of curing me of this malady.

In late spring, we planted a cherry tree near the fence in my honour and named it Kubus.

I helped till the land, sow it, look after cows, and perform countless other duties. For functions I couldn't do on my own, I would assist Mr Gogulka on a day he stayed home. But mostly he was away 'on business'.

We would anxiously wait for his return, and on days when he brought home a pig, the slaughtering would take place that very night.

By order of the German authorities, all animals had to be registered and tagged with a numbered metal clip affixed to their ears. It was forbidden for a farmer to slaughter an animal for his own use. Nevertheless, farmers risked their lives raising unregistered pigs and cows. Mr Gogulka dealt in these illegal animals, buying them and disposing the meat on the black market. If caught, he would have been shot on the spot, which is why the butchering always had to be performed at night and in secrecy.

The first time he asked for my assistance and saw me squirming as he raised the blunt side of the axe on the poor hog's head, he said, 'You've got to learn to kill son. It's part of life.'

In time, I became less squeamish and learned how to assist in the killing, how to cut the animal's stomach open, drain its blood, and carve the meat into sellable portions. Mrs Gogulka would make blood pudding, and with that, accompanied by some vodka, we would feast late into the night.

I took great pleasure performing these tasks, not because I enjoyed the killing, nor the taste of blood pudding, but because we were doing something illegal and undermining the occupiers.

Mr Gogulka praised me daily, making me feel secure and appreciated.

I also made friends. Once in a while I would visit one of them and sometimes they would visit me. We'd play cards, chase wild rabbits, and climb trees. And they, like everyone else in the village, came to know me as the 'Gogulkas' boy', and none asked questions.

'I need you to come to town with me, Kubus,' Mr Gogulka said one day.

This was a risk I would rather not have taken, but I decided to go. Not so much out of curiosity to see Siedliszcze again, but by trying to wriggle out of it, I was afraid of arousing suspicion in his mind.

We drove through the town, my heart beating and my eyes roaming from one side of the street to the other. I could barely recognise the town; German soldiers, a Polish police-man, peasants, and town folk. And when we came to the one-room row of shacks where I once lived, I refused to look in case someone noticed and recognised me.

SUMMER TURNED INTO AUTUMN, and then into winter. The snow came and covered the fields and roads.

It now seemed to me that I had never known any other life; that I had always lived with the Gogulkas and that, no matter what, I would always remain there. I could see myself grown up, getting married to one of the village maidens, and raising a family on a farm just like the Gogulkas.

The Germans, the war, fear, and being Jewish completely vanished from my mind. I continued to cross myself when required, and pretended to pray, but this too I accepted as part of normal life.

One Sunday, Mrs Gogulka and Lucja had gone to church, I remained to do some chores, and Mr Gogulka was still asleep. When he awoke, he looked for something to eat.

'How about we have some eggs and onions, Kubus?'

'Not for me,' I said, 'I've already eaten.'

'I thought you people liked onions,' escaped from his lips.

I stiffened as if waking from a bad dream. Jews consumed no more onions than anyone else, but for some reason it was said, 'You can always tell a Jew; he smells of onions.'

From that moment, I stopped singing. He knows. Otherwise, why would he have said that? Perhaps I didn't hear correctly! But if he knows, why is he risking his life by keeping me? Nightmares invaded my sleep.

Soon enough he called me to his side. His voice and manner were sombre. Gone was the infectious smile. 'It hurts me to say this; I've wanted to say it for months, but didn't know how.' He stared at his feet. 'Kubus – ' and he couldn't complete the sentence. Raising his eyes and taking hold of my shoulders, he resumed, 'You understand, son ... it's getting too dangerous. Word is out that the Germans are planning a house-to-house search.' I felt faint. 'You can't imagine what a loss this will be. You don't know how much you have meant to us, having a boy like you around. You're the son I've always wanted, and hoped that somehow, by an act of God, I could save you.' He pulled me to him. 'God only knows how I've tried. I've tried, but I'm afraid now.' He released me, choking on his words. I looked out the window and watched the snow blowing across the deserted fields.

'How long have you known?' I asked.

'I knew, Kubus, I knew from the first day. I remembered you from the Pejzak farm.'

Next morning the three Gogulkas stood at the entrance of the farmyard waving handkerchiefs and weeping at my departure. As I closed the wooden gate behind me, I glanced at the cherry tree, now so fragile, bedecked with snow and tormented by wind, and regretted that I would never pick cherries from its branches.

The following morning when Mrs Gogulka stepped out to scatter the chickenfeed, she found me in the ditch by the side of the house crying bitterly. Overcome with fear, her scream brought the other members of the family to her side. I wrapped my arms around Mr Gogulka's legs, beseeching him to allow me to stay. He implored me to be on my way, and when I didn't make a move, he swung me over his shoulders, carrying me the same way I had seen him carry a lamb or goat to slaughter.

'Leave! Go! Get away from here and don't come back,' he cried, tears cascading down his cheeks.

Deep was the snow, and far and wide where the earth meets the sky. Where to now?

I CROSSED VARIOUS FIELDS and soon stood in the doorway of a friend's home.

'How good to see you again, Kubus,' said my friend's father and invited me in. I helped my friend with his chores, we played tag in the barn and later engaged in a game of twenty-one.

When the family was ready to eat supper, the father said, 'Kubus, you'd better head home, it's getting dark and the Gogulkas will be worried.' I lowered my head and could sense his gaze throughout the long silence that followed. 'Would you like to eat with us, perhaps?' he finally asked. I nodded my head. 'What seems to be the trouble, Kubus?' he inquired later. Again I resorted to silence. 'Had a disagreement with your boss perhaps?' he probed.

'May I stay here for the night?' I asked meekly.

He motioned to his wife and son to leave the room, then sat down opposite me, rolled a cigarette, and said, 'You can confide in me, Kubus Nowicki.'

My eyes still downcast, I muttered, 'I'm a Jew and Nowicki is not my real name.' I waited for a reaction and when there was none, I continued. 'If you want, you can turn me in. I don't care anymore, I've nowhere to go and I'm tired of lying and hiding.'

'What happened to your family?' he asked.

I unburdened myself by telling him my true story: that we had lived in Pulawy, and when the Germans invaded and started persecuting Jews, my father escaped to Russia, and my mother, my brother, and I left for Warsaw to be with my mother's family, who lived in a basement on Pawia Street. One day when we woke up, we found ourselves imprisoned by a high brick wall surrounding our district: a ghetto, the Warsaw Ghetto.

Miraculously, we managed to escape, running from one town to another, stopping in Lublin. One winter day, we were rounded up along with other Lublin Jews and packed onto trucks to be deported to an unknown destination. Through another miracle, we escaped the net and returned to Lublin where there were still some Jews left who possessed special permits exempting them from deportation. When there was talk of a ghetto there, we fled and one night stumbled into Siedliszcze, hoping it would prove to be a safe haven. Later, my grandfather and his two youngest sons, my two uncles, left the rest of the family behind in the Warsaw Ghetto and joined us.

By the time I had finished my tale of woe, it was late. My friend's father wiped his brow and sighing said, 'I advise you to go ... as far away as possible, where no one knows you and start anew.'

'Where?'

He considered for a moment, and then said, 'Malinowka in the district of Chelm.'

ARMED WITH NEW HOPE, I set out the next morning. Once on the road, I took the rosary from inside my shirt and exhibited it over my coat.

Along the way, when I stopped a passer-by to ask for directions, he looked at me suspiciously, and broke out laughing.

'You're a Jew, aren't you?' He pointed to the cross hanging over my garment for everyone to see, and the prayer book in my hands. I didn't answer. 'You're too obvious,' he went on. 'A true Christian carries Christ close to his heart, boy. Do up your shirt and put the prayer book in your pocket.'

The roads were covered in bottomless snow and only occasionally did a sleigh go by, pulled by horses adorned with chiming brass bells, driven by shivering farmers wrapped in heavy garments.

Late in the afternoon I arrived at Malinowka. At the entrance to the village, I stopped to assess it and spotted a smithy. 'What do you want?' the blacksmith inquired.

'I'm looking for work,' I answered.

He extracted a piece of hot metal from the fire, and hammered on it, shaping it to his liking. Then he wiped his hands and said, 'I am called Alexander Tekalewicz. What do you call yourself?'

So as not to leave a trail behind, 'Zygmund Cybula,' slipped out of my mouth.

He led me into the adjoining house. 'This boy is looking for work.' He introduced me to his sister and mother.

'Sit down,' someone said, and then they hurled questions.

I answered, spinning my fabricated history. The sister, a tall, lean girl with a pleasant smile, became terribly emotional over how I was abused by my stepmother and had to take to the road to escape her brutal hand.

'I know someone who could use a boy like you, Zygmund,' she said, shedding tears.

At which point a tapping on the windowpane was heard and a German soldier's face popped up. The girl beckoned him to enter.

He greeted everyone cheerfully in German. The girl returned the gesture in broken German. He sat down beside me. The girl put on her coat and boots, picked up a purse, and then addressing me, she said, 'You wait here until I get back.' I nodded my head. The German stood up, clicked his heels, bowed, and they left.

Later, when the village was in darkness, the girl returned and immediately led me to a nearby house.

'I brought you a boy,' she announced when we entered.

The place was exceptionally filthy. The family sat by the stove. In a corner stood a Christmas tree with candles, cookies, and apples adorning it. Grimy dishes littered the table. On the floor, two half-naked children were playing with a black cat.

The man of the house, a sturdy figure in his underwear, sat on a stool picking his nose. His wife, a nervous woman with sharp, piercing eyes, was combing her long dark hair, hunting for lice.

'Who is the boy, Kazia?' asked the woman.

'A poor orphan,' she answered and left soon after.

I soon learned that my new employers, the Wajdas, were from Ukraine and had once lived under Soviet rule. As a result, Mrs Wajda hated the Russians bitterly, but even more, she hated Jews, whom she blamed for all the evil in the world. The Jews were responsible for the war, and all communists, fascists, bandits, swindlers, and the devil himself were Jews.

Before the German occupation, the dilapidated house in which they now lived had belonged to the only Jewish farmer in the village. No one knew what had happened to its owner, a Mr Goldman, except that he had vanished one night, leaving everything behind. Whatever was wrong with the house, the outer building, or the land, Mrs Wajda blamed on the former occupant.

I sat listening, agreeing, and sometimes even adding a few demeaning remarks of my own.

In comparison to his wife, Mr Wajda was tolerant, but extremely boorish in his manner. He talked so fast that one word overlapped the next; he constantly shouted, especially at me. Not once did I see him smile or hear him say a kind word.

The two had countless violent arguments, she threatening to break his head wide open with an axe, and he shouting back in half-intelligible sentences, made up mostly of profane, vile words.

'I should never have married you!' she would cry.

'Whore,' he'd call her, and spit in her direction. 'You slept with all the Bolsheviks.'

When they didn't go at each other, their two children, Wanda, aged seven, and Kazia, younger, romped about the house, tearing pillows apart and sometimes scratching at each other's eyes.

Christmas passed without much celebration, except for a few carols and Mrs Wajda's telling the Christmas story of how many, many years ago, Jesus, the son of God was born and later crucified by the terrible, terrible Jews. The candles flickered on the tree; the cookies and other goodies were soon devoured by all, and before long the tree was chopped for firewood and the holiday was over.

Another merciless winter had set in, and it refused to depart. Without gloves and with only wooden clogs on my feet, I was expected to fetch water from a neighbour's well a field away. Since there was no clear path to the well, my clogs, too large for my feet, would lodge themselves in the deep snow. I'd recover one, take another step, only to lose the other. An hour later I'd arrive back at the house, with only half a bucket of water, my face and hands numb from the frost, and my feet and legs frozen stiff.

'What took you so long?' Mr Wajda would reprimand me. And when I would sit by the stove to warm and dry my feet, again his boorish voice would shatter my ears with, 'Let's go, let's go boy. There's work to be done in the granary.'

There, for hours without rest, we would chop straw for the horse's feed. If I'd complain about the biting cold, or ask permission to rest, he would remind me that I was a hired hand and must pull my weight if I wished to eat.

He was an extremely fast eater. In fact, it was as if he didn't eat, but rather made his food disappear, like a magician. The fact that I took longer angered him. 'Let's go, let's go, Zygmund! The day is flying away.'

In time I learned to keep pace with him, and whenever he left the table, I followed, often leaving food on my plate.

Once during that winter the Wajdas went to Chelm. Mrs Wajda prepared a large potato pudding in the morning for our meals and instructed me to take good care of the children. I tried to entertain them with my full repertoire. But they were not interested, having witnessed my output many times before. The day seemed endless, and it was more from boredom than hunger that the three of us devoured the pudding before lunch. I searched the cupboards for more food, but there was nothing except some home-brewed vodka. The children egged me on to drink it, and so to offset their monotony, I took a sip.

'More,' they shouted, 'like Daddy.' I took another sip, then another. They laughed and jumped up and down on the bed.

The room felt warm and I was unafraid. Everything around me seemed so pleasant. I took another drink, and though it burned my insides, I continued.

The children applauded. 'You're drunk like Daddy,' said Wanda. But I protested that I wasn't, and proceeded to prove it by walking in a straight line and bumping into the cupboard, causing several plates to fall to the floor and shatter.

Wanda became alarmed, 'Wait and see what Mama will do to you!'

'Nothing!' I laughed. 'They're only dishes.'

The room swayed in front of my eyes, and sometimes turned upside down so that I thought I was standing on my head. The children seemed so far away that I only heard their faint laughter.

'I'm not drunk,' I slurred. 'I can walk a straight line.' And again I bashed into something. They giggled and began to throw pillows at me. I retaliated, and soon the goose feathers engulfed the room. 'It's snowing,' I yelled. 'Warm beautiful snow is coming down from heaven.' Then the door opened and my employers stood in the doorway with horrified stares planted on their faces.

'Your children think I'm drunk,' I said, beaming. 'But I'll show you I can walk in a straight line.' And I walked towards them. Mr Wajda's face seemed to get larger and larger, until I could see the texture of his pimply face and the hair protruding from his nostrils.

Someone was being whipped. Mrs Wajda was swearing, and Wanda and her sister were laughing and yelling, 'He's drunk!' More slaps, the room turned like a spinning wheel, and I heard myself joining the laughter, wondering who was being punished.

The next day, when I gazed into the mirror and saw a swollen face covered with black and blue bruises, I knew.

IN TIME, THE INJURIES disappeared and in time the snow melted and vanished into the ground.

All sorts of new faces now appeared. People who had only stared out of their tiny windows during the winter months now left their abodes and moved about the farmyards and roads. Soon they took to the fields and so did I, with the Wajdas' two cows and three sheep.

Occasionally Wanda would tag along, but most of the time I'd venture alone, and there I made new friends my age.

In late spring, a group of us were smoking and telling dirty stories when we heard shouts. A man was running towards us like a wild rabbit. Chasing him was a motley group of cowherds.

'It's a Jew, catch him!' the pursuing voices were yelling.

Someone in our group jumped to his feet and took off. 'Let's get him.' The rest followed. I hesitated, but a voice prompted, 'Let's go, Zygmund.'

And before I knew it, I was running with the others and shouting, 'Jew! Jew! Catch that Jew!'

The man was trapped; we had encircled him, but somehow he broke out of the ring and headed towards the forest. We pursued him. I caught sight of him, jumping over a ravine, stumbling, falling several times, and disappearing among the trees. At times I wondered if it wasn't me who was being chased, but I didn't linger on those thoughts.

'Jew! Catch that lousy Jew!' I shouted along with the others.

'He's gone now, we'll never get him,' I said when we were deep in the woods.

'We'll get him all right,' said a young bully.

'Forward,' ordered another, and they marched on.

'I have to go back,' I said, 'My cows.'

'The devil with the cows. We've got a live Jew to take care of,' said the bully. 'Come, Zygmund.'

'If my cows stray I'll be in deep trouble. I have to go back.' And I did. Who is this man? Where is he from? How much longer will he live? How will he die? And where will he be buried?

And then the mob returned, bitter and disappointed, with a damaged left shoe as the only reward.

'It got stuck in the mud,' said one. 'We'll get the other one next time.'

'We can play ball with it,' another suggested.

And we did for weeks after. A pang of guilt stabbed me every time it came my way and I had to kick it. The day the shoe fell into a pond and was lost forever, I was relieved. But this did not help to clear my conscience. Incessantly, I saw the runner in my sleep, limping on one foot and looking back. Sometimes his face was that of Moishe, sometimes that of my father, and sometimes the face was my own.

THREE

It was late summer and the days were humid and hot. At times I would forget who I really was, and sometimes I couldn't remember my real name. When it would come to me, I'd repeat it several times so as to lodge it in my memory forever.

Why, I didn't know, but something within urged me not to forget who I was, where I was born, and who my mother and father were. It was difficult recalling my real identity as, almost daily throughout that summer, I had spun fabricated stories of my imaginary life.

My friends would sit in a circle, mesmerised as my tales of mistreatment would unfold. On occasion these stories would evoke tears from my audience. They seemed so real that at times I too believed that my name was Zygmund Cybula, and that I had endured all these hardships at the hand of a despotic stepmother.

I was, therefore, quite shattered when a chubby young girl with stringy blonde hair said to me, 'My daddy says you're a Jew.'

I gulped.

'He says you're endangering the whole village and someone should turn you in.'

My God, they know! I'll have to run again, but where to?

I looked towards the forest, and the tall pine trees stared back at me. Deep inside the woods, I pictured fearless partisans brandishing rifles. Among them was the man with one shoe, my Uncle Moishe, perhaps even my father sent by Stalin to lead them! And Kisel with his mandolin, maybe he was there, too.

Adventurous stories circulated about partisans. Now and then a farmer would be found murdered in the middle of the night for collaborating with the enemy.

'Tell your father he should watch what he says,' I threatened.

'He's not afraid of you,' she replied, mocking me.

'He should be afraid of the partisans, though,' I warned. 'Perhaps he hasn't heard what they do to informers. First they kill the informer, then his whole family, and then they burn the house and barn. Tell that to your father.' I was amazed at my own words. The girl fell silent, and her eyes filled with fear. When I saw her next, she was still silent.

Occasionally I saw her father, and he too was silent; his eyes gazed past me, through me, but never at me.

The long summer days dissolved into cold autumn days. The farmers were gathering the harvest. The trees were changing colour, and the wind and rain became frequent visitors.

All summer I had gone barefoot without much trouble, but now several large white blisters appeared on the soles of my feet. It became impossible to walk, and so I had to alternate between treading on my toes and on my heels. I cried with pain and asked for help, but the Wajdas turned away unconcerned.

Stepping on freshly cut wheat fields became unbearable, but I had to, for that is where my cows and sheep grazed. Sometimes I begged my flock not to stray into neighbours' fields, and at other times, I simply sat down and cried, 'Mama! Mama! Help me ... help me!'

Nonetheless, every day without fail I had to take the animals to pasture; one day on this field, another day on that piece of land. Sometimes near the cabbage patch, Mrs Wajda's pride and joy.

'Watch those cows,' she would warn me. 'If they so much as eat one of my cabbage leaves, you'll be sorry you ever left your stepmother.'

With this kind of fear instilled in me, I guarded the cabbage patch with special care.

In the nearby field two young cows grazed, supervised by the chubby girl with the stringy blonde hair. She was constantly disappearing into her house, leaving the cows to their own devices. Without fail, they'd end up in Mrs Wajda's cherished cabbage patch. I kept driving them out.

'Mind your own business,' the girl would yell when I reprimanded her.

'I'll tell Mrs Wajda,' I'd warn.

'Go on, tell her. See if I care!'

I was afraid to provoke her, and so I watched the cabbage patch slowly diminish; some heads had vanished, others half chewed, and still others, stomped by cows' hoofs.

The day came when Mrs Wajda went to harvest her prized cabbages, only to find a ravaged field. That evening she was waiting for me with a long, heavy dried-out stick. Like an animal gone mad, she chased me around the room, into the barn, out of it, into the kitchen, and around the house, beating me with all her might, screaming and cursing with every obscenity imaginable.

I tried to explain, but she wouldn't hear me out.

'My cabbage, my cabbage! How I worked on that cabbage!'

she wept, covering my body, head, and face with blows until the stick broke in half. But even this didn't stop her, for now she attacked me with her bare hands, pulling my hair. 'My cabbage! My cabbage!' Her fingernails ripped into my skin and she hollered, 'I'm going to kill you ...! I'm going to kill you!'

Finally, her husband pulled her off me and led her into the house. I remained outside, resolved to leave.

I saw night descend and the moon appear. Still shedding tears and now shivering from the cold, I appealed to my mother, but the only reply was the distant howling of dogs.

I waited for someone to come looking for me, at least to be asked in for supper. And to protest, I decided I would refuse. I waited and waited. The sky got darker, the clouds moved on, the dogs stopped barking, and then the naphtha lamp inside the house was extinguished.

They don't care if I die, I realised. I have no one in the world who cares what happens to me, and this pained me more than the beating itself.

When next I saw the chubby girl, and she saw my bruises and welts, she said, 'That should teach you to keep better watch on your cows,' and laughed.

THE WAJDAS' CAT GAVE BIRTH to several kittens. Most of them died at birth or soon thereafter, but two little black ones survived.

At first everyone was happy with the new pets, but several weeks after their arrival, it became evident they were both sick. Some bloody matter protruded from their rectums, and on a neighbour's advice, the kittens were to be disposed of.

Kazia and Wanda protested and cried and delayed their

execution, but when the little creatures had not improved, and were getting worse, Mrs Wajda ordered me to get rid of them.

It's not nice for a Jewish boy, I seemed to hear. In what way am I different? Why is it that I'm repulsed even at the thought of killing two sick kittens? Perhaps it is true that Jews are cowards! It must be true, for deep inside me, I'm afraid. I'm scared not only of this, but of many things. I'll have to change. I'll have to become brave. I'll have to behave like the rest of them! How many times had I witnessed a farmer chopping the head off a chicken, without giving it a moment's thought? What do they possess that I don't? Is it the circumcision?

'Get rid of them, Zygmund,' growled Mrs Wajda.

'How?'

'What do you mean, how? Sometimes, Zygmund Cybula, I have the notion you weren't raised on a farm.'

My heart quickened.

'Drown them,' I heard her say. 'I hope you know how to drown kittens, don't you?'

Without hesitation I responded, 'I've done it many times.'

'Then do it,' she snapped.

I picked up the two pathetic creatures and walked out into the farmyard, past the barn, and through the fields until the Wajdas' house was out of sight. The kittens meowed and looked up at me. Cradling them in my arms, I felt like a third bleeding kitten, rather than their executioner. I wanted to flee with them, to keep going further and further, perhaps to the forest, perhaps to some distant land. The pond was now in front of me, and I saw my own sad reflection. I sat down and soaked my feet in the stagnant water. I hoped for some kind of miracle, but it didn't come. Then I thought of letting the kittens loose, but I feared they would find their way back home, and how would I explain that to Mrs Wajda?

The act has to be performed, but how can I do it? I'll have to be brave. Brave like the others. Brave ...

I stood up, closed my eyes, and threw the two kittens into the water, then turned my head. I heard pitiful mewing directed at me.

I imagined my forefathers for generations back, fanned around the pond, their heads bowed in shame.

Suddenly, I felt something brush against my ankles. I opened my eyes and looked down. The kittens were huddling against my bare feet, shivering. I reached and embraced them. Then I broke out crying and once more threw them back into the pond. They submerged for a split second, came up, and quickly paddled back to shore.

I became hysterical and flung them back, screaming, 'Please, you rotten kittens, drown! Drown!' And again they succeeded in saving themselves, and came to me for protection. I held them close to my chest and cried, burying my face in their wet furry bodies.

When I looked up, two boys stood on the other side of the pond observing the scene.

'What's up, Zygmund?' asked one.

I wiped my tears. 'It's these rotten kittens.' I tried to sound brave. 'They've scratched me ... Look, they're sick and I'm trying to drown them.'

The boys walked around the pond to where I was standing. 'You need a bag. You put them in a bag, fill it with stones, then you drop the whole mess into the water, and it goes down like a bomb.'

'I'll run home to get one,' I said.

'What for?' said the other boy. 'Here, let me show you.'

He picked up a couple of heavy stones, and with reeds from the pond, he tied the stones to the cats' necks. 'Watch this,' and flung the two kittens into the water.

For a moment they went under, but soon came up swimming towards us.

'I told you, you need a sack. These stones aren't heavy enough,' said the first boy.

'Don't let them out,' shouted the other, and he began hitting them with a stick preventing them from climbing out. The other boy joined in, and it only remained for me to follow their example.

We laughed, shouted, screamed, and watched the two helpless little black kittens struggle in the water, trying to survive, but, in the end, drown.

I am brave! As brave as they are! I thought on the way home, but I was still troubled, for I *felt* different.

Why, why can't I be like them? God, dear God, make me the same. Make me brave. As brave as they are.

THE COWS WERE TIED UP in the stable for the winter. Outside, the winds blew without mercy and inside the Wajdas' house, as in all the other homes in the village, the scent of burning peat bricks permeated the interior. Everyone huddled around the warm stove; some delousing, others reminiscing or weaving baskets from willow branches, and still others worrying about the Soviet partisan army, known as Kovpaks. It was said that by day they lived in the forests and by night they attacked the enemy, disrupting trains and telephone lines, and ambushing and blowing up army encampments.

Their reputation for invincibility was such that German detachments allowed them to do their mischief without resistance. Word quickly spread that they invaded villages, ravaging everything in sight.

Mrs Wajda became panic-stricken when listening to these rumours, and she would retell her own stories of rape and horror brought on by the Bolsheviks.

I listened silently, shaking my head now and then to denote my sympathy. Secretly, however, I hoped that the Kovpaks would raid our village and take me with them.

In my imagination I saw myself in uniform, riding a horse, a gun at my side and German soldiers fleeing, begging for mercy.

My father! Perhaps he is one of the Kovpaks! It's possible! Why not? I could easily see one of them smash into the Wajdas' house, find me there, and say, 'Your name is Jankele.'

'How do you know this?' I would inquire.

'I'm your father.'

At this point I would fall into his arms, 'Papa, Papa, I knew you'd find me.'

One night, as if swept by the tormenting wind, the village was invaded by the Kovpaks. The sound of horses galloping and the chaos woke us.

Mrs Wajda shook with fear and, pacing the room, she crossed herself and began to pray. 'The bandits, the rapists, we're finished,' she wailed.

There was a loud bang on our door. We waited in silence.

'Open up!' shouted a voice in Russian.

Mr Wajda trembled and hid in the corner like a child.

'Open it!' his wife ordered in a whisper. He didn't flinch.

Composing herself, she unbolted the heavy door. Two unshaven tired figures, automatic rifles over their shoulders, stumbled into the room.

'Welcome, welcome,' said Mrs Wajda in an artificial voice.

Her husband laughed nervously and repeated the greeting. The Soviets scanned the room and approached the hot stove. One took off his mittens and warmed his hands over the fire, rubbing his palms together. 'Please sit, sit,' said Mrs Wajda in amazingly good Russian. They obliged, gazing at us through wind-beaten eyes.

'We would like something to eat if you can spare it,' said one.

Immediately, Mrs Wajda cut several slices of her home-baked bread and two chunks of kielbasa. Without removing their quilted coats, they ate listlessly.

I studied the one sitting next to me; in the glow from the stove, he looked like my father. I sought to ask his name, his place of birth, his age, and whether he had children, but while these thoughts were skipping through my mind, I heard him say, 'I have two children at home. I haven't seen them or my wife in a God's age, and I don't know whether I'll ever see them.'

Everything fits, I concluded. I have to find out his name. Then his friend addressed him by a strange name, one I'd never heard before. He could still be my father, I justified; he may have assumed a Russian name. Somehow I have to let him know who I am.

And so I blurted out, 'I am from Pulawy, have you ever been there?'

In place of an answer, he pinched my cheek and said, 'Let's hope by the time you grow up there'll be no more wars.'

'When will the war end?' I asked.

'Who knows? Another year, maybe two or three,' came the reply. 'But I won't be marching in the victory parade. Our detachment started out with over two thousand men; there are fewer than half left. I don't think any of us will return alive.' He stood up and shook his comrade who had fallen asleep in a sitting position. 'You have a horse?' He addressed Mr Wajda.

'Yes,' answered my boss, and quickly qualified, 'but he's useless, he's old.'

'Not to worry,' said the warrior. 'He'll do.'

'Please,' begged Mr Wajda, 'if you take Chestnut, you might as well cut my arms off.'

'We'll give you a much better one in exchange. He just needs food and rest, and we can't spare that.'

Opening the door they headed for the stable. Looking out the window we saw our Chestnut resisting as he was led out.

Mr Wajda sank to the floor and cried.

Similar scenes took place in almost every farm in Malinowka that night. But in some instances, the Kovpaks did more than trade horses; they ransacked and plundered, grabbing whatever they could carry, especially pillows to use as saddles.

The next morning the village was quiet, and the previous night seemed like a bad dream. I cast my eyes along the road, but there was no sign of the invincible Kovpaks. The road, the field, the village itself, were deathly still. They had vanished as abruptly as they had appeared. And in their place came winter, blanketing the village with a coat of white snow.

'YOU NEVER TOLD US YOU were from Pulawy, Zygmund,' Mr Wajda casually mentioned days later. I fidgeted. 'The reeve has heard about you and wants to know why you're not registered. You do have documents don't you?'

'I neglected to take them when I left home, sir.'

Soon enough, a man with an overgrown bushy moustache

appeared. He was so tall that he had to stoop in order to enter the house. The Wajdas greeted the reeve with unusual cordiality.

Mr Wajda placed a bottle of his own distilled potato vodka on the table, and the two indulged, the reeve wetting his moustache whenever he downed one. They talked about the crop, the weather, the animals, the occupation, gossiped about neighbours, and eventually the official turned to me.

'So this is the boy, eh?' he said, and took out a pad of paper from a pouch and a pencil from an inside pocket. 'It's dangerous for you to be here without documents, boy. You could be picked up by the authorities, and without papers, they could mistake you for a Jew.'

They know. He knows and he's playing with me. 'Nothing to worry about, though,' continued the reeve, 'I'll send away for your birth certificate, and in no time we'll have you in the books, and you'll be issued proper credentials.'

Fear stabbed me. Where will he write to get my birth certificate?

'Now then,' I heard him say. 'What is your name?'

'Zygmund,' I answered.

The man scribbled on his pad, then lifted his eyes. 'Yes, yes, Zygmund what?'

I hesitated. If I give him my fictitious name and place of birth, should he write and find no such person ever born there, that could be my end. Then I recalled a Gentile boy with whom I had played, back in Pulawy. He was about my age. If I give his name, then surely they will find it on record, I reasoned.

'Well, boy, what is it?' the reeve tapped his pencil on the pad.

'My name is ...' All eyes were upon me. 'My name ... is Piotr Zielinski,' I managed to blurt out. Mr Wajda almost choked. His wife stared with wide eyes.

'I thought your name was Zygmund something-or-other,' exclaimed Mr Wajda, with a face as angry as a bull's.

'I'm sorry,' I said. 'I gave you a fake name, in case my stepmother tried to find me.' The reeve looked at me, and then shifted his eyes to the Wajdas. Turning to his pad, he jotted down my new name.

'Where were you born?'

'Pulawy,' I replied, assuming that my friend Piotr Zielinski had been born there.

'How old are you?'

'Twelve,' I answered.

'That's all we need,' he said. 'By New Year we should have a reply,' and he departed.

Mr Wajda now turned on me. 'You've been here almost a year and yet never, but never, in all this time have you written one word home.'

'I would write my father if I had his address in Germany,' I justified.

'Then why not write your stepmother and ask for it?'

'I don't want her to know where I am.'

'What's there to fear, boy? Why not write, and at least tell her you're alive?'

'I'd rather not have anything to do with her.'

'Maybe you can't write? Perhaps you want me to do it for you!'

'I can write,' I said with bravado.

'Then write. She's probably worried about you.'

I chuckled. 'You don't know my stepmother. She's happy to be rid of me.'

'Zygmund,' and he paused, 'or should I call you Piotr?'

'Piotr is my real name.'

'Are you sure about that? Perhaps you don't even have a stepmother?'

I looked up and he stared back. 'You think I'm a liar, Mr Wajda?' He didn't answer.

My sleeplessness visited me again, for I worried that Mr Wajda might try to take a peek at my penis while I slept. I now felt I was constantly being observed; at the table, while working, and at night by the stove. Where before there was lots of talk, quarrelling, and even fights, it was now unusually serene. No one looked directly at me, but I could feel their stares whenever I turned my back. They know! They know! I must dispel their suspicions. So I searched for paper and pencil, and sat down in close proximity to my employer and wrote:

Dear Stepmother:

It's been a long time since I left home, and you're probably worried by now not knowing what has happened to me. At present I am with a very good family. They are called Wajda, and they feed me very well and don't beat me ...

Just as I hoped, at this point my scribbling attracted Mr Wajda's attention.

'What's that?' he asked.

'A letter to my stepmother, sir.'

'I thought you didn't want her to know where you were.' He looked quizzically at me.

'You made me realise I was wrong,' I said and went back to my task at hand. He towered over me and, like an eagle, his heavy hand landed on the letter and he snatched it. This should convince him, I thought. How lucky for me!

He paced the room scanning the letter, and then dropped it on the table. Looking into my eyes, he said, 'You know something?' I waited. 'You don't write like one of us. You write like a Jew.' I turned my head sharply, for I knew the fear in my eyes would surely betray me.

Leave at once, something within urged. Before it's too late.

THE NEXT DAY, a middle-aged priest accompanied by an assistant knocked on our door. After Mrs Wajda opened it, the aide remained at the threshold while the priest shook hands, smiled, and asked questions concerning health and crops. Then, dipping a whisk into holy water and reciting a prayer in Latin, he misted the interior. With kind words for Kazia and Wanda, he then noticed me.

'Is this your boy too, Mrs Wajda?' he asked.

'An orphan from Pulawy, Father.'

The priest's face shone like the summer sun. He stroked my cheek with his palm, and then asked me my name.

'Piotr Zielinski,' I answered.

Again dipping the whisk into the sacred water, and blessing me, he sprinkled it over my head.

'Poor boy, poor boy!' he mumbled. 'May Jesus Christ watch over you!' He reached into a pocket and from a small wallet extracted a coin and forced it into my hand.

Mrs Wajda now forked out several paper bills and extended them to the priest saying, 'For the church, Father.'

The priest pointed to his young assistant, who took the money, bowed, and stuffed the notes into a safe box he was carrying. The holy man wished us all a Merry Christmas, bowed, threw me a wink, and set off with his aide.

'How much did you give him?' growled Mr Wajda.

'Why?' his wife shot back.

'They're all thieves, those charlatans. All year long when you're struggling, slaving, sweating, you don't see them.

Once a year at Christmas time he shows up with all that black magic.'

'Shut your mouth; show a little respect for God at least.'

'Since when have you become so pious, Holy Mary?' he came back at her. 'You haven't set foot in a church since the day you married me.'

I knew that the water the priest had blessed me with was the same holy water they used to baptise babies. By all rights then, I now thought, I am baptised. Unknowingly, the priest had converted me. I am no longer a Jew. I don't have to hide or lie anymore. But then again I felt that overbearing guilt and so I quickly washed myself to remove the Christianity.

THE OVENS IN EVERY HOUSEHOLD were busy with cabbage rolls, buckwheat cakes, cookies for the Christmas trees, braided holiday breads, and all sorts of other treats.

Boys and girls went from door to door singing carols, and their voices were heard until late into the night.

While the villagers celebrated, I was preoccupied as to where to run next. Deep snow had covered the landscape, so that the road was barely visible. If only I could fly! I mused. But then, even if I could, where would I fly to?

A sleigh pulled by two spirited horses appeared in the distance and now came closer and stopped at the smithy. From it stepped Kazia, the girl who had brought me to the Wajdas, escorted by her new husband.

In the meantime she had married, and her husband was now with her. I was pleased to see her, because before her marriage and departure to Piaski, she had always displayed a special affection for me. Sometimes she would cut my hair, or wash my shirt, or give me a freshly baked poppy seed cookie.

The villagers gossiped a great deal about her. They said that, in her youth, she had slept with every male in the village, and later, with every German soldier who would have her.

Tadek Krul, her husband; a muscular, handsome man, apparently knew all this, but had forgiven her. He had an underdeveloped right arm, like that of a child. As a result, he used his left to perform the most difficult tasks, and did them better than most could with both arms. In his brother-in-law's blacksmith shop, with hammer and steel he would display his one-armed prowess.

I stood among all the other children who had gathered at the smithy to gape. Kazia spotted me and came over to hug me.

'You're growing,' she said, and planted a kiss on my forehead. I blushed.

Later I noticed how her stomach had enlarged, and realised she was pregnant.

'How is everything, Zygmund?' she asked.

I told her of my mistreatment and that I wanted to leave, but didn't know where to go.

'I don't know where I'd put you. Our place is small.'

'I'd sleep on the floor,' I said, and tears came to my eyes.

She held me against her protruding belly, 'I hope I have a boy as handsome as you are!'

'Kazia,' I said, 'I don't want them to know that I'm planning to scoot.'

She smiled and whispered, 'It's our little secret. I'd like to see their faces when they find you've left.' She pulled out a flower-patterned hanky to wipe my eyes.

THE VILLAGE STILL SLEPT. The day was excruciatingly cold. The holidays were over; it was now one day into the New Year.

I opened the door and quietly tiptoed out of the Wajdas' house, wearing my Sunday suit, which the Wajdas had a village tailor make for me out of an army blanket. Over it, I wore what was left of my ever-so-tight coat, the only remnant I still possessed from home.

I walked into the stable and for the last time looked at the cows, the sheep, the traded horse, the pigs, the chickens, and several dozen rabbits that I had raised with special care and pride and was now leaving behind.

For a moment I recalled fondly how that past spring the Wajdas had presented me with a female rabbit, and how I had borrowed a male from a boy in the next village, and for days on end had tried to get them to mate.

Closing the stable door, I walked towards the blacksmith's shop. Kazia and Tadek were already seated on the sleigh, waiting for me. They waved me on, and I ran to them. Tadek extended his good hand and I found myself in the back of the vehicle.

I heard a whip crack, horses snort; little bells on the harness rang.

It was almost evening when we pulled into the little town. Piaski seemed to be overrun with German soldiers. Here one stood on guard duty; there another walked hand in hand with a young maiden; further on a truckload of them singing came from around the corner. We turned at a large, ornamented church and followed along a few narrow cobbled streets, one or more twists, and suddenly Tadek pulled at the reins and we stopped in front of a small cottage.

'Piaski,' said Kazia, and now I recalled being there once before.

'A town of thieves,' I remembered my mother saying. When we were on the run on our way to Siedliszcze, we had passed through here.

The man driving us had turned and smiled. 'In that case, let's get out of here before we get robbed.' And he whipped his bony horse.

'Is everyone here really a thief, Mama?' I asked in astonishment.

'I once had a friend living here. God only knows where she is now!' my mother mused.

'Was she also a thief, Mama?' I tugged at her sleeve.

My mother laughed. 'No, Jankele. It's only a myth. In Chelm people are supposed to be fools and in Piaski, thieves.'

'Zygmund! Zygmund!' the voice seemed to be coming from far away. The wagon driver's face vanished. My mother's image disappeared and my little brother Josele's sleeping body melted away. 'Zygmund, we're here. Help Tadek with the horses.' It was Kazia poking me, waking me from my reverie.

Days passed, then weeks, and there was little for me to do. In the morning, Tadek would leave for work and not return until nightfall. I would sit with Kazia and talk, peel potatoes, and fetch water from the town pump.

'Wait till the baby comes.' She patted her stomach. 'Then you'll be a big help.' She now held my face in her hands and looked into my eyes. 'Tell me, angel, what do I do to have an angel like you?'

I HEARD SCREAMING, crying, wailing, and sobbing. I awoke and saw a naphtha lamp burning on the table. Several women came out from the bedroom. Later Tadek sat silently gulping one glass of vodka after another. I was afraid to ask what was going on. I looked to Tadek, but he turned away.

'Come. You'd better come with me,' a voice said. I faced a matronly woman who lived across the street.

'Come to my house, child, they won't need you anymore.'

'What's happened?' I asked, with no response.

'Where's Kazia?' I demanded to know.

'Come,' and her arm wrapped itself around my shoulders leading me out.

It was still dark. We crossed the street and entered a tilting cottage.

'What's going on there?' I pleaded.

She motioned for me to sit. 'Kazia miscarried, giving birth to a boy,' she said. 'Only it isn't a boy.' She crossed herself. 'The body is that of a child, but the head, the feet ... are those of a pig.'

When dawn came, we drank tea and ate bread with marmalade made of beets. The woman recounted how lonely her life had been of late. How her husband had died years earlier and how her only daughter had been killed during the bombings.

In turn, I shared my fictitious orphan saga. When I looked at her again she was sobbing. 'You poor child,' she lamented.

If she knew my real story, I mused, would she cry more or would she throw me out?

By noon we were strolling along the streets of Piaski. Several armed Germans passed us. We entered a building and climbed stairs; the woman knocked on a door and it was opened by a little girl in a blue tunic.

'Is your mother home?'

'Yes,' she replied, and we entered.

The spacious room contained an upright piano, embroidered curtains, decorative carpets on the floor, and religious icons and ornaments throughout. From the kitchen came the aroma of food. In a corner of the room stood a cage with several birds in it, and asleep on one of the chairs was a furry yellow cat.

How fortunate a girl to live like this! I thought. I glanced into the bedroom and saw a large bed with huge goose-down pillows and coverings. On the walls hung a family portrait and souvenirs brought home from an excursion or holiday in some mountain region and a visit to a big city.

My eyes looked and my heart cried; I recalled our modest residence in Pulawy; above our bed hung a tapestry depicting reindeer in a forest. On another wall, a portrait of my mother painted from a photograph by a travelling artist. I remembered the scent of my mother's borsht; the kimono-clad ladies carrying parasols on the tin box of tea from China; my mother combing her long silken black hair; my father whistling, 'Si, si, si'; and the sound coming through the earphones of his homemade radio: 'one, two, three, one, two, three, one, two, three', the voice of a fitness instructor.

The little girl's mother now appeared, carrying a plate of steaming food.

'Mrs Kupinska!' she exclaimed upon seeing us.

'I have brought a guest,' she said, pointing to me.

'Sit, you're in time for lunch,' said our hostess.

We sat, ate the hot meal, and watched the little girl depart for school.

Mrs Kupinska went on to explain in detail how I happened to be in Piaski, how I had been orphaned, and how I now found myself alone and without a job.

Our hostess listened attentively, expressing much sympathy. Seeing my dilapidated clogs, she offered, 'The first thing I would suggest is that you take him to get shoes.' I looked up, so did Mrs Kupinska. 'Yes,' our hostess continued. 'If his father is doing forced labour, then he's entitled to a pair of free shoes.' Addressing me now, she asked, 'Your father is in Germany, boy, is he?'

'Yes, he is,' I answered, 'but how can I prove it?'

'Just give them the name, they will look it up. I'm surprised you haven't collected up till now. My husband is also in Germany and we've received many things.'

'Then we'll go; we'll get shoes for you,' I heard Mrs Kupinska say.

'As for work,' our hostess went on, 'take him to Adam Kozak in Gielczew. Tell him I sent you.'

When we left and once again found ourselves on the street, I was prepared to go to the Germans for the free shoes. If I refused, I reasoned, Mrs Kupinska would become suspicious.

At the same time I visualised the scene: unable to find the fabricated father's name in their files, their suspicions are aroused. They examine my face, my eyes, and pull down my pants.

'A Jew!' and empty a bullet into my head.

We now passed the same church and turned sharply off the main road, leaving the town behind.

'What about my shoes?'

Mrs Kupinska spat. 'Let them choke on them, the swine!' She reached for and held my hand as we made our way along the narrow pathway leading towards the village of Gielczew.

Humble little huts with thatched roofs lined both sides of the icy road. Now and then a horse would pass pulling a sleigh; a dog came out and barked at us as if we were thieves.

Mrs Kupinska knocked on a straw-insulated door and a voice from within beckoned us to enter.

The place consisted of one room with two small windows. In it were two beds, a table with chairs, and a brick stove in which burned a welcoming fire. A picture of Christ on the cross hung above a dresser.

The head of the household sat at one end of the table,

puffing on a pipe and weaving slippers out of strands of straw. He was a short, bowlegged man with a receding hairline, a handlebar moustache, and traces of oriental features. His wife, much taller than he with combed-back hair and an angelic face, sat beside him. Two grown boys nodded politely, and a girl, busily engaged by the stove, smiled shyly and returned to her task.

'I've brought you a boy,' I heard Mrs Kupinska say.

I removed my hat and coat and stood near the stove gazing at the flames.

What are the Wajdas doing now? I wondered. Perhaps they've informed on me and the Germans are on my tail.

'Whose boy is he?' Mr Kozak was asking, studying me. 'One has to be careful these days.'

'He's from the Pulawy area ...' And as if in confidence now, she went on, 'The father is in Germany. The poor child was being beaten daily by a witch of a no-good stepmother. When I heard of that, I said to myself, "As long as I'm alive, no flesh and blood of ours will suffer like that." I sent for him immediately. He's been with me these past months, but the poor boy needs to be on a farm; he loves animals.'

'So he's a relative, Mrs Kupinska?'

'Yes, yes, on my husband's side ... cousins.' She now smiled, then turned and forced a smile out of me.

'What's your name, boy?' Mr Kozak addressed me. My smile quickly vanished, and for a moment it seemed that I had no name.

My God! What is my name ... What is it? I can't remember. Zielinski. That's not my real name. What is my real name? I've got to think fast. If they look for me, they'll be searching for a Zygmund Cybula or Piotr Zielinski. I have to change my name again. But what about Mrs Kupinska? She knows me by my latest name. And so I didn't answer.

'Is he shy?' inquired Mr Kozak.

'You too would be shy in a stranger's home,' said his wife, and threw several logs into the fire.

'My name is Franek Kupinski!' I finally blurted out. I expected Mrs Kupinska to react, but the lady simply nodded and smiled.

Right there the Kozaks decided to take me on. Mrs Kupinska stood up, put on her coat and shawl and, embracing me warmly, said, 'Be a good boy, Franiu, these are good people ... I'll write your father in Germany and tell him that you are being well looked after.' She then turned to the others and said, 'May the good Lord Jesus Christ bless you and your entire household for the good deed you're performing.' She opened the door and before departing once again addressed me by the diminutive of Franek, 'Franiu'.

'Yes?' I ran to her.

'You won't forget to say your prayers and go to church every Sunday?'

'I won't forget auntie,' I promised.

She kissed me and I kissed her. 'May the good Lord Jesus Christ watch over you,' she whispered, and shut the door behind her.

FOUR

Adam Kozak was a quiet, patient, and methodical person. Unlike Mr Wajda, he never ordered, or even asked me, to do anything. Instead he would initiate a task, at which point I would jump in, begging him to let me help. We laboured quietly, for he wasn't one to talk. He'd puff on his pipe, clear his throat, and occasionally throw me a glance.

In many ways he reminded me of my grandfather, the baker from Pulawy, who could walk with me for kilometres and never utter a word, but somehow communicated by the touch of his hand.

Mr Kozak and I became inseparable. I rose when he did, I ate when he ate, I worked when he worked, and I went to sleep when he did.

'Go, Franiu, go and play with the boys,' he would urge. But I wouldn't budge, for his gentle nature and kind manner drew me to him like a magnet. It was a privilege to be his apprentice.

In time, little by little, he told me of his life. The two boys Stefan and Antek were not his, but his wife's from a previous marriage.

'They're lazy good-for-nothings,' he confided.

Cesia, his only child, close to Genia's age, but not at all like Genia, was distant and reserved. How I longed for Genia's sweet smile and zest for life!

Mr Kozak sat at the head of the table, and until he started eating, no one else did. Whenever meat or other delicacies were served, his wife placed the dish in front of him and he, like a little emperor, would divide it according to his best judgement. Due to his poor teeth, he could not chew the crust of bread, thus ate the centre only. Since I was the youngest, it was understood that I could help myself to a whole slice only when all the crust had been devoured. The little man had a healthy appetite so that the bread basket was constantly filled with crusts.

'How happy I am you're here!' Cesia said to me. 'At last I can have a proper piece of bread!'

My days were spent in the stable or the barn, and at night I would watch Mr Kozak and a handful of neighbours play cards, or talk about world events, or reminisce about their youth and the good old days.

During such conversations, the talk would occasionally touch on the plight of the Jews. And when it did, I choked inside, and pretended not to hear, and would busy myself with feeding the fire or stroking the cat.

On one such evening, a guest held us spellbound recounting what he had heard was happening at Majdanek.

'Jesus Christ, what has the world come to?' he was saying, coughing after inhaling a puff. 'The Germans have created a hell there. They've got Poles whipping Poles, Russians whipping Russians, Ukrainians whipping Ukrainians, Jews whipping Jews, and Gypsies doing the same to their own.'

THE WINTER MONTHS came to an end. The road was dry.
Butterflies fluttered in the garden, swallows busily constructed
nests on the side of a beam inside the stable, and I drove the
cows to pasture.

In the fields I met other boys, some about my own age, but
most of them older. They showed little interest in me, other
than wanting to know my name and who I worked for. One
day we were sitting around a fire roasting wild mushrooms.
Some boys were smoking cigarettes composed of dry grass
rolled in leaves. Wide eyed and open mouthed, I listened as
one by one, they told of witnessing sexual encounters between
a man and wife, girl and boy, neighbour with neighbour,
animal and animal. One outdid the other, by revealing more
than the last.

'What about you?' Attention was suddenly turned on me.
'Haven't you ever seen or done anything?'

I blushed, shook my head, and turned to check on my cows.

'He's too young,' said one.

'How old are you?'

'Twelve,' I answered.

'Probably doesn't even have hair yet,' scoffed another.

'Franiu, does it tickle you? Show us your little birdie,'
laughter all around.

A tall boy with half-closed eyes approached me. 'Let's see.'

And the rest echoed loudly, 'Yeah, let's see your pecker!'

'No!' and I retreated. They advanced. Hands were attempting to undo my belt. My shoulders were being pinned to
the ground. I turned, thrashed about, and screamed, 'No! Let
me go, let go of me!' The more I resisted, the more they were
encouraged. They laughed hysterically. I held on to my belt,
but not for long. As I struggled, they found the game more
amusing. In a snap my belt was gone. My feet were held;

someone was gripping my arms, and a hand was unbuttoning my fly.

'We won't hurt you, Franiu.' The laughter was deafening.

One button, two buttons, another button, laughter ... hysterical laughter. Someone was pulling my pants.

The rabbi at my brother Josele's circumcision appears; the knife cuts away foreskin, Josele cries, and the rabbi treats himself to a thin smile.

'Mazel tov,' the guests chant, and a bottle of sacramental wine and a large basin of chickpeas land on the table.

Why, dear God, did you set us apart? I pray.

'Let's see the tiny pecker,' voices taunt, and eager eyes loom above me.

With whatever strength I still possessed, I somehow managed to free myself. 'Leave me alone,' I cried. 'May our Lord Jesus Christ punish you for this!'

A deathly silence ensued. I buttoned my fly and someone threw me my belt.

'We were just having some fun, Franiu. No reason to cry.'

'We meant no harm,' added another.

For a time I avoided my tormentors but later reconciled and during the long summer evenings we would meet. Hide-and-seek was our favourite game, but as the summer progressed, we tired of it and changed to 'spy'. One of us chosen to play the spy would hide, and the rest had to find him. When this too became predictable, someone came up with a new game, 'Jew!'

'What kind of game is that?' asked one boy.

The one who suggested it then explained, 'The Jew hides, we count to ten, and then we search for him. When he is found, we frisk him, take everything we find, and shoot him.'

In the days and nights that followed, my friends and I

hunted for the pretending Jews, in barns, in fields, near the river, behind trees, and in haystacks. The game appealed to everyone, including myself. It offered a lot of excitement and suspense. When the Jew was discovered, he was required to surrender by raising his arms. We'd surround him, empty his pockets and remove his valuables. Pointing the wooden revolver, belonging to one of the gang, we'd shoot him with 'Bang! Bang!' Invariably, whoever played the Jew would immediately fall to the ground in a comical pose, and pretend to be dead.

Everyone fought for the privilege of playing the Jew. Everyone, that is, except me. I preferred the role of a hunter. But, so as not to arouse suspicion, I also lobbied to be the Jew.

After a lot of shouting, fighting, and arguing, I was cast in the coveted part. The group spun around, covered their eyes, and began to count, 'One ... two ... three ...'

Where should I hide? I left my playmates behind and took off ...

'Five ... six ... seven ...' I ran into the farmyard ... 'Eight ... nine.' I now found myself in the barn, and dug into the hay. 'Ten!' My heart pumped. I listened. Then I heard approaching voices, footsteps.

'I think I know where he is,' said one. It was no longer a game: the hunt was real.

I was back with Moishe at the Pejzaks' barn the night Staszek betrayed us. Moishe! Whatever happened to my Uncle Moishe? Is he alive? Will I ever see him again?

The door to the barn opened. Whispers, resonance. I lay still, my heart continuing to beat like a noisy clock. More whispers, other footsteps, and then, 'He's not here, let's go.'

It was now so quiet I could hear the silence. I fooled them, I thought, and smiling to myself I stood up to shake the hay off. Then I tiptoed to the open door and looked out into the night.

Where is my Uncle Moishe on a night like this?

'Got you!' a voice roared. 'Hands up, you dirty Jew!' I faced two of my playmates. One of them ran out and yelled, 'We've got him! The Jew is here!' The other approached and searched my pockets with one hand. With the other, he pointed the toy pistol at my temple.

When for a moment he turned his attention away from me, I dropped my arms, and ran.

'Bang! Bang!' his voice pursued me, but I paid no heed. 'Bang! Bang!' it repeated. My feet carried me further. 'You're dead!' the voice followed. 'I've killed you, Franiu!'

Far away I stopped to listen. Except for the crickets and frogs in a nearby pond, all was quiet. The moon above was bright and round. I looked at it in wonderment.

'I wonder if my Uncle Moishe can see you now too.' I addressed the moon, and leisurely walked back to the farmyard.

My friends were annoyed. 'I shot you three times, Franiu!' the one with the pistol complained. 'You're dead; you're supposed to fall down.'

'I ran away,' I defended myself.

'How could you run with three bullets in your head, stupid?'

'Because you missed every time.'

'You're crazy!' he shot back with anger. 'You don't know how to play a Jew.'

ONE RAINY DAY A GERMAN SOLDIER with a handful of grenades secured on his belt appeared at the narrow, winding river that passed through Gielczew. We followed him along the river's edge to see what he was up to. At one point he motioned for us to keep our distance and hit the ground. He then released the pin of a grenade, tossing it into the water and ducking for cover.

A small explosion followed, sending a mountain of water into the air. We leaped up and ran to the water's edge, and witnessed the stunned fish coming to the surface, floating as if dead. Several of our group quickly shed their clothes and jumped in to harvest the fish for the soldier. A little further down, he repeated the operation, and when his knapsack was full of fish, he left, the same way he had arrived, on foot towards Piaski.

We fell on the remaining catch, each fighting for the spoils, and then ran through the village, showing off, 'Look what we caught!'

This happened in the early spring, but by the time summer arrived and the days were extremely hot, no one thought too much about fishing, but a great deal about swimming.

On any hot summer midday a passer-by would have noticed a group of young peasant boys in the raw, diving into the river's refreshing water, coming out, and diving in again.

'Come swim with us, Franiu,' my friends begged.

'Maybe tomorrow, I have to help Mr Kozak,' I would invariably answer, or, 'I'll meet you there later,' or 'I'm not feeling up to it,' or 'It looks like rain.'

As the days passed and I ran out of excuses, I began to fear the consequences; my companions might grow suspicious.

I lay awake at night praying it would rain. I played with the idea of adding a piece of chicken skin to my penis, but how to go about it, I didn't know. I had to find a way. In the end, I'll have to go swimming, but how? Perhaps in my underwear! No, that won't work, I'll stand out.

On one of the hottest days, two of my friends came

looking for me. 'No more excuses. Today you're coming with us, Franiu,' they said, grabbing me by the arms.

'Sorry, I have to work ...'

'Go, Franiu, go swimming,' Mr Kozak's voice interrupted and I found him standing behind me. 'Go, boy, go. It's too hot to work. I'm going to have a snooze and you go. Enjoy yourself.'

On the way my two chums talked without stopping, but my mind was elsewhere. 'Isn't that right, Franiu?' I dimly heard one ask.

'Yes, yes,' I answered.

But in their place was the rabbi with his knife; he was cutting and the piece of skin fell to the ground. I now realised he wasn't a rabbi at all, but the Shochet, the ritual slaughterer, and that which had fallen to the floor was a chicken's head, bloodied, with its eyes open.

'What are you stalling for?' I was being pulled. 'Come on, the others are already there.'

I stood by the riverbank. Around me my friends, all nude, were diving into the water.

'Come on, Franiu!' they encouraged.

I began to undress. Slowly, I pulled the cotton shirt over my head and threw it down. I looked about; no one was paying the least bit of attention to me now. I sat, undid my belt, then one button, then another and the last.

'Let's go, Franiu!'

'What's taking you so long?'

Still sitting, I started to take my pants off with the help of my right hand, while with the other, I cupped my genitals. I now stood up, and with my free right hand outstretched, I dove in.

I'm safe, I thought, and swam from one bank to the

other. Someone splashed me, another offered to race me, someone dunked my head under, and still another asked if I could swim under water. They were no sooner in the water than they came out only to dive in again. I remained frolicking in the river, paddling like one of the kittens I had disposed of.

When it was time to leave, I climbed out discreetly, still clutching my privates.

From that day on, I frequented the river, and with each outing, I gained more confidence in nimble manoeuvres.

Then it happened! 'Why do you hold your dick, Franiu?' one boy asked curiously. All eyes focused on me.

'Why, Franiu, why?'

'What's the matter? Only have one ball, eh?' they heckled. 'Or no balls at all!' suggested another.

'Perhaps he's a girl,' and a gale of laughter followed.

I covered my penis with both hands and held tightly.

'What are you hiding?'

My first instinct was to take off, but then I considered lecturing them about modesty. Perhaps sharing with them what my father told me: only animals expose themselves in public. But what rolled off my tongue was something unexpected: 'I'll tell you why. Because if you run around naked you'll be cursed by evil spirits and your peckers will remain small forever.'

'Who told you that shit?' one raised his voice.

'My priest,' I answered emphatically.

'Bullshit!' cut in another.

'Oh yeah! Have you ever seen Jesus's dick?'

Dumbfounded, they stared at their nakedness.

From then on, a passer-by would have noticed a group of boisterous boys diving into the river, their right arms outstretched and their left hands covering their uncircumcised penises.

ONE EVENING LATE IN SUMMER, neighbours had congregated outside the Kozak hut and were deep in a political discussion when suddenly we heard from the sky above what sounded like a swarm of bees.

As we tried to guess how many planes there were and in which direction they were headed, the sky in the distance lit up with the most beautiful lanterns one could imagine. We watched in amazement, for the flares were obviously far away, yet so luminous, that our entire village, as if by magic, turned into day.

'It's over Lublin,' commented one.

'Must be some German holiday,' offered another.

'Maybe it's Hitler's birthday. May he choke on a chicken bone,' a buxom woman burst out laughing. Then we heard explosions, followed by more flares and more blasts.

'Lublin is in flames,' said Mr Kozak thoughtfully, puffing away. 'The Russians!'

The following day everything was back to normal. But shortly thereafter, while out in the pasture, I became aware of the repeated sounds of cannon fire from somewhere far away.

The Russians are on their way, I mused. Any day I'll be liberated. Perhaps my father, in a sharp uniform bedecked with medals, is behind one of those cannons.

For days I listened to the artillery and prayed they would move closer and closer. I asked Mr Kozak about it. He filled his pipe, twirled his moustache and, without looking at me, replied, 'It's the Germans. They're on manoeuvres not far from here.'

I didn't know whether he knew for sure or simply speculated. After all, he had said the Russians were bombing Lublin. Why couldn't it be the Russians now firing? But days later, when the cannons came to an abrupt halt, I realised Mr Kozak had been right.

Soon after, what seemed like the entire German army invaded our village. They were everywhere; by the river, along the road, in every farmyard.

Our yard was occupied by sturdy Belgian horses and massive wagons with iron-rimmed wheels. Soldiers were moving about, washing themselves at the well, shaving, shining their boots, brushing their uniforms, grooming their horses, and servicing their motor vehicles. They kicked a ball around, ate from mobile kitchens, and combed the village for willing young maidens.

Mr Kozak spoke to them in a fractured German and we learned that they had come from the Russian front and were only stationed here to rest.

'The front is far, far from here, deep inside Russia,' Mr Kozak translated. 'The Soviets are losing, and it's only a matter of days, at most weeks, before they surrender.'

He hadn't quite finished when we heard a hum and looked up. Far, far above, planes could be seen flying like wild ducks.

'They're ours,' boasted the German lieutenant, and proceeded to count, 'One, two, three ... ' When he reached thirty-two, the entire village shook, and in an instant everyone had vanished as if the earth had swallowed us all.

Several blasts followed. I found myself cowering in the stable, covered in manure. When I emerged, I saw red and orange flames and black smoke dancing above the town of Piaski.

'The cows, Franiu, the cows! Save the cows!' Mr Kozak called frantically.

I jumped and quickly unleashed the animals. 'Where to?' I
looked to him for guidance.

'Just take them to pasture, any pasture. They'll be safer there.'

I picked up my stick and drove the animals out and onto
the main road. All around there was chaos.

The Germans were packing their gear in great haste. It was
hard to believe how frightened they appeared. The smell of
diesel fuel emanating from their exhaust pipes permeated the
air, poisoning our lungs. In the middle of the road a young
soldier directing the panicky departure was reprimanding the
driver of a staff car.

I lashed the cows and hurried them on until we had left
the village behind and found ourselves in the valley through
which the river flowed. I had no idea where I was going, but
decided to stay when I saw a friend, Jerzy, with his herd.

The sky over Piaski was still black when a reconnaissance
plane appeared and, a short distance behind, a squadron of
planes in formation.

Jerzy and I fell to the ground, keeping our eyes glued to
the sky. We could clearly see bombs falling from the aircrafts,
like eggs out of a basket. The earth shook, more black smoke
billowed above, and the town of Piaski was again aflame.

'A town of thieves,' my mother's voice made itself heard.

I feared that at any moment a bomb would fall, ripping me
into smithereens and scattering the bits into the river for the
fish to feast on.

A circular red sun was setting when I sprang to my feet
and ran back to the Kozak house for safety.

My feet carried me as if by the wind.

The village road was deserted. I turned into our farmyard
– no one to be seen; I ran to the house – empty; I looked into
the stable – no horses.

'Mr Kozak!' I yelled at the top of my lungs. No response. 'Mr Kozak! Someone! Please answer me.' I revisited the road, and then back to the farmyard. I hurried behind the barn and, not finding anyone, I continued swiftly towards the back fields.

By now the sun was melting. 'Mr Kozak! Mr Kozak!' I faced deserted fields, but continued on.

By the edge of the forest I spied our mare and her filly grazing, and when I neared, I stumbled upon Mr Kozak and the rest of the family, with all their furniture displayed among the poplar trees. They stared at me in silence.

'Where are my cows?' asked Mr Kozak, visibly upset.

'By the river,' I answered.

'You left the cows?' his voice rose slightly.

'I'm afraid,' I blurted out. 'Sir, I'm scared of the bombs.'

'A bomb won't kill you, Franiu, but I will, if anything happens to my cows.' I drew back. I could hardly recognise Mr Kozak; his words were so out of character.

I turned and ran back through the naked fields to the desolate village, along the river, and back to Jerzy and Mr Kozak's cows.

Night descended quickly and a summer chill came with it. The cows lay down to rest and Jerzy and I huddled in a nearby ditch.

The next morning was quiet. The grass was wet with dew, and somewhere a single frog croaked. We watched the sun rise. The cows got to their feet and grazed. We knelt at the river's edge and washed our sleepy faces.

Bang! A shell exploded only metres away from where we were. Bang! Bang! Bang! A succession of explosions followed, shrapnel falling all about. We dove into the tall grass, shielding our heads with our arms.

'Franiu, let's get the hell out of here!' and crouching, he ran off in the direction of the ditch.

'Get down, Jerzy,' I screamed as another shell exploded. Raising my head slightly, I looked about through the blades of grass. Across the river I saw a German with binoculars on top of a tank, its nozzle pointing directly at me.

What's he looking at? At me?

I turned my head, and on the opposite hill I caught sight of a Russian soldier, also on a tank, observing his adversary through binoculars as well.

I stood up, but quickly fell to the ground as shells from both tanks landed in the valley, exploding. One slammed in the river, sending a fountain of water gushing into the air.

I was amazed at how the cows continued to graze, unaware and undisturbed.

Crawling, I made my way back to the ditch from where I could keep an eye on the cows, and jumped in. Panting, I crawled along the ground, and at a bend I came upon my friend, crouching.

'Jerzy?' I touched his arm. His body rolled over into the mud, his face streaked with blood. He was dead. A new barrage of shelling followed. Terrified, I fell to my knees, clutched the cross on the rosary around my neck. 'Dear Jesus,' I prayed, 'please save my cows and save me. If you help me one more time, I promise to believe in you for the rest of my life.'

Unexpectedly, the shelling halted. I peeked out of the ditch and checked on the cows.

I sat silently watching the smouldering countryside, and a horrible thought crept into my mind; perhaps I'm the only survivor left upon this earth!

The murky memory of a story once told to me by my Uncle

Shepsel, of a man with a foreign name, shipwrecked and all alone on an island, now came back to me.

At first the thought pleased me. I saw myself as the ruler of the entire world, owning all the houses, stables, cows, pigs, and roads, galloping on a white stallion through lands and forests. But then I dreaded the thought.

What would I do alone? I climbed out of the ditch, stood up erect and yelled, 'Hello!' Only the echo of my voice greeted me, followed by the sound of silence. I ran around the bend of the hill and called out, 'Is anyone here?'

A faint buzzing could be heard. I looked up, and as if diving directly from the sun, an airplane swooped down like a giant eagle, about to carry me off. I fell and shielded my head. Several bursts followed, and the rat-tat-tat of machine-gun fire filled my ears.

When I raised my head, I saw German soldiers along a back road hastily jumping off a truck. Next to it was another one, aflame and on its side. The plane circled several more times, then swooped down, targeting the escaping Germans with machine-gun fire, and cutting them down like stacks of wheat with a freshly sharpened scythe. The aircraft disappeared and the few surviving Germans got to their feet and ran to a nearby farmhouse.

The ravished, devastated landscape had an awful stench of gunpowder. High up in the sky the sun burned strongly and, though the attacking plane was not visible, I could still hear its hum.

Then from the farmhouse came a commotion of shouting, laughter, a woman's scream, and a pleading voice addressing the heavens. The door opened and a man stumbled out, heading my way. When he was close by, I realised he was weeping, his arms outstretched towards the sky, imploring God.

When he saw me, he wailed, 'She's five months pregnant,' and continued to walk without direction. 'Oh, Holy Mother, how can you allow this? The whole German army is raping my Jadwiga!'

Sometime later a single shot rang out, followed by a child crying, 'Mommy!'

At night Mr Kozak appeared out of the shadows, and after a long silence during which he counted the cows, he simply said, 'You can come home now, Franiu.'

The next day the heavens opened and a merciless rain descended upon us. In place of gunfire and bombing, there was thunder and lightning. We gathered inside the house to wait. I am not sure what it was we were waiting for. Perhaps it was for word that we were liberated, or perhaps only for the torrential rain to pass.

It was so quiet that the ticking of the clock seemed unusually loud. I sat near the little window and studied the raindrops pelting the panes.

What a fascinating world, all of its own!

Outside, the village road was a mass of mud, and beyond it, everything grey and hardly visible; not a man, nor a cat, or dog, or any other animal to be seen.

And then, diffused by the descending rivulets of rainwater running down the window glass, two figures appeared walking along the road. The others in the room must have sensed something, for without my signalling them, they one by one joined me to stare in disbelief. Their arms raised in surrender, two young German soldiers navigated along the mud-covered road as if through a minefield, fearing to take the next step.

A shiver ran through my spine. Not because I feared them, but rather because I felt sorry for them.

How different the enemy looked! So pathetic; their faces

gaunt, drenched, boots caked in muck, eyes full of fear. Suddenly the enemy didn't look like the enemy; more like my Uncle Moishe and me.

'Let's go and get them,' said Mrs Kozak's younger son, Antek, with an unconvincing voice. No one moved or bothered to reply. We simply watched the two Germans disappear down the road.

It rained for two more days, and when the downpour ended, word reached us that young Soviet soldiers, half drunk, brandishing machine guns and riding wild horses, had liberated the town of Piaski.

An old man wearing soaked trousers smelling of urine was limping along the road, pulling a goat on a rope. Stray cows, horses, and even pigs were roaming the fields, and now and then a stranger would appear looking for his animal. 'She has two black patches on her stomach.' But no one would listen. Everyone was busy trying to profit from the reigning chaos. There was great jubilation and celebration in the village, not so much because we had been liberated, but mostly because of the treasures that could be had from the half-burned town of Piaski. Many villagers ran to town, returning with all kinds of goods abandoned by the departed Germans, or ransacked from deserted homes. While the world burned, and with the Germans on the run with the Russians in pursuit, the villagers of Gielczew decided this was their opportunity to become rich.

I stood outside the Kozaks' hut and watched, and was sceptical that the Germans had really left. What if it's only a rumour, a trick to entice me to come out? I'll wait and see before making a move.

Before I knew it, six soldiers who looked more like Gypsy musicians than Soviet fighters were sitting at our table demanding food and vodka. I studied them closely, hoping one of them would have a scarred left cheek. They were Georgians.

Along the village road, Uzbek soldiers were setting up camp. An accordion was heard. Now and then a shot would ring out and whistle through the air. But above, the sky was clearing and the clouds dispersing.

From the next village, news reached us that the underground had apprehended the two Germans, imprisoning them in a cellar. The two detainees explained that they were ordinary foot soldiers and had never harmed anyone, not even a fly. Pleading for mercy, they displayed snapshots of their wives and children, and begged to go home to live in peace. Even kissing the boots of their captors did not save them.

In the darkness of the night, and in the presence of the animals in the stable, I knelt and prayed to Jesus to save the souls of the two German soldiers.

Their frightened faces loomed before me that night, and many, many nights thereafter.

TO CELEBRATE OUR LIBERATION, the town of Piaski held a fair. To my surprise and delight, Mr Kozak offered to look after the cattle, and gave me the day off.

He counted out eighty zloty and put the notes into my palm. 'You can stay the whole day,' he said.

I washed my face, combed my hair, dressed as if for church, and stuffed the money into my pocket. I set out early in the morning.

A few of the villagers greeted me along the road, others told me jokingly to bring them something back, and still others warned me in jest to watch out for pickpockets.

In Piaski the acrid smell of war was everywhere; empty cannon shells lay in the streets. Wherever I looked I saw rubble. The main road was congested with passing army convoys heading towards the front. A smartly attired female soldier was directing traffic like an orchestra conductor. The sidewalks were lined with soldiers, some bandaged, some limping, and others looking lost.

I studied each face closely in the futile hope of finding the one I was looking for. I thought I should surprise and drop in on Kazia and Tadek, as well as Mrs Kupinska. I wondered if they were alive, or if they had been killed by the bombs. In the end, I decided to go to the fair first, and visit them after, with souvenirs.

Except for the vendors behind the stalls, and a handful of early visitors like me, the fairgrounds were deserted. I had left the farm before breakfast and now I was enticed by the scent of steaming wieners reaching my nostrils.

I remembered the same aroma from the Warsaw flea market; wieners smothered with pungent mustard. Rumour had it that they were made from horse meat, maybe even diseased horses. As much as I hungered to sink my teeth into one, we could not afford it, and my mother would not have allowed it.

'How much?' I now asked.

'Five zloty,' the woman answered and moved to serve me. I walked away.

If I spend my money now, what will I do for the rest of the day?

My attention was caught by a man at a tiny table concealing a bean under one of three thimbles. I watched and was amazed by his nimble manoeuvres.

Further on, a one-legged man played an accordion and

a young boy, no older than I, a cigarette dangling from his mouth, was appealing for funds. Even though a voice within urged me to toss a zloty into his hat, I resisted.

The day is young, later ... later ... Then my eyes caught sight of a multicoloured drink. A sign read: two zloty a glass. It was Kwas, a sweet fruit-flavoured concoction that I remembered my Uncle Moishe treating me to from a vendor at the corner of Pawia and Smocza Streets. I could almost taste every flavour of every colour, and thirsted to treat myself to them all.

Later! Later! My voice hammered at me.

A clown busily blowing up balloons reminded me of a balloon I once received from a shoe store in Pulawy. When my father blew it up, it had the word 'Bata' imprinted on it.

The clown tried to interest me in one, but I held onto my money tightly, keeping my right hand in my pocket.

A burly lady was hawking sour apples from a large barrel; there was a blind man playing a fiddle; not far on were an acrobat and his daughter performing a sequence of contortions. I was astonished, but when the girl passed the tambourine around for donations, I quickly moved on to the next attraction.

By noon my stomach was growling from hunger; although I saw others bite into steaming, juicy wieners, I nevertheless still clenched my fist and held on to my fortune.

The longer I delayed my spending, I reasoned, the more I would enjoy it and the longer my day of pleasure would last.

Again I stood staring at the Kwas, and as much as I was tempted to quench my now dry throat, I couldn't bring myself to break up my even eighty zloty. I had never had that much money, and now that I did, I wasn't about to part with any of it so frivolously.

At a counter I decided to buy a bag of sweets to take home, but since it was only noon, I elected to delay this until the end of the day.

Suddenly an unshaven dwarf with a straw hat appeared. He produced a circular wooden disk, divided into four equal triangles of different hues. 'Place your money ladies and gentlemen!' he barked, and in no time he attracted onlookers, me among them. 'Place your bets, ladies and gentlemen!' and he rolled a single die painted in the same colours as the disk.

Bills quickly dropped onto the four colours. 'Place your bets! A winner every time.' Shaking the die, he rolled it. It came to rest. 'Red wins!' he trumpeted and paid double to the lucky one, pocketing the money of the losers. 'Place your money, ladies and gentlemen!' Again bills flew out of hopeful hands, obliterating the colours on the disk, and the die tumbled from the dwarf's hand. 'A winner every time.'

Without intending to, I reached into my pocket. You'll lose, an inner voice cautioned.

You could also win, said his opposite. Look at all those doubling their money!

The mere thought of it sent me dreaming. Why only doubling? Why indeed? There was no limit to what amount I could win at this magic wheel!

I felt my pockets bulging, my hat overflowing, and a sack of bills on my back – in fact a wagonload pulled by two straining horses.

I pictured myself buying a fancy new pipe for Mr Kozak, a dress for Mrs Kupinska, and for Kazia and Tadek, a cage with a rabbit. I was returning to Gielczew triumphantly, throwing bagfuls of candy to the villagers. The remainder, I spent erecting a monument, dedicating it to all those who had helped me survive.

'That boy is a Jew, but now we see that Jews are good after all. He has convinced us!' I hear the reeve addressing the assembled.

'Place your bets!' the dwarf continued.

I obeyed. And when I woke from my stupor, my face was dripping with perspiration, my stomach hungry, and my pockets empty.

'Place your bets, ladies and gentlemen! Move on, sonny, give other people a chance,' said the dwarf, prodding my stomach with his cane.

I withdrew from the circle and passed the two acrobats. The blind man was wiping his brow. At the Kwas stand, customers were downing glasses of the rainbow-coloured thirst quencher. The proprietress was doing a brisk business, filling and refilling, collecting money, giving change, as if she had ten pairs of hands.

My throat was parched now, and to add to my misery, the aroma of the steamed wieners reached my senses.

What will I tell Mr Kozak? And what will I bring home?

A dancing bear performed to the beat of a drum. Someone laughed and I felt they were laughing at me. I continued to circle the grounds and when I stopped I found myself at the entrance to our village. Judging by the sun, it was just past noon.

How can I return home so early? What excuse will I give them? I sat down on a rock, and could hear the sounds coming from the fair, one clearer than the rest: 'Place your bets, ladies and gentlemen! A winner every time!'

At sunset I picked myself up to walk home. No one paid me any heed along the way. When I entered the house, they were all at the table.

'Did you have a good time, Franiu?' asked one.

I nodded. They stared at me. I knew what they were waiting for.

'Come, sit,' said Mrs Kozak, pointing to my empty chair.

But before I took a step, someone else said, 'He's probably filled himself with all sorts of delicacies at the fair.'

'Goodnight,' I said, and left.

There will come a day yet, I told myself as I lay down to sleep, when I'll announce to all the villagers:

'My name is not Franek Kupinski, my name is Jankele Kuperblum; I'm a Jew, but as you can see, I'm not as bad as you think ... I'm good ... I'm good ... I'm as good as any one of you.'

FIVE

Wild geese flew in a V formation above us and the wind shook the leaves off the trees. We winterised the outside walls of the hut with straw and chained the cows in the stable for the long winter.

Thousands of soldiers had passed through our village, so many unfamiliar faces, faces that I had never seen before and would never see again; generals, officers, tall Soviet soldiers, short ones, dark ones, blond, people with slanted eyes, some with drawn faces, others smiling, and still others with broken limbs, or bandaged heads. Some played the accordion or harmonica, sang, danced, and then vanished like the others, only to be replaced by new ones.

Soon soldiers wearing Polish army uniforms appeared. Most of them were countrymen who had survived the war in the Soviet Union; others were Russians of Polish descent. To bolster their numbers, the new government called up all able-bodied young men.

Mrs Kozak cried bitterly the day Stefan and Antek received their conscription papers. She packed them each a bundle, and then Mr Kozak and I drove them to Piaski. They got off the wagon, patted the horse, shook hands with

Mr Kozak, winked at me, and soberly entered a building. Mr Kozak emptied his pipe, tapping it gently on the side of the wagon, clicked his tongue, adding a 'Giddy up,' to the horse, turned him around, and headed home.

Weeks went by without a word from either Antek or Stefan. The snow came, the river froze, and Mrs Kozak cried day and night. She hardly slept, and what little sleep she got was invaded with nightmares in which she saw her two sons being killed in action.

Almost daily Mr Kozak and I rode to Piaski to collect our mail at the post office. Invariably we returned empty handed only to find Mrs Kozak wrapped in a shawl, anxiously waiting for us on the village road far from home. She didn't have to ask, for she could read the answer on our faces. Slowly she would climb into the wagon and in silence we'd drive home. In silence she would enter the hut and remove her shawl, boots, and coat. Later, a faint, painful, suppressed cry could be heard coming from the corner of the room.

Then quite unexpectedly a letter arrived from Stefan in which he complained bitterly about the hardships he was forced to endure. He was in training in some undisclosed forest encampment and feared he would die of hunger or freeze to death as they were forced to sleep in trenches.

Mrs Kozak immediately dispatched a large parcel of butter, pork fat, bread, tobacco, underwear, and an assortment of treats.

In time, a similar letter arrived from Antek, and once again the mother packed a similar parcel and Mr Kozak and I delivered it to the Piaski post office.

Soon more letters came, revealing even worse conditions. Mrs Kozak shed more tears and refused to eat or talk. She busied herself with sending parcels.

One day a letter from Stefan arrived in which he related he had completed his training and was being sent to the front. He shared his fear of dying and worried that he would never see his mother again. He had touching words for everyone, even wishing me a good future in a better world.

His letter depressed all of us. Not only did Mrs Kozak cry, but so did Cesia and I, and even Mr Kozak was seen wiping away a tear.

We waited with great anticipation for his next letter, but none came, and when many weeks had passed and still no word, Mrs Kozak addressed a letter to the military in Lublin.

A reply came several weeks later; Stefan was missing in action.

About the same time, news reached us from Antek: he was now at the front, stationed on the Vistula River, waiting to liberate Warsaw. He described the hunger, the bitter cold, and his fear of death.

The Kozak household became a place of mourning. There was little conversation, and if one had to speak, it was done in funereal whispers.

Mrs Kozak continued to cry, and read and reread all the correspondence from her two offspring. The succeeding letters from Antek describing the intolerable conditions in which he found himself upset Mrs Kozak to such an extent that she packed several large bundles, and against her husband's pleas and advice, set out for the front.

'How do you know how I feel?' she asked him. 'You didn't carry him in your belly.'

We drove her to town and waited on the highway until an army vehicle stopped to offer her a lift. She climbed into the back of the open half-truck, shivering from the bitter frost, and managed a smile, the first in many months. The truck sped away, leaving a cloud of diesel fumes behind.

In her absence, Cesia cooked and looked after the household chores. We rose early, did our work, spoke little, and went to bed at an early hour.

On a snow-covered day, Mrs Kozak returned. After sleeping for three days and nights, she related, in halting sentences interspersed with tears, what she had witnessed.

'Antek has all this time been sitting in trenches near the banks of the Vistula ... bullets whiz overhead ... The Germans are still holding Warsaw ... The river is frozen ... now and then a few of our boys are sent across ... they usually don't come back, but they keep sending others ... Several conscripts died from frostbite ... Mines are everywhere, and many get killed or maimed that way ... Along the road you see dead Germans nailed to posts, an arm pointing to Germany and a sign reading, "This way to Berlin" ... Antek asked about everyone ... He's afraid ... he's so afraid that he may be next to be sent across the frozen Vistula ... Everywhere you look, dead bodies lying about.'

Friends and neighbours came to visit, listened, asked questions, and debated. Some said it was better during the German occupation, others opined that the officers and generals in the Polish army were either Russians with Polish names or Polish Jews, and were killing off the Polish soldiers on purpose. One was of the opinion that the Jewish officers had all deserted and left our fighters to the mercy of the enemy. This led to a discussion about Jews in general and more particularly what cowards they were and how they had never shed blood for Poland.

'We give our lives, they do business,' added another.

It's not true! I wanted to rise and protest.

Isn't it? teased my other voice. What about your Uncle Mendel?

And now my Uncle Mendel, one of my father's younger brothers, stood before me. His face radiant, he was hoisting me above his head.

'Jankele, you've grown!' he was saying. 'I can barely lift you.'

'Where is your uniform, Mendel?' someone was asking.

'It's this way,' my uncle explained. 'I say to myself, "With or without me the war is lost," so I get my hands on some civilian garb and the next outhouse I come to, the uniform, the gun, everything, I throw it where it belongs and come out looking like you see me now.'

That's an isolated case, I reasoned.

Isolated? mocked the voice. Didn't your grandfather Shie Chuen, the cobbler from Warsaw, have two missing toes?

What about it?

The voice laughed. Come now; fool everyone else, but not yourself. Don't you remember hearing that he had cut them off to avoid army service?

I now blushed with shame, for it was all true ... all true, and this cowardice is what I possess within *me*.

What is it that makes me so fearful? Why couldn't I kill the kittens? Why do I fear bombs, guns, and grenades? How is it that my Uncle Mendel deserted the Polish army while Stefan gave his life fighting for Poland? And Antek too, may never return. I had to track down and expunge whatever it was that made me like my uncle and grandfather; I had to become like Stefan and Antek.

WHILE FEEDING THE COWS one late winter day, I felt myself being watched. I looked around but couldn't see anyone.

My imagination, I consoled myself, when suddenly a bearded face popped up from the pigsty, startling me. A stranger climbed out and came towards me, eyes shifting from side to side. I let out a scream and backed away.

'Franiu, hush!' he said and advanced. 'Franiu, don't you recognise me?' the voice was familiar.

'Stefan?' And then I was truly frightened. Is this Stefan's ghost? I wondered. 'Is it really you, Stefan? You're alive?' my teeth chattered.

'I think I'm alive,' he said. 'Go tell my mother I'm here.'

I headed out when he called after me.

'Franiu!' I turned. 'You'll keep it to yourself, won't you ... my being here, I mean ...?' He looked so pitiful, and I saw something in his eyes that I had felt many times – fear.

A FEW WEEKS LATER, returning from her latest trip to the front, Mrs Kozak seemed unusually cheerful. She went about her business as if the war was over and she would have no need to set foot at the front again. Her changed demeanour was puzzling, until I entered the barn, and a pair of cold hands blinded me, and a voice asked, 'Guess who?'

'Let go, Stefan,' I giggled.

'Guess again,' said the voice.

The hands parted and I turned. Facing me was a Polish soldier with a shaven head.

'Antek!' I exclaimed.

'Go tell my mother to bring me some clothes.' I started to go. 'And Franiu,' he placed a finger to his lips, 'nobody's to know.'

By day, the two brothers remained in the stable and came out only at night to smoke a cigarette and stretch their legs. I brought them food, ran messages to and from the house, and kept them company in my free time.

In this manner the days and weeks flew by. But once the

snow had melted and the swallows reappeared, Stefan and Antek left their sanctuary, and their mother announced that her two boys had returned the previous night, honourably discharged from military service.

Almost nightly, neighbours would fill the Kozak hut to bombard the two valiant ones with questions.

Stefan and Antek obliged, keeping them spellbound with tales of danger and daring. In return, the villagers showered the heroes with words of admiration.

'As long as we have soldiers like you,' said one, 'offering your lives for our country, Poland will never again be suppressed.'

ALTHOUGH I HAD NOT SEEN a German soldier for months, and saw many indications of the enemy's defeat, secretly I still worried that my liberation might prove to be short-lived. I never divulged these fears, but in the dead of night I would lie awake and argue with myself.

Perhaps these soldiers aren't Soviets or Poles; only Germans in disguise.

At other times I wondered if I was in a deep coma and everything around me was simply a dream. I'll wake and find the Germans still here.

Desperately I wanted to be free of fear. I longed to tell someone, anyone, especially Mr Kozak, who I really was. I even practised for the occasion. 'Mr Kozak, I'm a Jew!' And yet day after day I kept delaying it, for not only did I still fear the Germans returning, but also the villagers themselves.

Horrific stories were making the rounds, of Jews who survived, came out of hiding and were murdered along a deserted farm road, upon returning to their former houses, and, worse still, in broad daylight in the Piaski market.

The villagers were hardly shocked by these atrocities. On the contrary. 'The nerve of them,' said one, 'the moment they emerge from their rat holes, they want everything back.'

'They inform on anyone who's done them the slightest injustice.'

'They're all communists ... Hitler was right.'

I pretended not to hear. On occasion, Soviet enforcers would descend on the village and haul out a member or two of a supposedly nationalist underground, after which the familiar venom would resurface.

'Some Jew turned him in.'

Perhaps they mean me, I worried. After all I'm the only one here and I know that gang. Did I inform on them somehow? If I did, I don't even know it.

Ever since my arrival at the Kozaks, I had attended church on Sundays. I understood little of what went on, but I mimicked; when others knelt, I knelt; when others stood, I stood; when the lady next to me turned a page in her prayer book, so did I; and when they crossed themselves, I followed. And when the priest read with a commanding voice: 'After these things Jesus walked in Galilee for he would not walk in Jewry, because the Jews sought to kill Him.' I too listened and pretended to despise the unbelieving Jews for their blindness.

Now that I was liberated, I wanted to end this charade but found myself going to church instinctively. My daily prayers were not simply to fool anyone. I was saying them with conviction and sincerity.

These revelations disturbed me, for I now realised how far I had removed myself from little Jankele Kuperblum. There were two of me: one Jankele Kuperblum, the other Franiu Kupinski. Franiu Kupinski I knew and could see well, but Jankele Kuperblum stood on the horizon. A blur!

Shame, Jankele! Shame! You're free, yet you make no attempt to return to the fold. Don't you realise what I'm saying to you? You have survived ... the game is over. The Germans left months ago ... the liberators are here. Jankele, don't you understand, the Germans have lost! You can come out now and return home.

Indeed I had survived, yet I had not recognised the victorious moment. I wanted to shout, to dance, to laugh, to jump into the river, to swim, to run, to leap into the air, and fly over the thatched rooftops. I wanted to do all those things, but in reality I couldn't squeeze out even a smile.

I have survived, I thought, but who has survived with me? Where are the others?

And now for the first time in months I remembered that I once had a mother named Edzia, a brother named Josele, and uncles named Shepsel and Moishe. Where could Moishe be?

I thought of my father and wondered if he was alive or perhaps buried somewhere in an unmarked grave.

My thoughts led me into a deep melancholy from which I could not free myself. I was pulled deeper and deeper into its vortex until I found no reason to go on living. I survived for nothing!

How did you survive? My voice interrogated me.

What do you mean, how?

What did you do? Whom did you betray?

No one, I swear. It was by chance ... luck!

Was it now? Come on ... the voice laughed. You left your mother.

How was I to know she'd be deported?

But did you go looking for her? Did you?

Where was I to look?

You didn't even try, did you? And your Uncle Moishe, didn't you let him go to his death?

I tried to stop him; you know that, you were there. But he wouldn't listen.

Weren't you pleased when he decided to turn himself in?

No! No! Why should that have pleased me? You're crazy!

Your Uncle Moishe looked Jewish and his Polish wasn't all that good. Without him you had a much better chance.

I loved Moishe, I defended myself.

Of course you did. But to survive you had to sacrifice him. Now, let's see, who else did you do in?

I didn't answer.

You're guilty, Jankele. You must be guilty.

I felt a pair of massive hands, hands so large and powerful that they could belong only to God, tightening around my throat.

'Holy Mother!' someone cried out.

A knife flashed in front of me and I fell to the sound of a thud. When I opened my eyes, I saw blurred faces looking down at me. I heard voices, but what were they saying? Everything seemed far, far away.

'WHY DID YOU DO IT?' asked Mr Kozak, towering above me in the barn and displaying two lengths of rope. 'Why?'

I was ready to unload, but when I turned to face him, he was gone and only the severed rope that held up my pants was there.

For days I waited for an opportunity to cleanse myself but the chance never came. Whenever we were together, someone else would intrude, or if we were alone he was in a bad mood, or I would get cold feet, and again delay.

Finally, one day when we were working, I said, 'Mr Kozak.'

He puffed on his pipe and kept turning the wheel of the chaff cutter. 'Yes, boy,' he murmured.

'Mr Kozak, I've been wanting to tell you something for a long time.' He didn't react. 'Mr Kozak,' I went on, 'I've kept a secret from you.' He carried on as if he hadn't heard me. We continued to cut and then brought the machine to a halt and refilled it with more straw. He was about to start turning the wheel again, when he glanced up and said, 'What were you saying, boy?'

'Mr Kozak,' I blurted out in a trembling voice, 'Mr Kozak, I'm a Jew!'

He gripped the handle and began to turn the wheel again. When the job was done, I expected him to question me or be angry, or delighted, but to my consternation, he was silent, as if my revelation meant nothing to him. This puzzled and later worried me.

During the days that followed, none of the family or villagers acted differently towards me. And since no one brought up the subject, I concluded that Mr Kozak, for whatever reason, had decided to keep my secret to himself.

Could it be that he didn't hear you? suggested my inner adviser, or he thought you were clowning.

He's silent because he plans to do away with you, offered the pessimist.

The first disagreed strenuously. No! He's silent because he's wise and ...

ON A HUMID EVENING, neighbours sat outside the Kozak hut gossiping. I was among them only half listening and wondering how it was that day turned into night and night turned into day.

From there my mind drifted to other questions for which I had no answers. At one point I saw a drunk approaching. He swayed from side to side, sometimes almost falling and then regaining his balance. He kept his right hand in his pocket and the left held an almost empty bottle from which he swigged.

'Look at him,' said someone. 'Poor devil! They took away his brother today.'

'They should arrest the lot of them,' another said. 'All they did for Poland was rob the poor.'

These same neighbours had sat on the same steps at the same time of day during the German occupation. A wagon pulled by two feisty horses appeared in the distance accompanied by male voices bellowing a patriotic Polish song.

'It's our fighters,' someone whispered with admiration. The entire wagonload of five or six, bedecked in a hodgepodge of Polish and German uniforms and brandishing rifles, were soon upon us. Their leader, sporting a four-cornered Polish officer's hat, making him appear taller, sat at the front with the driver. They saluted us as if we were on a reviewing stand, and the horses and wagon disappeared into the night together with the song.

The next day several strange horses were tied to a post in a neighbouring stable, and one of that gang would come looking for me.

'Franiu, be a good boy and get us some feed for the poor animals. Strictly between us, you understand?'

In summer, I would simply help myself to some drying hay in a field, and in winter I would do the same from a nearby haystack or someone's barn when no one was looking.

While attending to their animals, I overheard how the horses had been acquired; by force from some frightened farmer in a distant village made to believe that the soldiers were the Polish underground, and that what they were doing was for the cause of Polish liberation. They drank and laughed and showed off the gold rings taken from terrified Jews on the run. The horses would remain in the stable until they were sold. Subsequently, fresh horses would appear, and I'd be summoned yet again to hear their drunken laughter and listen to their heroic accounts of how they terrorised some unfortunate family. Or how they robbed some running Jew and killed him, leaving him naked in a field.

Once they bragged of having murdered a German officer and stealing his weapon. They displayed the piece and re-enacted the whole ambush for me.

I was terrified of this group, and could only imagine what they would do if they discovered my real identity. My security, I decided, lay in being as close to them as possible, and so I listened, laughed with them, and occasionally, at their insistence, took a sip of vodka. And although I was grateful that it never happened, to show their appreciation, they promised to take me along on one of their patriotic missions.

'After the war, Franiu, you'll be decorated for sure,' they promised. Momentarily I would forget who I was, who they were, and I would truly believe I was involved in the underground against the enemy.

The staggering drunk was now upon us, his eyes glazed and white saliva frothing from the corner of his mouth. He scanned the assembled faces and then hurled the empty bottle onto the roof of our hut.

'Have you heard from your brother?' inquired one of the neighbours.

He ignored the question, his eyes zeroing in on me. He looked so comical that I broke into laughter.

'Jew!' he shouted. 'You betrayed my brother, and the others.'
A revolver was suddenly in his hand. I jumped to my feet and
charged into the hut and onto the floor. I heard three succes-
sive shots, followed by a commotion. Mr Kozak did hear me!
They all know!

'He's gone,' said Mr Kozak after entering. 'He's a drunk
and doesn't know what he's saying. Come on out, Franiu.'

I didn't move and begged to be allowed to sleep in the
house that night. In my sleep, shadowy figures chased me
from place to place.

Days later a car pulled up in front of the drunkard's house
and two sinister-looking police types were seen entering and
exiting with the one who tried to kill me.

Soon word spread that it was their leader who had betrayed
them all. He was the first to be arrested and some swore
they had seen him in Piaski riding around with the Russian
Secret Police.

Unexpectedly, he showed up in the village wearing new
leather boots and sporting a fancy revolver under his belt. He
stood at the gate of his father's house, aiming the gun at a
squirrel high up on a tree.

Two days after his arrival someone targeted him, putting a
bullet through his head. His body lay like the dead squirrel;
face twisted, legs apart, eyes open, staring into the heavens.

'You have nothing to fear now,' said Mr Kozak.

'MR KOZAK,' I said, 'I think it's best for everyone if I left.'

'Not for everyone, boy,' he said in his quiet way. Then his
eyes bulged and he wagged his finger at me, 'You're not going
anywhere. Do you hear?' I was shocked at his erupting rage. 'I
saved your life, boy. Had you been discovered, all of us would

have been killed and everything we have worked for all of our lives would have been burned to the ground. You'll stay right here and work for me till your dying day.'

'You can't keep me here,' I surprised myself for standing up to him.

'I can and I will,' he snapped back. 'You owe me your life!'

I made plans to leave. But when I went to pack, my few meagre possessions were gone. How could I leave without my spare pair of long underwear, a shirt, one pair of trousers, and my coat?

A day or so later, I informed him that I had thought it over. 'The truth is,' I said, 'that I have nowhere to go anyway, so I hope I'm still welcome here and you'll allow me to stay. Forever!'

That same day my belongings were back in place.

The rest of that week was uneventful and on Sunday all of us drove to church.

Another week went by and again it was Sunday. Although it was a warm day, I put on my two pair of underwear, the two shirts, and both pairs of trousers. As usual, Mr Kozak prepared the horse, and everyone mounted the wagon for the short journey to the Piaski church.

'Franiu, we're waiting,' called Mr Kozak.

'Go without me,' I shouted back from the barn. 'I overslept; I'll go to late Mass.'

I heard the familiar, 'Giddy up,' then the horse's rhythmic trot, the screeching of dry wheels, and then silence.

I looked about me; my sleeping place, the familiar tools. In the farmyard I touched the worn handle of the axe, embedded in a dried-out tree stump. The clucking chickens blocked my path as I made my way to the stable to say goodbye to the pigs, the cows, the filly in the stall, the pitchfork that I had used so often to pitch the manure from the stable, the nest the swallows toiled so hard to build and then abandoned. And knew that this was the last time I would ever stand there ... the very last time.

To my astonishment when I entered the house Cesia was there.

'I'm going to church,' I said.

'You hungry?'

'I'd better be off or I'll be late.'

'Then take some cookies for the road,' and she handed me several. When I reached the door, she called, 'Franiu! Aren't you going to say goodbye?'

She knows, I thought.

'Goodbye, Cesia,' I said.

'Goodbye, Franiu.' And for the first time she kissed me, on my cheek.

'I'll see you later,' I said.

She nodded. 'Good luck Franiu.'

When I reached the road I turned to look back. She was leaning in the doorway gently waving her arm. I walked on, feeling her gaze behind me.

A Sunday quiet reigned along the village road. Every step I took seemed to echo throughout its length. A grubby dog standing at an open gate stared at me but did not bark. A flock of geese ran towards me. From behind a lace curtain I caught sight of an ancient woman's face, peering out.

When I approached the house where the gang's leader had once resided, I gave a cursory look at the spot where he had fallen.

Although there was no one to be seen, at any moment I expected a gun to be pointing at me from behind a curtained window, or barn door, and to hear the shot ring out.

Turn back. Right now, whispered the voice.

Keep going, said the other. Don't be afraid.

You'll be sorry, teased the first. You won't get out of this village alive. They're waiting for you. Remember, I warned you.

Alarmed, I would have turned back except that by now I was closer to the entrance of the town than to the Kozak farm. One careful step at a time, I moved on. Eight more houses and I'll be out, I comforted myself ... seven more houses ... six more ... I took several more steps. I looked to the left, and then looked to the right ... Five more ... four ... three ... two ... I now feared the worst. Perhaps they're waiting for me in the last house! I sneaked a glance. A door opened, and a man stepped out brandishing a rifle.

The voice heckled, you should have listened to me. It's too late now.

'Nice day,' said the man. 'Are you off to church?'

'Yes,' I answered, and when I dared to look at him, in place of the rifle, hc was gripping a walking stick.

The village of Gielczcw was now behind me and facing me was the town of Piaski. I'm out. I'm safe. I've made it!

Not yet, cautioned the voice. You might still get it in the back.

I'm safe, I'm safe ... I'm safe, I tried to convince myself.

The town was also deserted; hardly a soul to be seen and the silence interrupted only by chanting from the church. Staring at my feet stepping along the cobbled road, I moved on.

Suddenly the church choir stopped and so did I. It was eerily quiet again. The gleaming church loomed before me and in front of it the wagon and horse were parked, and sitting erect in the driver's seat observing me, was Mr Kozak.

I was stunned, trapped, ashamed, afraid, but I did not move. I stared at him and he stared at me.

Will he run after me? I wondered. Perhaps he has a gun! I'll have to find out. I took a step backward. Mr Kozak remained stationary. I took another step, then another and another, and he remained sitting, frozen to his seat, and simply stared at me, as if he was accusing me of ingratitude with his silence.

I turned and walked towards the highway. There I stopped to look back. Mr Kozak hadn't moved.

You're a dirty sneaky Jew, accused one of my voices. The poor man saves your life, and the first opportunity you have, you run out on him. So typical of you Jews!

I wish I could tell him how grateful I am for everything he taught me and how I truly love him, I justified.

Don't bother, Jew boy, said the voice, and then mocking me added, once a Jew always a Jew!

'Jump on,' a voice jolted me. I looked up to see a wagon with three men and a strawberry blonde woman. 'Where to?' asked the driver. I mounted but didn't answer.

The horses snorted, the wheels began to turn, and the wagon took flight. The town of Piaski, its church, and Mr Kozak became a speck in the distance, and then not even that.

THERE WAS MUCH CHATTER and laughter in the wagon, but my mind was elsewhere; on the stone-studded road, the bending trees, farms and fields speeding by. One dissolved into another so that structures appeared on top of trees, cows floating in the sky, and the earth turning, and we, it seemed, were flying through space, propelled by galloping horses.

An army truck full of soldiers staring blankly into the void passed us.

Signs proclaiming names of villages and kilometres to

towns flashed by. A bent figure, carrying firewood from the forest, stopped to adjust the heavy load. And now a boy fingering a flute was leading a solitary cow to pasture.

The road turned and twisted uphill, downhill, and by early afternoon I was in familiar territory. Every house, every tree, every bend of the road brought back memories. This was where I had wandered my first winter, begging for food and shelter. Where a farmhouse had once stood and now lay burned to the ground, except for the brick chimney, the woman asked, 'A bomb?'

'No,' replied the driver. 'The underground.'

Scanning the passengers, as one who knows more than he finds it wise to tell, he simply said, 'He was an informer,' and he spat onto the side of the road.

I've been in this village before, of course! The burned farm was owned by the very one who had examined my penis. 'How much further to Siedliszcze?' I asked the driver.

'Is that where you want to go?'

'I'd be grateful if you dropped me off there.'

He nodded, and about an hour later, pulled at the reins. I thanked him, jumped down, bid them all farewell, then proceeded down a dusty road.

I knew this road and yet didn't. I entered the town and here too everything seemed peculiar, as if I had visited there, but not in real life. Perhaps in a dream! Here too everyone seemed to be in church. The town looked desolate. I feared for my life.

I worried, and walked ever so cautiously. What if I'm recognised? I wanted to talk to someone, anyone, ask questions, but thought better of it in case my words might betray me.

A street, another, a turn, and to my left I expected to see the tiny one-room row cottage where I last saw my mother.

I so much wanted to go in, examine, inquire, but I was terrified of even glancing in that direction.

I must look, I must, I kept repeating to myself. Perhaps my mother is there! Perhaps everyone is there! Perhaps they've all returned and are waiting for me!

But I didn't stop; I did not dare. I only shifted my eyes to catch a glimpse. A parquet of a few saplings and an empty park bench stared back at me. 'Dear God!' I whispered. 'Dear God!' and walked on, as if the transformation was of no concern to me.

I continued to journey without knowing where I was heading or for what I was looking. And yet instinctively I took certain turns, passed a windmill, jumped across a brook, and as the sun was setting, found myself at the entrance of a farm, admiring the blossoms on a cherry tree.

I bent to inhale its fragrance when a voice disturbed my pleasure. 'Hey! What are you doing there?' Mrs Gogulka appeared from the barn carrying a bucket of milk. 'Holy Mother, it's our Kubus!' she screamed and crossed herself, allowing the bucket to slip from her hand, and spilling the milk. She embraced me warmly, and passed me like a football into her husband's arms and then into Lucja's. Their joy was overwhelming. They bombarded me with questions, touching me to make sure I wasn't only a mirage.

In the morning, Mr Gogulka took me aside, cleared his throat, and began: 'Kubus, chances are that your family has perished, and as you know, we always thought of you as our own. Stay with us and accept our name. When the time comes, this place will be Lucja's and yours.' When I didn't reply he added, 'You don't have to decide now, Kubus, think about it.'

How wonderful it is to be wanted, to have a home! I thought. Kubus Gogulka ... sounds good!

Looking out the window I gazed at the wet fields in the direction of Kulik.

Moishe! My God, Moishe may be alive, and if he is, he'll look for me at the Pejzaks'.

'I have to find my uncle.'

Mr Gogulka turned white. 'If you don't find him, Kubus, promise me you'll return to us.'

I promised without hesitation.

With wet feet and a heavy heart pounding with antici- pation, I cut across the flooded fields. My legs ached, but I resolved not to rest, for I was certain that at the end of my journey, my Uncle Moishe was waiting for me, perhaps even my mother ... perhaps ... perhaps ...!

SIX

I stood on the driveway leading into the Pejzak farm. There was the house, the barn, the orchard behind it, and the sound of a rooster alerting my arrival. A smile curled my lips. I have made it! Mrs Pejzak didn't think I had a chance and here I am, about to prove to her that I've outwitted the entire German army.

The weeping willow trees lining the road looked like the honour guard for the returning hero. A dog began to bark as I entered the farmyard and soon a tall, lean farmer with a weathered face and creased felt hat came out of the barn. He studied me, 'Where are the Pejzaks?' I asked, my voice betraying the anxiety I tried to disguise.

He stuck his head into the barn. 'Someone for you.' A woman with greying hair stepped out and, straining her eyes, attempted to bring me into focus. I moved closer to her. Mrs Pejzak had aged and looked troubled.

'Don't you recognise me, Mrs Pejzak?'

Her mouth opened wide, and she covered her face with the palms of her hands. 'I can't believe it! You're alive!' and she kissed me all over. 'We heard you were shot at a roadside,' she said. 'Is it really you, Kubus?' And once more covered me with kisses, whispering, 'My beautiful little boy!'

'And Genia, where is she?'

'She's visiting her papa's grave.'

'And what about Staszek?'

'In the field. Go, he'll be happy to see you.'

I went behind the house and found Staszek planting potatoes at the bottom of the hill. In spite of everything, I was ready to forgive him, to show him I didn't carry grudges, nor did I seek revenge.

'Staszek!' I called and cautiously moved towards him. He glanced at me. 'What are you doing here?' and continued with his work.

'Aren't you happy to see me?' I asked, poking for a soft spot in his heart. He didn't respond.

Soon after, Genia, dressed in a stylish coat, high leather boots, and an elegant hat, entered, accompanied by a young man. She held tightly onto his arm. She was laughing, and suddenly her face shone like the sun and her smile almost melted my heart. We fell into each other's arms.

I soon learned that the farmer was Mrs Pejzak's new husband, and the young man, Genia's fiancé. They were to be married shortly.

When we were alone, Genia confided that although he was a decent and hard-working man, and good to her, she did not love him.

'Then why are you marrying him?' I asked.

She smiled, 'Because I got tired of waiting for you, Kubus.' And we both giggled. 'Remember,' she spoke quietly, 'the good times we had?' I blushed. 'I have to marry him, Kubus,' she continued as if resigned; 'It's mother's idea. That way, she thinks I'll be saved from deportation.'

'Deportation?' I frowned.

'Haven't you heard? All Ukrainians are being deported from Poland and everyone says they'll ship us to Siberia.'

'Why?'

'Because of those Ukrainians who helped the Germans. Mother says if I marry him, because he's Polish, the farm and I will be saved. She's also been after Staszek to find himself a Polish girl. But he's stubborn. That's why mother remarried, to a Pole. It seems, Kubus, that Jews and Ukrainians have the same bad luck.'

With no sign of Moishe, I decided to return to the Gogulkas. Both Genia and Mrs Pejzak encouraged me to stay longer.

'He may still show up, Kubus. Wait,' said Genia.

I waited, peering through the window, at every approaching figure, hoping that every speck on the horizon would turn out to be my Uncle Moishe. But I was not so lucky.

In the meantime, I made a visit to my grandfather's grave in the village of Dobromysl. I didn't exactly know what I would do there, but I felt I should pay my respects.

From the distance I recognised the dead tree, but when I came closer, I could not find the grave, or the stone that used to mark it. Instead I met an elderly farmer planting tomatoes.

I desperately wanted to know why the grave had been obliterated and the marker was gone, but I feared showing interest in a Jew's grave.

On the way back I stopped to rest, and wondered if I was lying on someone's grave! Perhaps all the fields around me are packed with victims! Maybe the whole world is one large cemetery; no graves, no headstones, and no survivors to mourn for the dead.

UPON MY DEPARTURE MRS PEJZAK reminded me that she still had a few of my mother's belongings and offered them to me. The pots would have been too cumbersome to carry. I opted for the bedsheet, now slightly torn, folded it into a neat bundle and tied it with string. Throwing it over my shoulder, I intended to set out to the Gogulkas', but unconsciously I headed in another direction.

By sunset I stood once more at the entrance to the smithy in the village of Malinowka. Upon seeing me, Mr Tekalewicz the blacksmith nodded and resumed work as if I had never been away.

'Aren't you surprised to see me?' I asked.

'I was rather hoping you'd show up,' he said when he stopped to reheat the metal he had been hammering. 'I'm married now,' he said. 'Wait until you see the farm I have acquired. Want to work for me?'

'I just came to see how everybody is faring,' I said.

'Not for a few more beatings from that bitch Wajda?' and we both broke out laughing.

'Come!'

He closed his shop, then hopping onto his bicycle, he pointed for me to jump on the back. As we rode through the village, he waved to neighbours and they looked on with envy at the treasure transporting him.

He turned into an estate boasting an elegant white house, an orchard dotted with fruit trees, a sound stable and impressive barn. The courtyard was spacious and orderly. Flowering shrubs fronted the property. Mr Tekalewicz, bursting with pride, watched me admire his newly acquired wealth. The property had once belonged to a Volksdeutch. When the Germans invaded and annexed western Poland, they deported the Polish peasants from that area and gifted their lavish farms to the ethnic Germans. In turn, the evicted Poles were offered the abandoned properties of the Volksdeutchen. Thus an exchange took place. When the German army retreated, with the ethnic Germans right behind them, the dispossessed western Poles returned to their former estates, leaving many highly desirable farms in Malinowka for the taking. Mr Tekalewicz wasn't one to miss such an opportunity, nor were others. Everyone tried to upgrade.

He led me into the house and introduced me to his wife. 'Sweetheart, Zygmund's going to work for us.'

'I can't,' I said apologetically.

'What a shame, Zygmund. I was counting on you. We would treat you well, get you some decent clothes, pay you a salary, and even let you sleep in the house.'

'I'm already committed. Someone is expecting me.'

'What a pity, especially now, with a baby coming,' and he playfully patted his wife's belly. 'If you could at least stay a month or two, it would be a great help.'

It was he who had welcomed me to Malinowka when I looked for shelter. How could I refuse him?

What about the Gogulkas? a voice gnawed within me. Is that how you keep your word?

I'll write them, I'll explain that I've been delayed, the other voice defended me.

You'll write? When?

Tomorrow, the next day, soon, and I went to bed with visions of the Gogulkas patiently waiting for me by the gate near the cherry tree, not knowing where I was or what had happened to me.

By the time I sat down to write, weeks had gone by and so I resolved that it was too late. I was embarrassed.

THE COWS GRAZED IN A FIELD on the adjoining village road where the grass was green, thick, and tall. Barefoot, I'd sit in this luxurious pasture, keep watch on my flock or follow the flight of a butterfly, and I'd sing.

Passers-by would often stop to listen, and on days when I rested my voice, they'd call out to me, 'Sing something!'

'It's a gift from God,' some told me, and others predicted that I'd become a singer of great renown and give concerts attended by royalty all over the world.

Mr Tekalewicz liked to drink and was proud of the vodka he distilled himself in the winter months. He was always of good cheer and forgiving if I made a mistake or neglected to carry out a task. I was comfortable with both him and his wife and happy that I had decided to remain. But the fact that I continued to live a lie eroded my soul. One evening my employers became involved in a bitter quarrel that led Mr Tekalewicz to hit his pregnant wife, storm out, and shut himself in the stable.

He emerged hours later with a sheepish smirk on his face and so drunk that he tried to enter the house through the window. He held a small antique revolver, which he tried without success to point at his wife's protruding belly.

'I'll shoot it out of you!' he guffawed.

The very next time we worked together in the field, I came to the point: 'Mr Tekalewicz,' I began, 'what would you say if I told you that I'm a Jew?' I felt tremendously relieved.

'Is that a fact? That's good, very good. Do you know Goldman?'

I shook my head.

'He's the Jew who owns the Wajdas' place. Now he has a farm, almost as nice as this one. When he came out of hiding he had himself and his daughter baptised, even changed his name, though everyone still calls him Goldman.'

A day or so later I made my way to the Goldman farm, and from behind a raspberry bush, stole a look into the house.

At the table sat a girl braiding her long black hair, and beside her sat an elderly man with a book in his hands. I expected him to resemble my grandfather the baker, with a beard, hat, and black caftan, but instead, he looked very much like any other peasant here or in any other village.

At night I lay awake thinking of them; driving to church on Sunday, interacting with others as equals, without fear, without having to lie, hide, or pretend. Blending in rather than sticking out. And I envied them! These musings led one of my persistent voices to ask, how is it that you, and only you, survived?

Luck, I guess.

Luck? It scoffed. Think hard.

A suffering Jesus descended from a colossal cross and with outstretched arms came to embrace me. Jesus Christ saved me, I affirmed.

I shared my decision to convert with Mr Tekalewicz and asked for his assistance.

'I'll speak to the priest about it,' he said dismissively.

On Sunday, he and his wife, dressed in their finery, mounted the wagon, and as on every other Sunday, departed for church.

Waiting for their return I fantasized how life would soon change for me. And when they did return I quickly ran out in anticipation of the good news.

My boss expected me to unhitch the horse, but made no mention of having consulted the priest.

'What did the father say?' I asked anxiously.

Mr Tekalewicz struck his forehead with the palm of his hand. 'Zygmund, I apologise, I completely forgot!' and he put an arm around me trying to console me. 'Next Sunday for sure.'

Not discouraged, I began to prepare by studying the catechism and memorizing the prayers.

The following Sunday seemed like a lifetime away, but it came. Again my employers went to church. This time the priest had been too occupied to give them an audience.

In the weeks that followed, there were other excuses and more than once he questioned the wisdom of my becoming a Christian. I argued, persisted, and as a last resort, wept and begged.

'I'll tell you what, Zygmund,' he said. 'Let's wait until the baby comes, and then we'll have a double christening,' and added, 'I promise.'

I counted the days and prayed nightly for the baby to arrive. Mrs Tekalewicz's stomach seemed gigantic now, and yet still no baby. It was only when I had given up all hope and had even stopped praying for its delivery that I was awakened one moonlit night by a shrill cry from the next room.

'It's a boy!' shouted Mr Tekalewicz. 'On Sunday I'll make all the arrangements.' And to fortify himself, he emptied a full glass of his homemade vodka.

I counted the days, the nights, the hours. In my sleep the words from the catechism seemed to come off the printed pages and dance in my head.

At long last, the appointed day arrived. I rose early and watched a warm sun appear. I looked at the tranquil sky and listened to the birds chirping in the trees. I prepared the wagon, harnessed the horse, and packed some feed for him.

There was celebration in the courtyard; family and friends arrived in decorated wagons and waited for the Tekalewiczes to emerge and lead the convoy to church. Neighbouring children stood by to catch a glimpse of the newborn infant being carried by his mother.

'Giddy up,' my employer yelled, ready to pull out for the long drive.

Nimbly I jumped onto the end of our wagon as it was pulling away.

Mr Tekalewicz brought the horse to a sudden stop and stabbed me with his eyes.

'Where do you think you're going?'

'But you promised,' the words struggled to leave my lips.

'I don't remember. Perhaps I did and perhaps I didn't. We can't leave this place unattended. Someone has to stay behind.'

'Let him come,' said Mrs Tekalewicz.

Her husband threw her a vicious look. 'You just hold the baby and let me handle this.' She bit her lip and suppressed whatever she felt for me.

I slid off the wagon and watched them pull out. The children ran after the convoy screaming and shouting. I sat down on the decaying bench by the well and cried.

Midweek I put on my Sunday best, my shoes dangling over my shoulder, and left the village of Malinowka in the early dawn. With an optimistic heart, I headed across fields, along a potholed road, closer and closer to the church, on the way to Chelm, to the priest, to be baptised, to be a Christian, to be free, to be good, and to live like all others.

The day was hot and the journey arduous. Kilometres later, I could see the church; a massive structure made of grey stone and surrounded by shrubs and flowers.

Hungry, thirsty, and sweating, I arrived at the wooden gate leading into the garden and spotted the bent figure of the priest. His back was turned to me, but then, as if he had sensed my presence, he straightened up, swung around, and slowly came towards me.

Without saying a word, he extended his hand, which I gladly took, and he led me into the rectory. There he pointed to a chair and disappeared behind a curtain. I sat studying the many images on the walls; of Christ, the Holy Mother, and many saints. Soon he returned carrying a tray with bread, cabbage, meat, and a glass of milk.

'Please eat.' He sat down and watched me. Between spoonfuls I studied his kind face and now I remembered him. He had come to bless the Wajdas' home and had tossed me a coin.

When I had finished eating, he cleared the table and then returned to his chair. Looking deep into my eyes, he said, 'I know why you're here.'

How does he know? I wondered. Do priests speak to God?

Momentarily he closed his eyes, took my hands into his, and said, 'You've come to be baptised.' I nodded my head. 'Why?' he asked.

'I want to be a Christian and believe in Jesus.'

'But why, my child? Why not remain a Jew?'

'No ... no!' I protested. 'You must convert me.'

'You're too young to know what's best for you.'

'I'm already thirteen,' I answered. 'Jesus saved my life, and I promised Him.'

He reached for my face and stroked my cheek. 'You must not turn to Him out of debt, but out of love.'

I gripped his arm. 'I beg you, please! Father, you must. I know the entire catechism by heart. I love coming to church,' I implored and started to cry.

'You don't realise what you're asking me to do, but if your parents agree ...' He looked at me with sorrowful eyes. 'I thought not. Come back to see me when you're twenty-one,' and he attempted a smile, 'but then chances are, you'll understand more and most likely be far away from here, perhaps in a distant land!' He held me by my shoulders and looked deep into my eyes. 'God's spirit rests upon all, Jew or Gentile. His hand extends to all who seek Him. There is no monopoly on Holiness.' He handed me a clean freshly pressed handkerchief, of a sort I hadn't seen since leaving home, and motioned for me to wipe my tears. 'Allow me to tell you a story:

A fox came alongside a stream and said to a fish:
'I came here to give you a warning.
Some fishermen are coming so beware!
Why don't you come out and they'll never catch you?'
The fish replied; 'You're not as wise as you're supposed to be old fox.
If I come out of the water, I'll die right away, but if I stay in the
water, I can at least try not to get caught by the fisherman.'

So you see my child, one who abandons his heritage is like a fish out of water.'

'But Father, I just want to be normal,' I pleaded.

'Normal?' he joined his hands in prayer and looked heavenward. 'Oh Heavenly Father, how we have sinned!'

Night fell and I was still some distance away. The road was barely illuminated. I looked at the dark sky and wished I could grow wings and fly away into the heavens and be lost among the stars.

It was very late when I arrived home; Mrs Tekalewicz was feeding the baby.

'We were worried about you,' she said. 'We didn't know where you were.'

I undressed and went to sleep and dreamed that a priest was

baptizing me, and with needle and thread, sewing a piece of skin onto my penis. A Christian at last! I was flying above the village and below the peasants were threatening me with clenched fists. The shouting became louder. I covered my ears, but it wouldn't stop. It was coming from somewhere in the village. I awoke in a sweat, cleared my eyes, and shook my head, hoping to free myself of the nightmare. I looked out the window, and saw orange flames dancing in the air in the distance.

The next day the story spread like wildfire: vandals had shattered the windows and broken down the door of the Goldman household, shouting, 'Jews to Palestine.'

Goldman and his daughter barely escaped, while the hooligans torched their farm, reducing it to ashes.

No one went looking for the Goldmans and they were never seen or heard of again.

LEAVE AT ONCE, URGED THE VOICE, but I refused to listen. I had to prove that I had purged myself of fear.

One evening when I was left to babysit and helped myself to a glass of milk, Mr Tekalewicz entered and grabbed the milk jug out of my hands. 'There's a baby here now.'

When on the subsequent Sunday, inebriated, he ordered me to perform a task, I saw an opportunity to test my newfound confidence, and refused.

'I don't work Sundays.' He was stunned, as if he hadn't heard me correctly. So to make sure, he repeated his request. I stood my ground.

'I'll ask you one more time,' threatened Mr Tekalewicz, clenching his teeth.

'No!' I replied. 'It's the Lord's Day.' I climbed a tree and popped a cherry into my mouth.

'I'll ask you for the last time.'

I looked down. Framed between branches stood my outraged employer, his outdated revolver pointing directly at me. With a sadistic grin on his face, he ordered me to come down. I jumped. He came closer, his revolver pressing against my forehead in his wobbly hand. 'How dare you disobey me,' he slurred.

'I'm no longer your slave.'

This unbalanced him. 'You dirty, lice-infested son of a dirty bitch of a Jew. I'll kill you! God is my witness, I'll kill you right here, right now!'

How ironic to have survived Hitler's Germans only to have a bullet pumped into my brain by a drunken blacksmith.

Placate him, the inner voice advised, but the words that spewed out of my mouth were hardly conciliatory.

'Go on, shoot me!' I answered. 'It doesn't matter to me anyway. I've no reason to live. Pull the trigger and be done with it.'

He closed one eye and aimed. 'I'll count to ten. If by then you're not on your way to what I'd ordered you to do, you're dead. One ...'

I'm not sure what prompted me to laugh, but I did. 'Mr Tekalewicz,' I said, 'you have a wife and child to live for. But if you kill me, you can be certain little Zbigniew will grow up knowing his father was a murderer.'

'Oh, so now you're threatening me, Jew boy?' He lowered the gun. 'If I see you here again, I swear by Jesus, I'll shoot your brains out.' He spun around and tottered away.

I leaned against the tree, embracing it, and began to sob. 'Dear Mother,' I cried. 'Why was I chosen to remain? Why didn't they take me with you? Where is there for me to turn to? Oh, Mommy, if only you were alive! Without you, what good is my life?'

I cried until I could cry no more. And now I heard the baby's wails coming from inside the house. Night had descended and the wind was chilling my scantily clad body. I shivered and tried to keep warm by hugging myself. I'll get my things, I thought, and started for the house, but stopped midway. 'Where should I go then?' I whispered to myself. And although I knew there was no one to hear me, nevertheless I expected an answer. None came. I started to walk, passing trees which in the dark looked like monstrous creatures poised to consume me.

I stopped on the road, and looked back to the house. It was quiet; even the baby's crying had faded. Not another soul along the road. I scanned the dark fields. There too was deathly silence, except for the blowing wind bending the tall wheat to one side then to the other.

I lay down in the wheat watching the dark clouds traversing the sky, and I tried to decipher the faces in them. Then I listened to the wind, and the longer I did so, the more I recognised the melody: it was my mother's song. I could make out her striking face in a cloud, gently, sweetly singing, and next to her, Kisel strumming.

> Giddy up, my horses, Giddy up my eagles
> Hold your heads high
> Carry the passengers, the bones are shaking
> Giddy up, raise up a cloud.

The driver in the song materialised, sitting on a wagon, pulled by six galloping horses. He lashed them across their rumps and lightning struck, followed by thunder, and then the driver and horses receded and disappeared behind the clouds, along with his passengers; Kisel and my mother. And from the heavens came rain.

Drenched, I woke in the morning and peered through the

stems of wheat to check on the Tekalewicz house across the road. The sun too was just waking, ready to cast its warm rays. The faint cry of the baby accompanied the passer-by traversing the road, interrupted by a barking dog, a door opening, a cow mooing, and Mr Tekalewicz on his bicycle heading to his smithy, wearing a smug smile.

Imagining I had a rifle, I closed my left eye, aimed at his head, and pulled the trigger. 'Bang!' I whispered. He fell off, his face lodging deep into the mud, blood trickling from his mouth. When I opened my eye, he was peddling his two-wheeler, disappearing around the bend.

I made my way to the house and faced his frightened wife. 'I came for my things,' I said enunciating each syllable. 'Take whatever is yours,' she answered, visibly upset. 'I'm truly sorry for you, but what can I do? I'm also afraid of him.'

'He doesn't frighten me with that stupid pistol of his.' I stood erect, like a soldier.

'Take my advice and leave before it ends in a tragedy.'

'I want the money that's owed to me.'

'If I had it, I'd give it to you.'

'If you don't pay me, you'll see what will happen,' and gathering my belongings I headed for the door.

She followed me. 'Zygmund, don't do anything foolish. I'll get you the money. Give me a little time.'

When I reached the road I realised that I had no destination, but I felt good about myself.

The sun warmed me and I inhaled the fresh air. How good it was to be alive!

I stopped to wash my face at a pond. Tossing pebbles into the water, I was hypnotised by the whirls they created. A bullfrog stuck its head out of the pond, as if wondering who I was and what business I had to be there.

'Caught any?' A lean, barefoot boy, much older than me, sat down beside me. He wore grubby linen trousers and a frayed shirt. He was in need of a haircut and had a face that was sprouting hair. One of his eyes appeared to be damaged.

'I'm not fishing,' I answered.

'Good. This is my fishing hole.' I now noticed a wicker basket in his hand. 'What are you staring at?' he asked.

'Nothing,' I shrugged.

'That's all right kid,' he said. 'I don't mind you looking. Here, take a good look.' And the hand that had held the basket was now in front of my eyes. His thumb and index finger were missing. 'My name is Bronek,' and he offered me the same hand for me to take.

'Zygmund,' I said, and I shook his three fingers.

'Want to know how I lost them?'

'If you want to tell me.' I threw away the words as if I didn't care, but in reality I was dying to know.

'A mine, one of our own, an accident.'

'You were in the army?'

'With the partisans. Two years.'

'Did you ever kill?'

'Many.'

'How many?' I asked.

'I never counted. Mines were my specialty.'

'Didn't you have a gun?' I asked.

'That too,' he replied, and reaching inside his belt he withdrew a Luger and tossed it to me. 'Careful, it's loaded,' he said as I caught it.

He taught me how to take it apart, clean, aim, and fire. The basket was for catching little fish, and in a nearby field, we dug up new potatoes. After this, Bronek led me to a house, only a stone's throw from where I had lived at the Wajdas, in which he occupied the smaller of two rooms.

We dumped the fish and the potatoes into a pot on the stove and boiled them together. By the time the meal was cooked, night had fallen and we ate in the dark.

A dozen or so older men occupied the adjoining room. 'All drifters,' informed Bronek. 'One hardly knows the other, just like you and me. Tell me about yourself.'

I hesitated to tell him everything and so revealed only my grievance with the blacksmith.

'We'll fix him good with this,' and I could hear the Luger's safety latch being disengaged.

'You mean kill him?' I gasped.

'If you tell me to,' came the calm reply from the dark.

Our conversation was cut short by the sound of music coming from the next room.

'Isn't it beautiful?' I remarked.

He pushed open the door. Although a candle illuminated the room, little was visible due to pipe and cigarette smoke.

A man with hollow cheeks and large bony fingers was sitting by the window, playing a concertina. Around the faint flame four men were playing twenty-one, others were sleeping, someone coughed, and another snored. The room reeked of human odours.

We returned to our room and lay down for the night.

Through the window I fixed my eyes on the stars above. I'm lucky, I thought, to have found Bronek. God keeps an eye on me.

I tried to sleep, but couldn't. I felt uneasy not having told Bronek the complete truth about myself.

Still afraid, aren't you? the ever-present inner voice taunted.

And to prove it wrong, I shook Bronek. 'Wake up!' In an instant the muzzle of the Luger was pressing against my chest.

'Don't move or I'll blow your head off, whoever you are.'

'My name is not Zygmund, and I'm a Jew ...' I said.

'And my name is Adolf, and I'm the Führer!'

I felt relieved. Obviously he didn't care.

We returned to our sleeping bags, but neither of us slept. Bronek lit a cigarette and talked about his days with the partisans in the forest. Relishing every incident, attack, explosion, and ambush so that it came to life in the present darkness. It was so real that I fell into believing I had been there, partaking in all these risk-taking operations.

I began to yawn. His voice became fainter and fainter. I thought I was dreaming when he asked, 'You're really a Jew?'

Half asleep, I sat up. He asked questions and I supplied answers. I spoke and he listened, and by the time the sun rose that morning, he knew everything. Rubbing his eyes, he now let out a laugh. 'Why are you still here?'

'Where should I go?'

'To Lublin, the big city,' he replied, spreading his hands.

'I don't know anyone there, and no one knows me.'

'But you're a Jew, and there are other Jews there. I'll tell you what – ' His excitement accelerated. 'We'll both go. We'll do well there. I'll pretend to be a Jew, and the rich Jews will look after us. Better still, you'll tell them I saved you and that should be worth plenty in gratitude.'

'Then let's go.'

He chuckled. 'No, no my friend. You don't go to the big city dressed like we are; no shoes, empty pockets. We couldn't very well steal potatoes or go fishing in the streets. And what about train fare?'

'But you said other Jews would help us.'

'It takes time to make the right contacts.' He ran his tongue across his teeth, then asked, 'Didn't your family leave you anything?' He stood up and looked out the window. 'That Mrs Pejzak you told me about. I bet she has it all. For sure! I have it all figured out.' He clapped his hands. 'Sure, your mother gave all her possessions to this Pejzak woman for safekeeping. Now, once your mother is taken away, what does this whore do? She tells you to give yourself up, right? When you refuse, her son threatens you. They don't want you alive.'

I stared at him in disbelief.

'I say we attack!' He ran outside, then burst back into the room pointing the Luger at me, and in a threatening voice, said, 'All right, Pejzak, let's have it or I'll blow you to smithereens.' He jumped, touching the ceiling, and then fell to the floor convulsing with laughter. 'Look at you,' he said. 'You're trembling like a leaf in the wind.'

'We can go to the Pejzaks, but not with a gun,' I said. 'You can ask her yourself, and see what she says.'

'What kind of a dope are you?' he looked up. 'What will I ask? "Mrs Pejzak, may I *please* have his mother's gold and silver back?" And she'll say, "Certainly, my dear boy," and hand it to me just like that!' He flicked his wrist at the side of my head. 'I know,' he went on, 'the only thing people understand and respect is this.' And he held up the Luger. 'Tonight we strike and tomorrow we'll be in Lublin smoking real cigarettes.'

Instead of feeling protected by Bronek, I hoped the night would pass without me getting killed.

There was a long pause during which Bronek got to his feet, opened the window, looked out at the round moon, and in a forlorn tone said, 'I know what you told me is the truth. I was just hoping for some real action tonight. Oh, God, how dull life has been of late!' He played with the Luger, emptying and reloading bullets. A stray black cat suddenly appeared on the windowsill and meowed. Bronek aimed the gun and emptied the full load of bullets into the animal. A high-pitched scream burst from the cat; it shot up into the air, and limply fell to the ground.

I WAS DETERMINED to go to Lublin and, to raise money for the journey, I decided to sell my mother's bedsheet.

Bronek laughed. 'You'll get nothing for it.'

Early in the morning, the bedsheet under my arm, I set out for Chelm. By noon I had arrived, and in the midst of a war-scarred town, found a busy marketplace of shouting, haggling, and bartering; a lady offering a man's suit, a peasant woman selling bread, here an old farmer displaying eggs, and there a young boy, no older than I, holding up a bird imprisoned in a homemade cage. Further on, a circle of onlookers had gathered. I pushed my way through. A blind man was working a large accordion, and beside him stood a slender boy with greasy hair singing a Russian war song.

The spectators cried, applauded, and dropped coins into the hat on the ground. I admired and envied. If only I had an accordion, then I could play and sing, and earn my living in Lublin!

I moved on, and the voice and music followed. Someone was feeding a horse, a pretty girl held a chicken under her arm, a drunkard was vomiting against the wall, and from the distance came an alarming cry: 'Thief!' And now a young barefoot urchin was pursued by a bald, heavy-set man with a Hitler moustache.

There were all sorts of pungent odours here. It smelled of

manure, of freshly baked bread, of new potatoes and fruit, and also of decayed flesh and gunpowder.

'Shoes! Shoes! Shoes!' I heard a voice. I followed, thinking I would see a used-shoe cobbler like my grandfather. 'Shoes!' My eyes caught sight of him; he was a tall emaciated figure of a man with a hungry look. 'Shoes, shoes!' He displayed a pair of brown ones. They had seen better days, but were now reconditioned and shiny. 'Shoes!'

I approached and gaped at them, then looked at my bare feet and tried to determine if they were my size. At first he ignored me, but then he cast a glance and said, 'Perfect for your feet.' I moved on.

'Bedsheet! Bedsheet!' I chanted, unfolding my inheritance for everyone to see. 'Bedsheet for sale!' People milled about, but none threw so much as a glance in my direction. I studied their faces to guess if any of them were possibly Jews. 'Bedsheet!' I looked in their eyes, the giveaway. But those who passed my inspection lacked the sorrowful look, acquired through generations of oppression and suffering.

Where are the Chelm fools, then? How often in the past had I heard stories about the fools of Chelm?

The Chelm fools, as they were referred to in the stories, were not to be seen. The little Jews with black caftans and white and blue phylacteries were gone. The ones with the long beards and sidelocks were not here. I vaguely recalled the tale about the Chelmite who was asked what he would do if he found a million rubles in the marketplace and knew who lost them. The Chelm fool replied without hesitation, 'If I knew that the money belonged to Rothschild, one of the richest men in the world, I would keep it, but if I knew that the million rubles belonged to the poor rabbi of the old synagogue, I'd return it to the last kopek.'

From the distance, sounds of the accordion and the boy's haunting voice reached me:

The night is dark
Only the bullets are wailing in the Steppe,
Only the wind is droning through the wires,
Dimly, stars are winking.

'Bedsheet! Bedsheet for sale!' I called out again and again, and began to circle. A sour-faced woman stopped for a moment, examined my goods with gnarled hands, and dismissing it with a flip of her hand, moved on without comment.

'Shoes! Shoes for sale!' once more the vendor. 'Shoes! Shoes!'

'How much?' I asked.

He looked me up and down assessing me, and concluded, 'You can't afford them.' Then back to, 'Shoes! Shoes!' When I walked on, he called, 'You!' I turned. 'I'll let you have them for five hundred.'

I walked away.

'Bedsheet! Bedsheet! As good as new.' I scrutinised the ever-changing faces, no longer in search of the Chelm fools, but of my Uncle Moishe.

Wouldn't it be a miracle if I ran into him here? It's possible. Why not? Everything is possible. One only has to believe and have faith.

'How much for this torn sheet?' a young woman, her head wrapped in a floral kerchief, asked.

'Five hundred zloty,' rolled off my tongue.

Good-naturedly she pinched my cheek. 'You're so very good looking,' and walked away.

If I could realise five hundred zloty, I figured, I would

return to Malinowka looking like a city slicker wearing the polished brown shoes. Suddenly I had a thought, and ran to locate the shoe peddler.

'You want five hundred zloty and I want five hundred. Why don't we trade?' I proposed with a big grin.

'Get lost kid!' he growled.

'Shoes!'

'Bedsheet!'

'Shoes!'

'Bedsheet!'

'Shoes!'

'Cigarette holders!' A fresh voice joined the chorus, and it was my own. In my mind, I was back at the corner of Pawia and Smocza Streets in the Warsaw Ghetto. 'Cigarette holders! Cigarette holders!' I sang.

People bustled by. A horrific scream sounded. One pedestrian asked another, 'What's all the commotion?'

'A girl committed suicide. Jumped from her window.' Both shrugged.

'Cigarette holders!' I begged to be heard, and a woman carrying parcels stopped, eyeing my goods. 'How many would you like, madam?' I asked. 'They're very fine and made of glass.'

'If you help me carry these to my apartment, I'll make it worth your while.' I seized the parcels and followed her. She led me along the street and at the next intersection, turned into a courtyard. Then we entered a building and walked up four flights. Outside her door, she offered me a few coins. I thanked her and quickly returned to my corner, and bought an apple square from a vendor.

Once I had devoured the delicacy, a terrible guilt set in. I'm stuffing my mouth with luxuries, while at home there's not enough bread.

I moved to the opposite corner in the hope of changing my luck.

'Cigarette holders made of glass!'

I thought of my father in Russia. I wondered when the war would end and tried to imagine what it would be like to kiss Esther, with whom I was secretly in love and who lived in the same courtyard on Pawia Street.

As the day passed, the chaos of buyers and vendors subsided and the bustling corner became deserted, save for an elderly gentleman kneeling at the iron fence encircling the statue of the Holy Mary. How strange they are! I thought. Not only do they eat pork, but also pray to Gods made of stone and mortar!

Though tired and discouraged I resisted going home. I was ashamed to return empty handed. I was also waiting for a miracle.

'How much?' a young man stood before me.

'One for five groszy, three for ten,' I answered.

He furtively examined the merchandise, and said, 'A kid down the street sells the same ones for three groszy apiece.'

'He probably buys them from a different supplier,' I answered.

'Don't give me your grandmother tales,' said he. 'I know you pick them up for nothing in the ruins of the bombed glass factory.' I remained silent. 'I'll tell you what,' he went on. 'How many have you got there?'

'Fifty, a hundred, maybe more,' I answered.

'Excellent,' replied the man, 'I'll take the lot at three groszy apiece.'

I could hardly believe my ears. Indeed, this was a real miracle!

'The only thing,' said this angel from heaven, 'I haven't got the money on me, and so if you don't mind walking me home,

I'll pay you there.' I readily agreed and we proceeded. 'Just a little further,' said the man every so often. I didn't mind the walk in the least. For this kind of miracle, I would have walked to the other end of Warsaw and beyond. 'Just a little further.' We turned into this street and went up that street and at last arrived at his address. 'Wait here and I'll be down in a minute with the cash.'

I leaned against the gate of the courtyard and began counting my goods, trying to figure how much money I would go home with. The numbers swam in my head and the figures confused me. I could see my mother's face beaming with pride as I handed her the money to buy bread and potatoes. Perhaps she'll even write my father. He too will be proud!

I was convinced it was God who had sent this messenger to me. I waited and waited and heard doors opening and closing, but no sign of the angel. The courtyard turned dark; here and there a light appeared in a window. I shivered and worried, but never lost hope.

At long last, he appeared. 'I'm very sorry to have taken so long, but I had trouble finding my money. I don't know where I hid it. Just so it won't be a complete waste for you, here's three groszy and he helped himself to one cigarette holder and disappeared like a rabbit into a magician's hat.

'How much?' asked a voice.

'What?' I was back in Chelm, clutching my bedsheet.

'How much do you want for it?' the voice repeated.

'Five hundred,' I said.

'It has a hole in it,' said the young lady examining the sheet. Beside her, silently looking on stood her husband, I guessed, cradling a squawking duck. 'Two hundred zloty, that's all it's worth, and that's all I've got.'

I hesitated, then handed her the sheet. Raising her skirt,

she pulled a wad of bills from inside one of her stockings and counted off two hundred, pushing it into my hand.

I held the money tightly. 'Shoes! Shoes!' The voice beckoned me.

'I'll give you two hundred,' I said, and revealed the currency in my hand.

He threw me a vicious look. 'Not enough.' I started to leave but he called me back. 'I'll tell you what, because I see you're barefoot, I'll let you have them for four hundred.'

'Two hundred is all I have.'

'You don't want to buy them, you want to steal them. Get away scum, and don't let me see you again.'

I strolled among the wares.

Two vendors were quarrelling. A Russian soldier, with a disfigured face like a deflated football, was examining a child's doll. A Billy goat escaped his noose and ran through the market, pursued by his owner.

I walked, gaped, and, without meaning to, ended up at the shoes again. This time I stood admiring them from a distance.

The peddler noticed me and beckoned with his forefinger.

'Look,' he began, 'it's getting late and I've been here since early morning. I'm tired and hungry. Give me three hundred and let me go home.' And he offered them for me to take. I smelled the fresh polish, reminding me of my grandfather's workroom in the cellar on Pawia Street.

'I only have two hundred,' I repeated.

'I'll kill you!' he shouted, and snatched them from me.

I walked away. He followed after me like a puppy. 'Make it two hundred and fifty.' I shook my head and left him standing, still shaking his fist.

As the sun fell to the rooftops of Chelm, the crowds began to disperse. The rickety stalls were dismantled, the goats were

driven home, the horses were harnessed, the blind accordionist packed his instrument, and the young singer counted the
take. The place was littered with garbage.

I turned up my collar. My hands in my pockets, I set out
for the return journey to Malinowka. I had taken only a few
steps when a recognizable voice called, 'Wait! Wait!' He was
running towards me. 'All right, you win,' he said, breathing
hard. 'You're stealing them from me, I tell you.' And once
more he extended the shoes for me to take. Again the shoes
were in my hands. 'Let's have the two hundred, sonny.' He
jiggled his fingers.

'First I want to try them on,' I said. 'What if they don't fit?'

'For two hundred they have to fit yet?' he growled. I stepped
into the shoes with my filthy feet, tied up the laces, and paraded
around him. He looked at me with contempt. 'Well?'

Slowly I unlaced and took off the shoes and began to
inspect them, turning them every which way. 'What now?' he
gritted his teeth.

'The soles feel like wood.'

'Are you blind? Can't you see they're leather? Let me have
the rotten few zloty. I have a long way home.'

I found no fault with the shoes, but there must be something wrong, I reasoned. Why else would he be selling me a
five-hundred-zloty pair of shoes for only two hundred?

I gently placed the shoes back into his shaking hands and
took off.

He pursued and caught up with me. Gripping my arm, he
pleaded, 'I swear by Jesus the shoes are perfect, all leather.'

'I don't want them.'

'Make it one hundred and fifty then.'

I shook my head. 'I don't want them at any price.'

The sun had already set when I left him standing in the

empty marketplace of Chelm, his head bent, the shoes hanging limply in his hands, and his voice still to be heard calling, 'Shoes! Shoes! Shoes for sale!'

LEARNING OF MY NEWFOUND wealth, the collection of vagrants in the next room became friendlier and began asking for handouts. One needed medicine, one vodka, and a third cigarettes. Another offered to sell me a pair of suspenders, another, a worn wallet, and still another, a soiled hat. When I didn't bite, they appealed to my sympathies. After all, we were all lost, destitute, homeless drifters, and should help each other.

Bronek suggested I give him the money for safekeeping, but I declined. He laughed menacingly and asked, 'Don't you trust me?'

I kept the bills in my trouser pocket and checked on it frequently to make sure it was still there. At night I held it tightly in the grip of my fist.

Every sound, the smallest movements, made me think they were intending to rob and do away with me. Bronek also distanced himself, and on one occasion even accused me of being a 'stingy Jew!'

I knew that if I didn't share the money I would fall victim to this lot. And so I exchanged my two hundred zloty for the concertina. While they celebrated, I sat in the dark trying to imitate the blind accordionist in Chelm.

Leave for Lublin, the voice rang in my head. Go, escape! Don't wait for Bronek. He'll never take you!

Returning to the wheat field I waited for Mr Tekalewicz to leave for work then made my way to his door. His wife seemed pleased and even relieved to see me.

'I've been waiting for you,' she said, and took out bills from an earthen jar and handed them to me. 'If my husband knew, he'd probably kill me.'

'I'll never forget you for this,' I said.

'Go, Zygmund, go! And don't judge us too harshly.'

Along the way, making sure I was alone, I counted the money. She had given me three hundred zloty. I tore an opening in the lining of my hat and hid the cash there.

'I'm going tomorrow,' I told Bronek.

'If you wait until next week, I'll go with you.'

'I'm leaving tomorrow,' I said firmly.

'How do you plan to get there?' he asked. 'By foot perhaps?'

I was not about to tell him of my new wealth. 'I'll use my thumb,' I said.

'And what about the squeeze box?'

I was puzzled. 'What about it?' He summoned a few of the drunks from the other room.

When Bronek told them of my plans, they laughed hysterically.

'What's so funny?' I asked innocently.

'The Russians will take it from you in a flash,' said the one who had sold it to me.

'Why?'

'No reason. They don't need a reason. Lucky you don't have a watch, or they'd pilfer that as well.'

'That's right,' chorused the others.

'Better get rid of it while you can,' advised the previous owner. 'I'll give you fifty zloty for it.'

'Fifty!' I exclaimed.

'Fifty is better than nothing.'

I knew not to believe what they were telling me and so I turned to a sympathetic widow, who lived in the former

Wajda house with her horde of children. She confirmed the rumour of the Russians confiscating musical instruments, watches, and whatever else caught their fancy. To help me out, she offered to take the concertina off my hands.

'But as the Good Lord Jesus is my witness, I have no money,' she added, 'unless of course, you would accept this in exchange.' She pulled out an army coat of a greenish colour with polished brass buttons.

'Belgian army,' she offered. How it came into her possession I didn't bother to ask. The coat looked as if it had never been worn and the fabric was sturdy. 'It will make a good suit for you,' she said. I left the concertina and returned with the coat.

'You had no right doing that!' hollered the former owner.

'Where are you going?' asked Bronek the next morning when he saw me grabbing my coat.

'I told you, I'm going to Lublin.'

'Not today, you're not,' he answered. 'In a few days we'll go together.'

I extended my hand to him. 'Goodbye, Bronek.'

He looked at it but didn't take it. I opened the door, stepped outside and headed for the road. The musician followed me with his sad eyes and bitter expression as I passed the window.

'Take one more step and you're finished.'

I froze and slowly, very, very slowly, turned my head to look back. Bronek was pointing the Luger at me. 'I thought we were to help each other, Jew boy,' he said. 'And now you're running out on me.'

An inner voice urged me to run but I felt compelled to leave with my head up high. I walked on, taking measured steps, and never looked back, not even once.

SEVEN

'Which way to the train?' I asked an aged farmer leading a lame horse on a leash.

'Follow that road. Make a turn to the right at the next one.'

In front of me was an open horizon. A bright sun shone above, and the sky was friendly and wide. Now and then I would stop to rest. Taking off my hat, I would feel its lining to be sure the money was still there. Once I even counted it; three hundred zloty.

Fields of wheat swayed gently, and potato and cabbage patches bordered the roadside, with scattered figures, bent over, weeding and hoeing.

'Which way to the train?'

A young girl pointed, 'Straight ahead, maybe two kilometres.'

The sun inflated and turned reddish as it prepared to disappear for another day. How strange, I thought, that it rises from one side and sets on the opposite, and yet the next day appears again from the first side! How is that possible?

'Which way to the train?'

'Over there.' In the distance a small station came into view. The sun was about to disappear completely; the road in front

of me was clear. I was overjoyed to see the tracks and hear a
train whistle in the distance. As I began to run, I noticed a
group of boys converging upon me from both sides of
the road.

I slowed down and silently prayed. I masked my fear by
whistling, though I worried what might happen.

The station was just in front of me. The sun had disappeared, and the boys, all barefoot like me, with sticks in their
hands, blocked my way.

'Where you going?' asked one.

'To the train,' I answered.

'What you got there?' asked another, pointing to the
Belgian Army coat, draped over one of my shoulders.

'It's just a coat,' I answered

'Let's see,' and he moved to snatch it.

Though my legs trembled, I tried to sound tough. 'Get lost.'

To further provoke me, one snatched my hat.

'Give it back,' I panicked.

He hid it behind his back, and when I jumped to retrieve
it, he tossed it to another. I leaped after it and saw it soaring
through the air. Again I attempted to catch it and failed. The
hat went from one to the other and I, like a caged animal, ran
in a circle, my face covered with sweat, my heart pounding.

'Please!' I begged, 'I'll miss my train.' And the more desperate I became, the more they seemed to enjoy it.

'Here, here, come and get it,' said the one holding the hat
now, as if taunting a kitten.

I reached and almost had it in my grasp, when my three
hundred zloty inside took off like a bird.

And soon another voice rose behind me, 'Here, come and
get it.' I couldn't move. It was more than I could bear. I simply
sat down and cried.

'Here, here,' their taunting voices continued. 'Come and get it.'

'I can't fight all of you,' I began. 'In fact, I'm not strong enough to fight any of you. But there is a power that watches and judges, and He will make sure that you're damned for this.'

Their goading turned into stony silence. The youngest among them, with scarred legs and crossed eyes, came forward and handed me my cap. The last I saw of them, they had dispersed in the adjoining fields, herding their cattle.

Except for a well-dressed youth, about my own age, there was no one to be seen at the station. He wore short trousers, knee-length socks, and sandals, and his blond hair was neatly trimmed. Beside him rested a large suitcase. In his right hand he held a leather leash at the end of which was a muzzled brown boxer dog.

When the animal made a move to jump me, the youth yanked the leash and ordered, 'Sit, Adolf.'

How I envied that boy! He reminded me of how I used to look when my mother would dress me to go visiting, or sit in the park and watch kites flying in the wind.

'Where do you get tickets?' I asked.

'Inside at the wicket,' the boy answered, pointing to the interior.

Behind the little cage sat a uniformed man wearing glasses that kept falling down on his nose. 'I want to go to Lublin.'

'That will be two hundred and thirty zloty.' He adjusted his spectacles. I took off my cap, self-consciously counted the exact amount, and handed him the bills.

He wrote something in a ledger, produced a ticket, and punched and stamped it. Handing it to me he said, 'Don't lose it now.' Then, after glancing at the large clock on the wall, he added, 'It should be here any minute.'

The youth with the dog was still there when I came out. 'Are you waiting for the train to Lublin?' I asked.

'Yes,' he replied.

'On your own?' I inquired, hoping to have some company.

'My mommy is over there.' He pointed to an outhouse a short distance away.

'You live here?' I went on.

'No,' he answered. 'We've been visiting my grandparents.'

'Ah, so you live in Lublin.'

'Yes.'

I now worried if Bronek had lied to me. What if there are no Jews in Lublin? Perhaps the war isn't over!

'I guess the Germans are no longer in Lublin, eh?' I spoke as if the answer to my question was of no importance.

'Where have you been?' He looked at me quizzically. 'The Germans are kaput, or don't you know that either?'

I swallowed the insult. 'What about the Jews?' The word wedged in my throat.

'What about them?' asked the boy, perplexed.

'Well, are the herring merchants back in Lublin?'

The boy contorted his face, and said, 'The city is crawling with the lice carriers.'

A shiver went through my body.

'My father says,' he went on, 'that Hitler made one big mistake in not getting rid of all of them.'

'You can say that again!' I concurred.

'Not to worry, though,' he continued, raising his nose into the air. 'We'll finish them off. My father knows everything.'

The train suddenly appeared and so did his mother. She combed his hair, straightened his jacket, and picked up the suitcase.

It was almost dark when we boarded the train. I watched

the boy, his mother, and the dog board a coach, and then made sure not to enter the same one. I ran towards the back and jumped into a carriage occupied by Russian soldiers. I found a window seat and suspiciously ogled everyone. Some were sleeping, others were playing cards or downing vodka from flasks, still others writing letters. I covered myself with my Belgian coat. Nobody even looked at me.

The train began to inch its way out of the station. Outside it was dark. Through the window I could see faint lights shining in the distance. I leaned back and closed my eyes.

Thousands upon thousands of images flashed through my mind. My whole life was before me in fragments, the last of which was the intimidating face of the boxer dog, growling, wishing to devour me.

'LUBLIN! EVERYBODY OFF!'

I opened my eyes. Half the coach had already cleared, and the remaining passengers were pushing towards the exit. Outside the window, silhouettes of people burdened with baggage moved swiftly by. Sounds of engines hissing, churning wheels, and high-pitched whistles came from all directions.

'Lublin! Everybody off!' A man in a blue uniform was pushing through the disembarking passengers.

'Are we in Lublin?' I asked, rubbing my sleepy eyes.

'Didn't you hear me? Everybody off!' And he disappeared into the next car.

Quickly I adjusted the hat on my head, reached for my coat, and joined the exiting line. I stepped out into a gloomy night and found myself standing on railway tracks.

'Get out of there!' I could hear the voice but couldn't see

the face. I crossed onto another track and now faced an approaching engine. I jumped out of its way and into the arms of a railway worker with a smeared face and a lamp in his hand.

'Watch where you're going, sonny,' he growled angrily.

A short distance away another engine was belching out smoke. Flames twisted and turned, and lights danced in mid-air. Bizarre noises could be heard all about, but there were no faces to be seen. I was petrified.

Is this really Lublin? I wondered. Or perhaps the train had derailed and this is the world below!

'Somebody help!' I cried in distress. 'Where do I go? Where is the city?'

'Follow me,' said a voice. A man in a long coat, carrying two heavy suitcases, materialised. 'It's easy to get lost here,' he mumbled. I could hardly keep up with his pace. After crisscrossing more rails and making turns this way and that, we mounted steps to a huge building. All about were people rushing, yelling, screaming, crying, and scurrying with their baggage. The whole scene was frightening.

I looked ahead, but the man I was following had been swallowed up by the other onrushing bodies.

If only Bronek was with me, he would know where to go. Dear God, I now prayed, here I am all alone, lost. I don't even know where I am going to spend this very night. What about the next night? And the night after that? If only, dear God, you would take mercy upon me and guide me. Please help me, I'm lost.

As if from infinity, a faint voice rose, 'Beds for the night! Nice clean beds for the night!' I turned and followed it and soon came upon a woman, calling, 'Beds for the night! Clean beds! No bedbugs!'

Smiling, I marvelled, God looks after me. He heard my plea!

Moving closer to her, I said, 'How kind of you!'

'A hundred zloty.'

I was shocked that one had to pay to sleep. 'Where do people sleep who have no money?' I asked.

'Over there,' she pointed.

I followed the horde moving in that direction.

A loudspeaker announced departures and arrivals. A soldier with a bandaged face pushed by me. A little girl with a brace on her leg cried for her mother.

At last, I entered the station's enormous waiting room illuminated by large lamps suspended from a high ceiling. The stench was unbearable. Yet, in spite of its size, there was hardly enough room to walk, for every bit of space was occupied by sleeping bodies curled up on the floor. Newcomers rushed about in search of a corner, anything, just enough room to sit down.

Carefully, so as not to disturb anyone, I made my way to the far side. The sounds of snoring and groaning provided background music. I looked around, but hardly anyone looked at me.

With luck, at long last, I found a standing spot against a wall. Dropping the coat on the floor, I fixed it between my feet and shut my eyes, hoping to drift off. Soon, however, I lost my balance and fell onto an obese woman. Stunned, she woke and attacked me with a volley of insults. Standing up, I looked across the vast field of bodies and caught sight of the blond boy being carried in the arms of a Polish officer bedecked with shiny medals. He was showering the boy with kisses and his son beamed with happiness. The mother walked beside them, the boxer leading her.

'Here,' a voice called in Russian. 'Over here.'

When I turned, I saw a Russian soldier beckoning me. I hesitated at first, then, bent over to pick up my coat and approached him. 'There's enough room here for both of us,' he said cheerfully. 'Make yourself comfortable,' and he moved his satchel to make room for me.

I thanked him shyly and sat down beside him, studying his face. Wouldn't this be another miracle if he turned out to be my father? He looks a lot like him.

There you go again, laughed my voice. I see no scar, do you? Everyone you meet you think is your father. Are you sure you remember what your father looked like?

Of course I remember.

I examined his face in detail. His teeth were of uniform size; his eyes were dark and sad, and seemed to penetrate the soul. The soldier was neatly shaven, his hair was trimmed, and his tunic freshly pressed. An army blanket covered him from his waist down. He now reached for his luggage, flipped it open and, turning to me, said, 'You must be hungry.'

'No, thank you,' I lied, although I was weak from hunger.

'Don't be shy,' he said. 'We can share everything that's here.' And he placed the open satchel between us, allowing me to see inside: a ring of sausage, a loaf of bread, and several chocolates. He extracted a knife from his pocket, flipped open the blade, and began cutting. He tore apart the bread, and handed me a chunk. Then stabbing the knife into a length of sausage, he held it up for me to take. As we were eating, he kept his eyes on me, forcing a smile out of me. 'That's much better,' he said.

'Where are your parents?' he asked between bites. When I didn't answer, he added, 'I'm sorry for asking.'

'My father is in Russia,' I said, 'probably in the army. His name is Zelik Kuperblum. Do you know him?'

He shook his head. 'Here, have some German chocolate. Those criminals make the best.'

'Were you in Germany?'

'I fought in Berlin.'

I lay back, using my Belgian army coat for a pillow. 'Go to sleep, boy,' said the soldier, and covered me with his own coat. The lights above blinded me; someone nearby was crying.

Through all the snoring, groaning, wailing, and general tumult, a familiar melody reached my ears. Someone was whistling Schubert's *Serenade*, exactly the way my father whistled it.

The next morning, the first thing I saw was a one-legged man hopping about on a crutch. My eyes travelled up, and settled on his face; the face from the night before.

'Did you sleep well?' he asked, gathering his things into the satchel.

'Yes,' I answered. 'Are you leaving?'

He nodded. 'What about you? Where are you headed?'

'I don't know where to go.'

He now noticed someone and waved. Out of the moving throng, a beautiful young female soldier appeared and saluted him. She immediately picked up his coat and satchel, and he whispered something into her ear. Her attention now shifted to me. 'Come with us,' she said in a melodious voice. I reached for my coat and, after much manoeuvring, we made our exit from the waiting room, and were soon descending the steps of the train depot.

An army car was waiting at the curb.

'Come,' said the female soldier as she entered it. 'Come with us. You'll join our detachment, and be a mascot.'

'I want to look for my people,' I answered.

She embraced me, and then got in behind the wheel.

'Good luck,' said the soldier tossing the crutch into the back and, hopping on his one foot, made his way into the passenger seat.

I started to walk away when I heard his voice calling me. I ran back. 'This is for you,' and he gave me the remaining chocolates.

He smiled and saluted me, and the car drove off.

THE DAY WAS JUST BEGINNING and the mist that set upon the city made visibility impossible. I began to walk, seeing only a few metres in front of me. I heard echoes of footsteps and motor vehicles coming from all directions. I walked slowly, uncertain and afraid. It was eerie.

Soon a glowing sun appeared from behind the buildings, and later a full street came into view. How vulnerable and terrified I felt! If only I could, I would have gladly returned to Malinowka.

In a street mirror I caught an image of a young boy with closely cropped hair, torn cotton trousers, and bare feet caked in mud. The face was serious, too serious, and over his shoulders was a greenish Belgian army coat with gold-coloured buttons.

Is it really me? I asked myself. I wonder if my family would recognise me now.

Pedestrians walked about and, as the sun rose higher, the streets came to life. Many trucks and horse-drawn carriages traversed the cobbled road. Military, civilians, hungry-looking vagrants, and cripples mingled and moved about with no more certainty on their faces than on my own.

Where shall I go? Though I had spent time here with my family before moving to Siedliszcze, the city looked unfamiliar. And the faces too, did not resemble the people I once knew. I approached a stranger but, before opening my mouth, I walked on. If I ask him about Jews, he'll immediately suspect who I am, I worried.

Such fears crossed my troubled mind. In the end, I took a chance on a candidate heading in my direction, and casually asked, 'Where do the Jews live?'

'You're a Jew?' he asked.

'No!' I protested. 'I was just curious,' and I quickened my pace so as to lose him.

'Wait!' he caught up with me. 'I'll show you.' We walked in silence. We turned one corner, and then another, crossed a street, then along a boulevard. 'Look, over there!' said my guide, pointing to a passing horse-drawn taxi with a moustached driver and two non-descript passengers. 'Those two are Jews.'

I stared and in my mind they acquired long hooked noses, shifty eyes, and tailored suits. I made the wrong decision in coming here. I have nothing in common with those people. I don't want to be a merchant or usurer, sell herring or be chauffeured in fancy carriages by Gentile drivers. I want to walk like other people. I want to farm and live honestly by the labour of my own hands.

'Come! Come!' called the stranger. I looked up and saw him ahead of me. 'I'm in a hurry,' he said when I caught up with him. We crossed a bombed-out section and soon were walking on a downhill street.

My mind was still idling: I should turn and go back to Malinowka, or why not to the Pejzaks'? What a fool I was not to have stayed with the Gogulkas! I wonder what Mr Kozak is doing at this moment? I think I'll make my way to the highway and hitch a ride to Piaski.

'There!' The stranger disturbed my daydream, shoving me towards a hefty man with a broad nose and short fuzzy black hair, leaning against a gate. 'One of yours,' he said to the man, and continued down the street.

The man popped a cigarette between his lips, and looking at me with suspicion, lit it.

'Are you a Jew?' I asked, focusing on him as if he was some extinct specimen.

'What do you want?' he asked nervously, exhaling a puff of smoke into my face. Then, turning, he entered the courtyard.

Following him, I said, 'I too am a Jew.'

'Be on your way, boy!' he retorted angrily. 'We don't need your kind here,' and he was about to enter a door when I gripped the hem of his jacket.

'Please, you must believe me,' I pleaded. 'I'm a Jew.'

He then said something in Yiddish.

'I don't understand,' I explained.

Filled with doubt, he said, 'Wait,' and called, 'Esther!' An attractive young woman appeared.

'He says he's a Jew.'

The woman sized me up, and then her doubting turned to laughter, and in a flash, the two bolted the door behind them. Desperate, I banged on it.

'Go away or we'll call the police,' their voices threatened in unison.

Nevertheless I continued pounding until it opened. 'I'll take down my pants so you can see that I'm a Jew.' The couple exchanged glances.

'Where do you come from?' asked the man.

'Pulawy,' I answered.

'Come with me, and we'll soon know if you're telling the truth.'

The woman kept shaking her head and repeating. 'He looks like a peasant if ever I saw one ... he looks like a peasant ...'

He led me down a hallway and knocked on a door.

'Come in,' said a guttural voice from inside. We entered a tiny room. The only source of light came from a solitary window covered with a lace curtain.

Occupying most of the room was an iron bed, on which lay a gigantic man with curly red hair. Jumping on top and all around him were three or four children of various ages, who reminded me of little cubs romping on a big bear. The man was giggling. Eventually, pointing at me, he said, 'What's this?'

'He claims he's a Jew from Pulawy.'

Papa Bear sat up and motioned for me to come closer. 'Who's your father?' he inquired.

'Zelik Kuperblum,' I answered.

'You're Zelik's son? You're Chaja-Eta and Shloime's grandson?'

I nodded.

'In that case,' he said, 'you have family here, in Lublin. They live down the street at number thirty-one.'

Surely this must be a dream or a mistake, I thought. Who would have survived?

'Follow me,' said the man who had brought me there, and soon we were entering a barbershop and I was introduced to the young proprietor. He had a pleasant demeanour, and was busy shaving a customer.

One glance at me and he said, 'How can you be Zelik's son? You don't even look like a Jew.' Then immediately regretting his words, he changed his tone. 'This is wonderful!' he said when he had finished with the customer. 'Zelik's son has survived!' He ran out of the shop and in a loud voice called, 'Sarah! Sarah!' A young vivacious woman stuck her head out of a window behind a balcony and looked down. He motioned for her to come.

She rushed down the metal staircase and entered the barbershop panting. 'What's the trouble?' she inquired with concern.

'Guess who he is?' And he pointed to me.

'How should I know?' she responded.

'Take a guess. Who does he look like?'

She looked again, 'What's to guess? A peasant boy. What else?'

Later, the barber and his wife interrogated me as to how I had survived. What happened to my parents? When did I last see my grandfather, the baker?

In turn, he explained how we were related. It seemed to me that the relation was very distant, but I wasn't about to point that out. On the contrary, I was more than pleased to have someone claim me as a cousin.

'I remember you,' the barber said, 'when you were still in your mother's belly. Ah, your mother. Let me tell you, she was a real beauty with a voice like a canary. And your father too, he was nobody's fool. He played the mandolin, taught dancing, and always had more girls on the string than on the mandolin.'

'Shmuel, shame on you,' said his wife.

'That was when he was still single, of course!' Cousin Shmuel rectified.

The apartment on the second floor walk-up was tiny: two miniature rooms, one a kitchen, the other the bedroom. A vase with a bouquet of fresh flowers adorned the dining table; several framed photographs of elderly people in traditional garb decorated the dresser, and on the wall hung a faded drawing of a cat playing with a ball of wool. The floors had been freshly scrubbed and were now covered with newspapers. A long-forgotten aroma from the stove brought back vivid memories of my early life. Cousin Sarah chopped fish on a board, and the reverberation pulled me back to the Friday afternoons when my mother did the same. The scent of simmering chicken soup also resulted in a multitude of awakenings. I sat and watched silently.

Early in the evening, while I washed my hands and face, and attempted to cleanse my feet of the caked dirt, she bedecked the table with a white linen cloth, and placed two silver candlesticks on top. When the sun had set and Cousin Shmuel had locked up the shop below, we all sat down to eat. I automatically crossed myself and blushed when I noticed them exchanging glances. Sarah lit the candles and covered her head with a shawl. Closing her eyes, she made circles with her hands, and blessed the candles. Something stirred within me and, looking at Sarah, I saw my mother.

First we ate gefilte fish with horseradish and challah, followed by chicken soup with noodles and lima beans. The tastes were so familiar and yet so foreign, so very foreign. I looked at the shimmering candles, and then shifted my gaze to my hosts. They were staring at me.

'What's the matter, Jankele? Don't you like it?' asked Cousin Sarah when I had stopped for a moment.

Quickly, I resumed spooning the broth into my mouth, and now tears from my eyes fell into the soup. I did not wipe them, I did not want them to see me crying, and so I kept my head down, eating soup mixed with tears.

'You'll stay with us,' said Cousin Shmuel. 'You'll be like our own.'

'We'll buy you a pair of shoes,' added Sarah. And later she handed me a pair of her husband's pyjamas.

I looked at myself in the mirror, and saw a clown looking back at me. It made me laugh and on this jovial note, I was ushered into the bedroom and tucked into bed. For the first time since leaving home, I laid my head on a real pillow and covered myself with goose-feather bedding.

The room was in darkness. Within earshot of the kitchen, I could hear Yiddish conversation. What are they saying? They're probably discussing me.

My eyes closed and sleep overcame me. When I awoke early the next morning, I found myself crammed between two sleeping bodies. I wanted to run, to escape, not to face them, but could hardly move without disturbing them. If only I had wings, I would fly out the window, for beneath me everything was soaked with my urine.

Slowly, I wiggled out of bed and, tiptoeing, got dressed and made my way down the stairs and out to the street. I ran until I came to an open-air market. Merchants were setting up their stalls for the day.

The sun was rising, the city was waking, and the day was unfolding. I stared at the people and buildings, and recognised one of the streets. A castle hovered above it.

Instantly the scene changed: the street was snow laden. My mother, carrying a bundle in one arm and Josele in the other, kept repeating to me, 'Hold on to me, Jankele.' At the intersection, German soldiers with pointing rifles were herding us to the waiting lorries to deport us to God only knows where!

'Faster! Faster!' they barked.

'Hold on to me, Jankele,' pleaded my mother's voice.

In a split second the snow melted, the sky rotated, and the sun's glare attacked my eyes. Pedestrians with blank faces like potatoes, walked backwards. 'Mommy,' I called for all to hear. 'I held on to you. Where are you now?'

People gathered around me and stared. I was embarrassed and wanted to run, but a sharp pain in my knees prevented me. I couldn't even manage one step. A fever raced through my body and without warning I vomited, splattering the cracked sidewalk with pieces of gefilte fish and fragments of the once-sweet chicken soup with lima beans.

FOR SEVERAL DAYS I STAYED IN BED. A doctor with bulging eyes visited me. I was aware only of endless glasses filled with tea and lemon, whispers from the other room all in Yiddish, and the room spinning around me.

Upon my recovery, Cousin Sarah led me to the registry office of Jewish survivors. We climbed countless stairs to the third floor of a shabby office. In this room a strange collection of people sat, patiently waiting, pacing the floor, puffing on cigarettes, and staring into space.

How despondent they looked! One smiled at me, holding up a candy for me to take, but I turned my head.

Our waiting was interrupted now and then by a young girl opening a door and calling, 'Next!'

I noticed a wall covered with scribbled names and messages. The ones in Yiddish I could not decipher.

Chaim Zigleboim was here, read one; *Ania Melman*, was another; *Szmil Zaifman was here and left for Lodz.*

I became dizzy scanning through the maze of names, but could not find Kuperblum, or Chuen.

'Why don't you add your name?' Sarah suggested. 'You never know, this way someone might find you.'

'Next!' called the girl and Sarah pulled me by my sleeve. We entered an office and the man behind the desk pointed to chairs for us to sit.

After conversing with Sarah in Yiddish, he turned to me and, licking his pen, asked in an accented Polish, 'What is your name? Where and when were you born? Your father's name ...?'

He shot one question after another, stopping only to ink the pen. When I had finished recounting my entire history, giving dates, names, and places, he flipped back a page, showing particular interest in Mr Tekalewicz.

'You say he threatened you with a gun?' and he looked at me through his thick glasses. 'We can have him arrested,' he said, and scribbled a note on another piece of paper.

I jumped up and screamed, 'No!'

He slowly removed his glasses and, wiping them with his handkerchief, said, 'But that fascist threatened to kill you!' He replaced his glasses on the bridge of his nose and, leaning across the desk, he looked into my eyes. 'We could have him in jail by tomorrow.'

'No!' I repeated.

'Why not? Why are you protecting him?'

'Because,' I began, 'I don't want him to think badly of me.'

'What do you care what he thinks?'

'I'm not a Jew informer!'

The two exchanged startled glances, followed by words in Yiddish. And then we were on our way. As we entered the outer office, Cousin Sarah again pointed to the wall.

'Let's go!' I said, pulling towards the door. I ran down the three flights of steps, leaving her calling after me.

'Jankele, wait, wait for me!'

I heard her, but I didn't stop or slow down.

My days were now spent accompanying Sarah to the market or sitting in the barbershop watching Cousin Shmuel trim hair and amuse his clients. Sometimes I would walk the streets and peruse faces, hoping and praying one of them would be my mother, my father, my Uncle Moishe, or anyone at all from my family.

Not finding any of them, I had visions of capturing Hitler. I was now on the lookout for the monster with the small moustache.

What would Hitler be doing in Lublin? That gnawing voice mocked me.

Because if I was Hitler, that's where I would hide. Who would ever think of looking for him here?

I followed many suspects, with embarrassing results. In spite of it, I did not give up hope. I'll unearth him, no matter how ingenious his disguise.

ONE EVENING MY COUSINS, their eyes staring at the floor, tried to tell me that perhaps it would be better for me to be placed in a children's home.

'Don't think we don't want you, Jankele,' said Cousin Shmuel. 'You can stay here if you wish, but we're thinking of you. We'll miss you terribly, but at least we'll know we've done the best for you.'

'There'll be other boys and girls just like you,' reinforced Cousin Sarah. 'They'll send you to school. You'll have a bed of your own. Our place is so crowded.'

'You'll come to visit us often, Jankele,' consoled Shmuel.

'And we'll visit you,' added his wife.

The very next day she led me to an address on a wide elegant avenue, and there in an office, we were told to wait. Behind a desk sat a brunette with long wavy hair, attired in a white blouse, and around her neck on a dainty gold chain dangled a Star of David.

I stared at the little star and could clearly see my mother in the Warsaw Ghetto sewing the compulsory armbands with the Stars of David upon them.

'Sorry, he's not acceptable,' I heard an irritating woman's voice. An imposing woman with short wiry hair, in a white smock and shoes, was addressing Cousin Sarah. 'What am I to do?' Sarah pleaded.

'We cannot admit this child in this condition.' She bent at the waist, and examined me at close range, with disdain on her face. 'Look at him,' she bristled. 'He needs a good bath, a change of clothes, and his feet, my Lord, no shoes!' She ran a pencil through my hair. 'Probably infested with lice!'

'That's why I've brought him here. I have no facilities.'

'My good woman, we cannot allow a carrier of lice to mix with the many other children in our care.'

Sarah lost her temper. 'Are you telling me that the children you have here came out of forests, attics, and death camps dressed in tuxedos with white shirts and clean fingernails? This boy is an orphan like the others, he needs your help.'

The woman hardly twitched. 'The others have no one, this boy has you!'

Back at the apartment while Sarah scrubbed my body with a stiff brush, hoping to loosen the imbedded dirt, I kept crying, 'Please don't send me there.'

'Don't worry, they'll be kind to you,' she consoled, and submerged my lathered head into the basin of hot water.

I said goodbye to Cousin Shmuel, and once again Sarah led me back to the Children's House. Again we waited and again the same woman in white appeared and examined my hair, asked to see my hands, and looked disapprovingly at my bare feet.

'Still dirty,' she concluded.

'I tried my best,' Sarah's eyes begged for understanding.

The woman fingered the clean white shirt I was wearing, and asked acidly, 'Isn't it too large for him?'

'My husband's, but it's been washed and pressed,' replied Sarah.

'Very well,' said the woman. 'It will have to do.' Then turning to me, she ordered, 'Say goodbye and follow.'

I looked up at Sarah. 'Jankele,' she began, 'believe me, we're doing this for you. You don't really know how much we'll miss you, but it's really best for you.' With tears in my eyes, I nodded my head. She embraced me. 'You'll come to visit us, won't you?' And releasing me, she left.

'Come!' ordered the woman. I trailed after her.

From the other end of the long hallway came an onrushing group of boys and girls, laughing, and shouting in Yiddish. I spun around, wishing I could run back into Sarah's arms, but she was not to be seen.

ON THE STREET BELOW, a colourful victory parade was in progress. Flags and banners shimmered in the wind. Tanks, cannons, and horsemen with swords all moved along the boulevard. Foot soldiers, their heads high, their uniforms gleaming and medals reflecting in the sunlight, paraded to the beat of a large brass band behind them. A mascot, about my own age, and beating a drum, led a contingent of female soldiers displaying automatic weapons across their inflated chests. The pavements were lined with cheering spectators, some tossing flowers at the veterans. Onlookers applauded from balconies and open windows. Mammoth-sized portraits decorated the parade route. I was unfamiliar with most, but one was well known to me, that of the great Josef Stalin. His

gigantic face hung on a wall opposite my window. His imposing image stared directly at me, his eyes locked onto mine.

The dormitory was deserted, as the others had elected to
watch the parade from a higher floor. I alone stayed behind.

Although I had been there for some time now, I still felt
nervous and afraid of the others.

They sang songs, laughed, and played games. Most spoke
Yiddish at will, while I sat on my bunk and observed, knowing I didn't belong. In turn, they seemed to ogle me with
suspicion, and as time passed things worsened rather than
improved. They often played football and, because I didn't
know how, I declined the first invitation and was never
asked again.

Instead, I would wander through the Lublin streets,
window gazing, looking into open doors, scrutinizing anyone
and everyone who passed me by.

I'll run away, I thought.

Where to? asked one of my voices.

If only I had an accordion, I'd know what to do!

And I'd envision playing and singing 'Dark Night' on a
Lublin street. People would gather around, listen, applaud,
and drop coins into my torn hat. In one window, I had spotted an accordion, and some days I would stand looking at it
for hours and dream.

One evening while the others played ping-pong, chess, and
dominoes, I stared out the window at the imposing portrait
of the great leader.

If only he knew your torment, he would send you an accordion, my inner voice assured me.

Armed with paper and pencil, I wrote a long and detailed
letter to Comrade Stalin telling him about me and why I
needed an accordion. After dropping the envelope into a

mailbox, I returned to the orphanage to wait for the parcel to arrive.

While I waited, the others went on excursions, kicked a ball around, and played practical jokes. At night, the boys' dormitory with two rows of double bunk beds would come to life the moment 'Lights out!' was called.

Finding their way in the dark with a flashlight, several would sneak up to a sleeping body, insert scraps of paper between his fingers and toes, and then ignite the papers. This prank was called 'Bicycle', because once the flames reached the flesh, the victim would frantically move his arms and legs as if peddling.

At other times, a prey would wake in the morning to find his penis painted in bright colours. To make the game more thrilling, the painters invaded the girls' dormitory and performed their artistry on the girls' faces.

To retaliate, the girls entered our quarters when we were sleeping, and the next morning when the wakeup bell rang, and we went to jump into our trousers, we found the legs had been sewn together.

In turn, the boys tied strings to the girls' blankets and then to a master cord. At an appointed time, the cord was yanked, pulling off the covers and leaving the exposed girls screaming in the middle of the night.

One boy was nicknamed 'Horse'. He was older than many of us and preoccupied with his penis. At night when we heard his bed rattling, we killed ourselves laughing, knowing what he was up to. Once, a thread was tied to his organ, and the other end to the dormitory door. Early the next morning when someone opened the door, Horse jumped with an agonizing yelp.

The most spectacular prank was named 'The Destruction

of Stalingrad'. This was accomplished by angling the bed boards. When the unsuspecting ones jumped into bed for the night, they fell onto the floor or onto a sleeping body below on the lower bunk.

I tried to stay up for as long as I could, for fear I would be their next prey. But to my relief, I was bypassed as much at night as during the day. I felt like an island, or worse, a shadow, a ghost, or perhaps even less than that. It could be that I don't exist! I once thought. Perhaps I'm only a memory in someone's mind! In time, however, I realised they were more than interested in me.

'How come you can't speak Yiddish?' asked Partisan, an olive-skinned boy with sturdy legs and our star football player, who claimed to have served in a partisan unit in Lithuania, and to have killed a German with a butcher knife.

'I forgot my Yiddish,' I answered.

He eyed me with his black, piercing eyes and said, 'Perhaps you never knew it!'

'You call yourself Jankele, but you don't look or act like a Jankele,' said a tall boy with glasses, the possessor of a stamp collection. It was said that he had survived hidden in a closet.

'Are you sure you're a Jew?' joined Curly, who had outfoxed the Führer dressed as a girl, thus hiding his circumcision.

'Don't you believe me? Why else would I be here?'

'Then what's this about?' said another one, smiling mischievously and displaying my rosary, which I had hidden under the mattress since my arrival.

'Give it back,' I said and stretched to retrieve it.

'Hey, he wants his Jesus back.' He threw it out the open window, and they all had a good laugh.

'"Jesus", that's a good name for you,' weighed in Partisan.

And the name stuck.

Perhaps they're right. Perhaps I'm not a Jew after all and that's why Jesus saved me.

One day, while sitting at the window, facing the courtyard of the building and listening to the clamour of the others playing football below, at another window I noticed a new face staring into space.

'Who are you?' I called out to him.

'I came yesterday,' he replied in a peasant Polish.

His name was Mietek and his survival was similar to my own, except for the fact that his parents had paid a large sum of money to the farmers who kept him as their own.

'I was really happy there,' he told me. 'Then this jerk appears, claiming he's my uncle and drags me here.'

I soon discovered that we shared other things in common; one of which was that Mietek, like me, could not speak one word of Yiddish. It didn't take long for the bullies to nickname him 'Holy Ghost'.

'There goes Jesus and the Holy Ghost,' they would ridicule when they saw us together.

'I'll tell you a secret,' said Mietek one day. I listened. 'I don't like this place. I don't like any of them.'

'Neither do I,' I confessed. I was jubilant to have someone who shared my sentiments.

'You know something else?' He looked around to make sure no one was about. 'I still believe in Jesus Christ.'

'I do too,' I said. 'When the lights go out I still pray to Him and cross myself.'

'Me too,' he said. 'I sneak out and go to church every Sunday.'

One day he went off by himself and, when he returned, he took me aside, 'It's all arranged. We can escape.'

'Where to?' I was very interested.

'I talked to the priest and told him about you. He wants to meet you and said he can baptise the two of us and send us to some place where we'll never be found.'

'When can we go?'

'Tomorrow, when the others leave to play football, we'll sneak out.'

Once the lights were switched off and Horse's bed began to squeak, I knelt in my bunk and thanked Jesus for not forsaking me. Except for a few whispers and isolated chuckles, it was unusually quiet. My eyes closed, sleep came easily, and I slipped into a dream. I was being baptised; the priest sprinkled holy water upon me, and I heard the congregation snickering. I looked up and was horror-struck; the assembled were my entire family. Why are they here in a church? Ashamed, I turned to the kindly old priest, now wrapping a piece of chicken skin around the head of my penis.

'You see, my son, even that can be corrected by the power of Jesus. You're now a true Christian!'

'He's a Jew,' whispered one in the audience.

I opened my eyes and was blinded by a flashlight. Faces were peering between my legs.

'He's a Jew!' repeated the same voice. It was Partisan.

I jumped out of bed and began swinging my arms in the dark. The group quickly scattered. I followed and stumbled. Somehow I managed to find the switch and flicked on the light. Eyes peeked out from under blankets. Others snored, feigning sleep.

In my mind, I was back in Pulawy, being chased home from school by a Gentile boy shouting, 'Jews to Palestine!' Now, enraged and out of control, I pulled at the blankets, tore pillows, and smashed whatever was in my path. They were trying to escape from me, and I was in pursuit and ready to kill. 'Jews to Palestine!' I screamed. 'You cut off dicks! You cowardly bastards! Bloody Christ killers! Hitler should have made soap out of all of you.'

Stunned by my violent outburst, they stared in silent disbelief.

'No! No one will ever call us names like that again. No one! Do you understand?' It was Partisan again. Suddenly I felt a blow in my stomach, another in the head. I fell, hitting the floor. He picked me up and slugged me, then kicked me. Others joined in, kicking and punching me, accompanied by their infuriating voices: 'Bloody Jew hater! Let him have it! Christ-loving anti-Semite! The dormitory swayed and their distorted faces spun around. I hit the floor. Silently I prayed, 'Dear Jesus, help me!'

When I awoke the next morning, everyone was gone. My pillow was drenched with blood. I sat up and studied my bruised face in a cracked mirror. My right eye was half closed and swellings covered most of my face. My entire body was racked in pain. I got dressed. The door opened and Mietek entered.

'Are you ready?' he asked. I nodded. He reached under his bed and pulled out a bundle. 'Aren't you packed yet?'

'There's nothing to take,' I answered.

'What about that?' he pointed to my Belgian army coat.

I hesitated, then reached for it and flipped it over my shoulder.

Using the back stairwell, we calmly walked down onto the street.

'Does it hurt?' he asked when we had gone some distance. I didn't answer.

After another lengthy silence he said, 'I'm sorry I didn't come to your aid.' We crossed a street, turned a corner, and passed a monument. Mietek stopped in front of a building to tie a shoelace.

It was the same building to which Cousin Sarah had dragged me to register. People were going in and out. Some greeted each other and exchanged pleasantries in Yiddish. I listened and understood some of what they were saying.

'Come,' said Mietek, pulling me. Soon a magnificently beautiful church with many steps and a bell tower appeared before us. Mietek winked and we began our ascent. From above came the clinging and clanging of bells, and as we were reaching the exquisitely carved oak door, the bells seemed to get louder and louder and louder. Then suddenly they stopped. And so did I. 'Come,' said Mietek, pulling my arm. I didn't move.

'It's too sudden,' I finally said. 'Let's go back and talk it over.'

'We did talk it over.' His voice betrayed his annoyance. 'I'm going in,' he announced firmly. 'If you want, you can follow me.'

He walked up to the welcoming door. There he stopped, turned, and looked down at me. He waited for a split second, then turned and disappeared into darkness. I waited in vain for him to come out.

Slowly, I made my way down the steps and for a while waited again on the sidewalk. 'Mietek!' I yelled several times. I started to walk, turning back often in the hope that he would be trailing behind me, but soon the church and the street faded from my view.

I now spotted a bearded man coming towards me. Could he be my grandfather the baker? I wondered.

As we neared each other, I noticed a turban on his head and what looked like a flimsy bedsheet wrapped around his body, hardly sufficient to keep out the morning chill. Arms outstretched towards passers-by, he kept repeating the same phrase in a language nobody understood. He was a portrait of desperation; eyes filled with fear, body frail and undernourished. Hardly anyone paid attention to him except a few children who tailed and laughed at him.

'Who is he?' I asked one of them.

A boy shrugged.

'What is he saying?' I continued.

'No one knows,' answered a little girl. 'He's been walking around like this for weeks. He seems lost.'

I reached for my coat and draped it around his shoulders. He looked at me and said something, but I couldn't understand.

I had nowhere to go, but I worried that I'd be late. My instincts led the way. I crossed the street into a building and then upstairs, higher and higher. Panting, I fell into a room filled with waiting people. They looked up and smiled, as if they had been expecting me.

It was the registry office. In a corner sat a young woman with a beautiful baby crying in her arms. She tried to pacify the child with a nipple, but the infant continued to cry. Softly the woman began to hum a lullaby. The melody was familiar:

Giddy up, my horses, Giddy up my eagles
Hold your heads high
Carry the passengers, the bones are shaking
Giddy up, raise up a cloud.

Perhaps my mother taught her the song! Is it possible she knows where my mother is? I have to find my mother, my father.

But where? chuckled one of my ever-present voices. Everyone is dead. They're all dead. You'd better face it.

A man was writing his name in a small space on the wall, and when he finished, I asked to borrow his pencil. After locating a clear spot, I noticed all the people were staring at me. Blushing, I turned back and carefully wrote: 'Jankele Kuperblum is alive.'

Perhaps someone will find me now! I thought on the way back to the orphanage. Perhaps my mother is alive! Perhaps she and Josele escaped and hid somewhere ... and Moishe, he's probably looking for me ... and my father ... he's no doubt in the army ... but soon they'll release him and he'll find my name on the wall. I began to skip and now looked up at the bright sun shining from above.

It's possible, I told myself. Everything is possible.

ABOUT THE AUTHOR

Jack Kuper escaped Poland and emigrated to Canada at the age of fifteen. He has been an actor, playwright, author and filmmaker. His film, *RUN!*, was honoured by the Venice Film Festival and he is the recipient of a Gemini Award for *A Day in the Warsaw Ghetto: A Birthday Trip in Hell*. He lives in Toronto with his wife, former dancer Terrye Lee. They have four children and thirteen grandchildren.